PEOPLE
in Time and Place

VIRGINIA

HISTORY AND GEOGRAPHY

AUTHORS

Parke Rouse, Jr.
Virginia Historian and
Retired Executive Director
of The Jamestown — Yorktown Foundation

Dr. W. Frank Ainsley
Professor of Geography
University of North Carolina
Wilmington, NC

The first edition
of this text
was published
in conjunction with
the Virginia State
Department of
Education.

SERIES CONSULTANTS

Dr. James F. Baumann
Professor and Head
of the Department of Reading Education
College of Education
The University of Georgia
Athens, Georgia

Dr. Theodore Kaltsounis
Professor of Social Studies Education
University of Washington
Seattle, WA

LITERATURE CONSULTANTS

Dr. Ben A. Smith
Assistant Professor of Social Studies Education
Kansas State University
Manhattan, KS

Dr. John C. Davis
Professor of Elementary Education
University of Southern Mississippi
Hattiesburg, MS

Dr. Jesse Palmer
Assistant Professor, Department of Curriculum and Instruction
University of Southern Mississippi
Hattiesburg, MS

SILVER BURDETT & GINN

MORRISTOWN, NJ • NEEDHAM, MA
Atlanta, GA • Dallas, TX • Deerfield, IL • Menlo Park, CA

SERIES AUTHORS

Dr. W. Frank Ainsley, Professor of Geography, University of North Carolina, Wilmington, NC

Dr. Herbert J. Bass, Professor of History, Temple University, Philadelphia, PA

Dr. Kenneth S. Cooper, Professor of History, Emeritus, George Peabody College for Teachers, Vanderbilt University, Nashville, TN

Dr. Gary S. Elbow, Professor of Geography, Texas Tech University, Lubbock, TX

Roy Erickson, Program Specialist, K–12 Social Studies and Multicultural Education San Juan Unified School District, Carmichael, CA

Dr. Daniel B. Fleming, Professor of Social Studies Education, Virginia Polytechnic Institute and State University, Blacksburg, VA

Dr. Gerald Michael Greenfield, Professor and Director, Center for International Studies, University of Wisconsin — Parkside, Kenosha, WI

Dr. Linda Greenow, Assistant Professor of Geography, SUNY — The College at New Paltz, New York, NY

Dr. William W. Joyce, Professor of Education, Michigan State University, East Lansing, MI

Dr. Gail S. Ludwig, Geographer-in-Residence, National Geographic Society, Geography Education Program, Washington, D.C.

Dr. Michael B. Petrovich, Professor Emeritus of History, University of Wisconsin, Madison, WI

Dr. Arthur D. Roberts, Professor of Education, University of Connecticut, Storrs, CT

Dr. Christine L. Roberts, Professor of Education, University of Connecticut, Storrs, CT

Parke Rouse, Jr., Virginia Historian and Retired Executive Director of the Jamestown-Yorktown Foundation, Williamsburg, VA

Dr. Paul C. Slayton, Jr., Distinguished Professor of Education, Mary Washington College, Fredericksburg, VA

Dr. Edgar A. Toppin, Professor of History and Dean of the Graduate School, Virginia State University, Petersburg, VA

GRADE-LEVEL WRITERS/CONSULTANTS

Sharon H. Adams, Grade Teacher, Liberty Middle School, Hanover County, Virginia

Dr. Deanna Gordon, Director of Elementary Education, Roanoke County Schools, Salem, Virginia

Dr. Norma Jean Peters, Supervisor of Social Studies and Foreign Languages, Roanoke County Schools, Salem, Virginia

Michael G. Sams, Social Studies Department Chairperson, Lafayette High School, Williamsburg, Virginia

ACKNOWLEDGEMENTS

Virginia State Library, Richmond, VA; Virginia Historical Society, Richmond, VA; Valentine Museum, Richmond, VA; National Tobacco Textile Museum, Danville, VA; and John Quarstein of the War Memorial Museum of Virginia for their generous cooperation in ferreting facts and illustrations.

Grateful acknowledgement is made to the following publishers, authors, and agents for their permission to reprint copyrighted material. Any errors or omissions in copyright notice are inadvertent and will be corrected in future printings as they are discovered.

Misty of Chincoteague by Marguerite Henry. Copyright © 1947, renewed 1975 by Marguerite Henry. Used by permission of the author.

"In Coal County" excerpt from *In Coal Country* text copyright © 1987 by Judith Hendershot. Reprinted by permission of Alfred A. Knopf, Inc.

Pocahontas by Ingri and Edgar Parin D'Aulaire. Copyright © by Doubleday, a division of Doubleday Dell Publishing Group, Inc. Reprinted by permission of the publishers.

To Be A Slave, Text copyright © 1968 by Julius Lester. Reprinted by permission of the publisher, Dial Books for Young Readers.

"I Have a Dream" Speech. Copyright © 1963 by Martin Luther King, Jr. Used with permission.

CONTENTS

UNIT **1** VIRGINIA:
OUR HOME

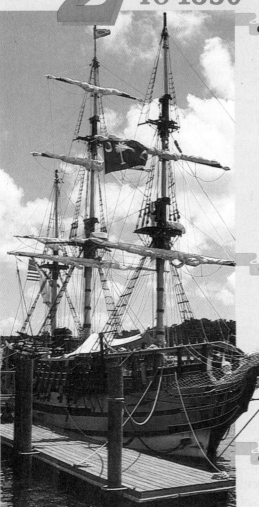

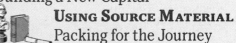

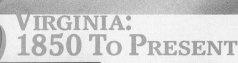

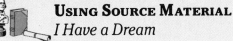

RESOURCE SECTION

MAPS

ATLAS

TIMELINES

GRAPHS

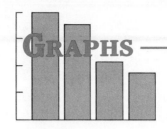

TABLES

CHARTS

DIAGRAMS

SKILLBUILDER

SPECIAL FEATURES

USING SOURCE MATERIAL

LITERATURE

CITIZENSHIP AND AMERICAN VALUES

LET'S TAKE A LOOK AT VIRGINIA

My family lives in Virginia Beach. My parents own a restaurant near the beach. Sometimes I help out there. I like living so close to the Atlantic Ocean.

Barbara

Many people visit Battlefield Park, near my home in Richmond. Parks like this one help people understand the important events that took place in Virginia.

Julio

I live in historic Williamsburg. When I am older, I want to dress in colonial clothing and tell visitors about this famous place.

Lisa

There are many things to do in Washington County. I like living here because we are close to the Barter Theatre. My family goes there often to see plays.

Margaret

The golden crescent is the most populated area of Virginia. There is much to do here, including a visit to King's Dominion.

Rich

We have many teams to cheer for in Chesterfield County. I like football best. Maybe when I am in college, I will be a great Virginia athlete.

Marcus

If you like apples, come to Winchester in May for the Apple Blossom Festival. If you come later, you can pick the apples off the trees.

Christie

My family comes from Korea, but I was born in Virginia. I live near Mabry Mill. Many people who travel on the Blue Ridge Parkway stop at Mabry Mill.

Joey

Dear Student,
As you enter the fourth grade, you will begin studying about our state, Virginia. You will find out many things about this great state and why it is so popular.

Many famous leaders came from Virginia. Eight presidents were born in this wonderful state. Virginia led the thirteen English colonies in their fight for freedom and independence. These colonies later became the United States of America.

I hope you enjoy reading this book and learning about our great state.

Sincerely,

Amy Layman
Glenvar Elementary School

MAP SKILLS HANDBOOK

Knowing how to work with maps is a social studies skill that everyone must have. You can't learn history and geography without being able to read maps. Maps, however, have uses that go beyond what you are learning in school.

Watch the nightly news. How many times are maps used? The next time you are in the library, take a copy of a weekly newsmagazine and count the number of maps that accompany the articles. Are maps used in any of the advertisements in the magazine? Keep a record over a week of all the times you see or use a map.

As you study United States history this year, you will be using map skills that you already have. You will also be learning some new map skills. All the map skills you will need appear in this Map Skills Handbook. Study the table of contents on these pages to see what you will learn.

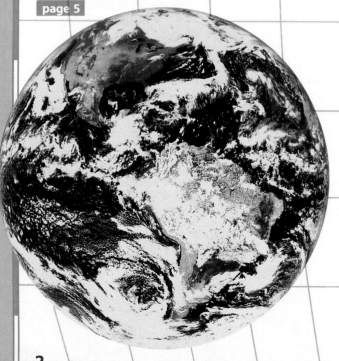

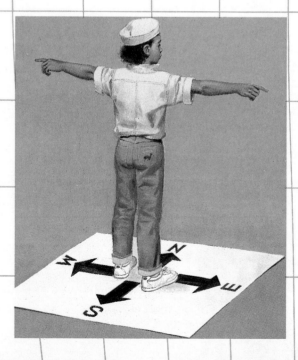

2

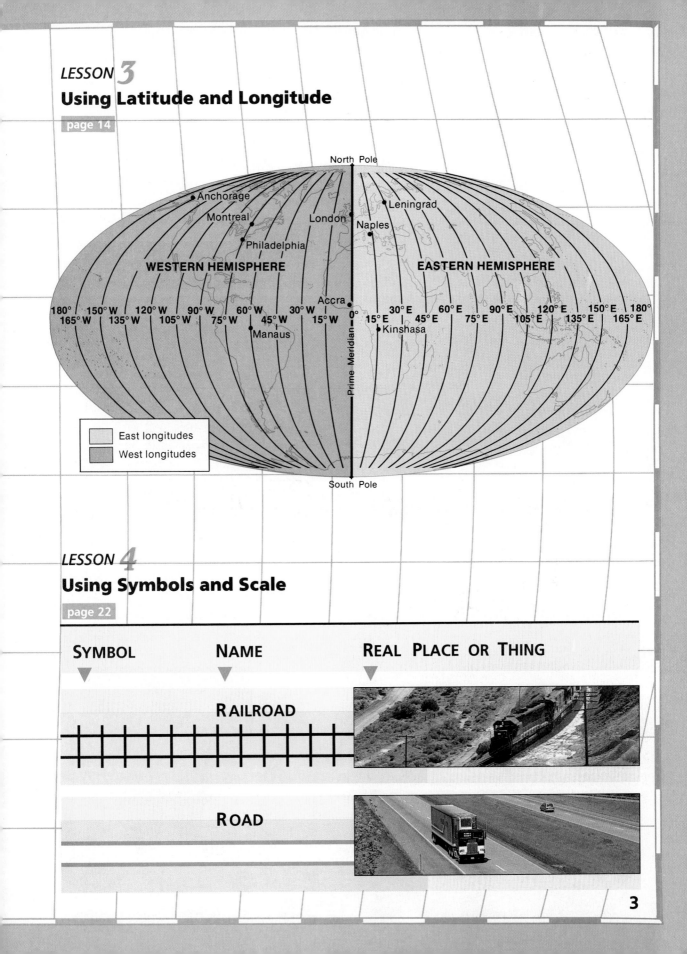

LESSON 3
Using Latitude and Longitude
page 14

North Pole

• Anchorage

Leningrad

Montreal

London

Naples

Philadelphia

WESTERN HEMISPHERE

EASTERN HEMISPHERE

Accra

| 180° | 150° W | 120° W | 90° W | 60° W | 30° W | 0° | 30° E | 60° E | 90° E | 120° E | 150° E | 180° |
| 165° W | 135° W | 105° W | 75° W | 45° W | 15° W | 15° E | 45° E | 75° E | 105° E | 135° E | 165° E |

Manaus

Kinshasa

Prime Meridian

□ East longitudes
□ West longitudes

South Pole

LESSON 4
Using Symbols and Scale
page 22

SYMBOL ▼	NAME ▼	REAL PLACE OR THING ▼
	RAILROAD	
	ROAD	

Learning How to Describe Where Places Are

THINK ABOUT WHAT YOU KNOW
Make a list of any states you have visited outside of Virginia.

STUDY THE VOCABULARY

location	ocean
map	continent
sphere	geography
globe	history

FOCUS YOUR READING
What do we need to know to study the geography of Virginia?

A. Looking at the Earth

Locating Places on a Map. Yolanda ran into the living room clutching the letter. "I have been accepted," she shouted. "I am going to school in France next year."

Yolanda's mother and younger brother Carlos congratulated her. They knew how excited she had been when she applied to the foreign study program at school. But they had not known whether she would be accepted or which country she would go to if she were accepted.

Carlos asked Yolanda to tell him everything she could about the place where she would be living. She explained the location of France and of the town she would live in. A place's location is where it is compared with other places around it. Yolanda said, "France is part of Europe. It is across the Atlantic Ocean from the United States. I will be living with a family in a small town."

"I have heard of France before, but I am not sure where it is," Carlos said. "Can you show me?"

"Sure, Carlos," Yolanda replied. She went and got a book with many maps in it. A map is a special kind of drawing that shows the earth or part of the earth on a flat surface. On the front of the book there was a picture like the one you see on the left on page 6.

> A map is a special drawing that shows the earth or part of the earth on a flat surface.
> ▶ Why do people use maps?

These are two ways of looking at the earth. One is a photograph taken from space. The other is a model of the earth.
▶ What can you see in these two pictures?

"Do you see the picture on the cover?" his mother asked. "It shows what the earth would look like if you were flying very high above it. You would be looking down on it."

"The earth looks round, Mom," said Carlos.

"That is because it is round. You could also say it is shaped like a sphere," his mother replied.

A Model of the Earth Yolanda got out a basketball. She asked Carlos, "How much of this basketball can you see at one time?"

"Only half," Carlos answered.

Yolanda turned the basketball around. "Now you see the other half. The earth is like this basketball. Even from outer space, you can see only half of the earth at one time."

"Yolanda, why don't you go get your globe," her mother said.

Carlos's mother explained that a globe is a model of the earth. A model is a small copy of a real thing. The picture on the right above shows a globe like the one Carlos's sister brought back. The globe showed Carlos the shape of the earth's land and water.

B. Oceans and Continents

Carlos's mother used the globe to explain many things. She told him that about two thirds of the earth's surface is covered by water. Much of that water is found in **oceans.** Oceans are the largest bodies of water found on the earth. There are four oceans. They are the Atlantic,

Arctic, Indian, and Pacific oceans. She pointed out to Carlos that the Arctic Ocean is the smallest and the Pacific Ocean is the largest.

Carlos's mother explained that the other one third of the earth is made up of land areas. These land areas are divided into **continents.** Continents are the largest areas of land on the earth. There are seven continents. Carlos's mother turned the globe slowly as she pointed to each one and identified them: "Africa, Antarctica, Europe, Asia, Australia, North America, and South America. Asia is the largest, and Australia is the smallest."

"But Mom," said Carlos with a puzzled expression on his face, "it looks like Europe and Asia are one big continent."

"You are right, Carlos, it does," his mother replied. "Actually, they are two separate continents. But we sometimes speak of the total land areas of Europe and Asia as Eurasia. That word combines letters from both the words *Europe* and *Asia*."

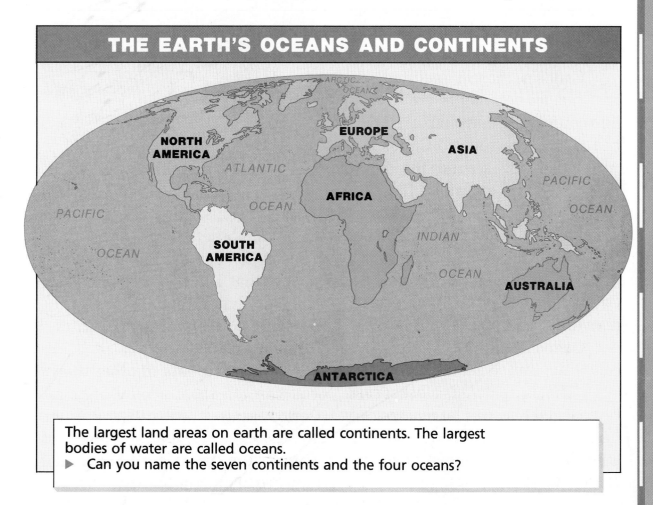

THE EARTH'S OCEANS AND CONTINENTS

The largest land areas on earth are called continents. The largest bodies of water are called oceans.
► Can you name the seven continents and the four oceans?

The geography of a place often determines how the land will be used. The people who live in Virginia use the land and the water in many different ways.
▶ What are some ways Virginians use the land and water?

C. Countries

"What is France, if it is not a continent?" Carlos asked.

"It is a country," his mother said. "Most continents are divided into smaller parts called countries." She explained that continents are large bodies of land, whereas countries are regions that have been organized by people. She continued, "There are over 170 countries in the world. Here is France, between Spain and Germany."

Carlos's mother pointed out that not all continents are divided into countries. For example, Antarctica is not. She showed Carlos that Antarctica lies around the South Pole. Then she explained that it is covered with ice and is very cold. "People visit Antarctica, but no one lives there all the time," she said.

She went on to explain to Carlos that Australia is both a continent and a country.

Carlos said, "Our country is called the United States, right?"

"That is right," his mother said. "And it is the second largest country on the continent of North America. Only Canada is larger than the United States."

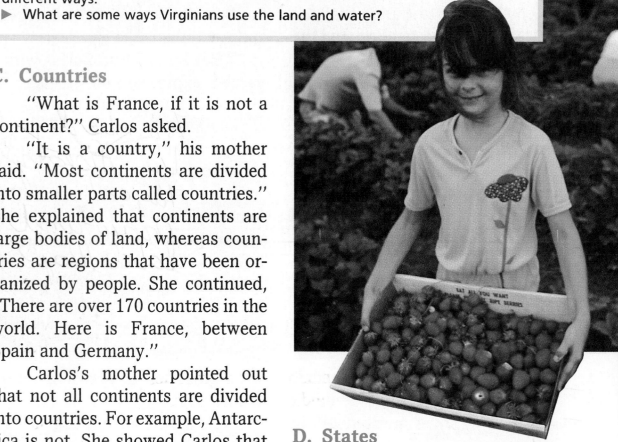

D. States

"Our country, like many others, is divided into even smaller regions. Those regions are called states," Carlos's mother said.

"When I go to France, I will tell people that I live in Virginia. I can also say that Virginia is one of the 50 states in the United States," Yolanda said.

"There are lots of other things you can tell them about Virginia," Carlos said. "You can tell them stories about Virginia's people and events. An event is anything that happens that is important."

"And, of course, I can explain Virginia's **geography**," Yolanda said. "Geography is the study of the earth and how people use it."

"Don't forget to tell them about Virginia's rich and colorful **history**," their mother said. "You have stud-ied a great deal in school about our state's past."

"And, of course, you will want to tell them what a great brother you have," Carlos said as Yolanda and their mother followed him into the kitchen to get ready for lunch.

LESSON **1** *REVIEW*

THINK AND WRITE

A. In what ways is a map different from a globe?
B. What are the names of each of the seven continents?
C. Which of the seven continents is also a country?
D. Why is it important to study the geography of Virginia?

SKILLS CHECK

MAP SKILL

Locate the following places on the map on page 7: Asia, Africa, Antarctica, and the Atlantic Ocean. Which one of these places does not belong in this group? Give a reason for your choice.

Learning How to Use Maps

THINK ABOUT WHAT YOU KNOW

Describe a time when you saw someone use a map. What did the person want to know? How did the map help?

STUDY THE VOCABULARY

boundary   **compass**
compass rose   **rotate**

FOCUS YOUR READING

How do we describe where places are on a map?

A. Using Maps to Get Around

Planning a Trip "Dad, do you really mean it?" Gillian asked. "Can we really go to North Carolina to see Aunt Margo's new farm?"

"Yes, Gillian, we can go. In fact, I thought you might help me plan a route to get there," her father said.

"Sure, Dad. But first, can I invite my friend Valerie to go with us?" Gillian asked.

"Yes, as long as it's OK with her parents," Gillian's dad answered.

"I'll be back in a minute," Gillian called as she skipped into the kitchen to call her best friend. When she came back five minutes later, her father was reading the newspaper. "Do you still want me to help you plan a route to Aunt Margo's?" Gillian asked.

Her father put the paper down. "Of course I do," he said.

"How do we start?" Gillian asked her father.

"Well, the first thing we need to do is look at a map," her father answered. "The map will show us where places are and how far places are from one another."

Boundary Lines Gillian walked to the desk and got a map out of the top drawer. The map she found of the United States was like the one on

The North Pole and the South Pole are opposite each other.
▶ Which is the most northern place on the earth?

this page. "On this map," she said, "it's easy to see where Virginia ends and North Carolina begins."

Notice that lines on the map are used to separate one state from the next. These lines are called **boundary** lines. A boundary is a line that separates one state or one country from another. A boundary can also be called a border.

"Will we go over a line like that when we go to North Carolina?" Gillian asked.

"No," her dad replied, "those lines are only on maps. They are not really marked on the land."

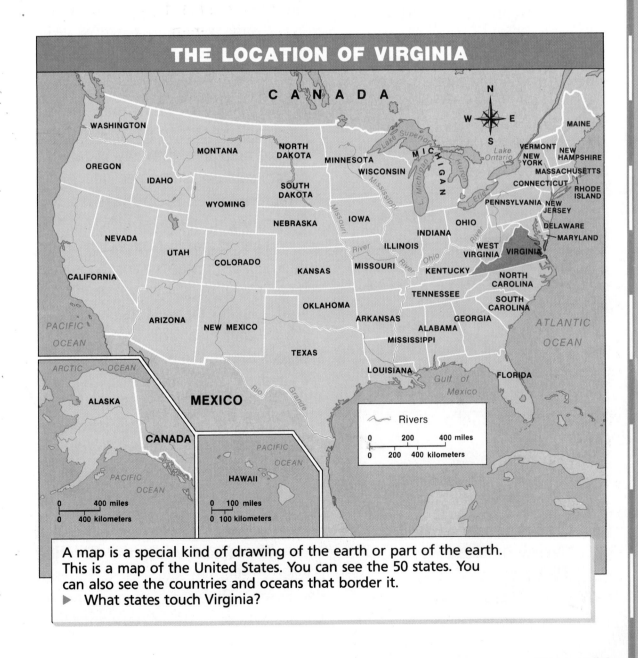

THE LOCATION OF VIRGINIA

A map is a special kind of drawing of the earth or part of the earth. This is a map of the United States. You can see the 50 states. You can also see the countries and oceans that border it.
▶ What states touch Virginia?

B. Using Directions

Which Way to Go "To plan a route, you need to know something about directions," Gillian's dad said. "There are four important direction words you can use to locate places on a map. These words are *north*, *south*, *east*, and *west*. The letters *N*, *E*, *S*, and *W* are often used to stand for north, east, south, and west."

Gillian's father got a very large piece of white paper out of the desk. On it he drew a diagram like the one shown below. He asked Gillian to stand in the middle of the diagram and face toward the letter N.

If you face north, south is behind you.
▶ Which direction is on your left, and which is on your right?

"OK, Gillian, what direction is to your right? What direction is to your left?" her dad asked.

"East is on my right, and west is on my left," Gillian said.

Then Gillian's father asked her to turn and face toward the letter W. "OK, now tell me where the other three directions are."

"East is behind me now. And north is to my right and south is to my left," Gillian said.

A Special Rose Many maps have a drawing like this to show directions on the map. The drawing is called a compass rose. Some people call it a direction finder. A compass is a tool for finding directions.

The diagram of the earth on the facing page contains a compass rose. It is used to show where north, south, east, and west are located.

Sometimes you need to find places that are in between two of the four main directions. For instance, the direction of a place that is between north and east is northeast. A place that lies between south and west is southwest.

C. Understanding Directions

"I see how to use the direction words," Gillian said. "But I'm not sure what they really mean. Who decides where north is? Or south?"

Gillian's father explained that north is the direction toward the North Pole. The location of the North Pole is shown in the diagram on this page. If Gillian were to travel north a very long way, she would come to the North Pole. Part of this journey would be across the Arctic Ocean. Actually, the North Pole is just a point on the map. Like a boundary, it does not really exist on the surface of the earth.

Then Gillian's mother said, "Imagine that you are going south from Virginia. You would cross the state of North Carolina, then South Carolina and Georgia. If you continued on for a very long distance, you would at last get to the continent of Antarctica and then would reach the South Pole."

Gillian's dad brought over their globe. He pointed to the North Pole and the South Pole on the globe. Then he took the globe off its stand

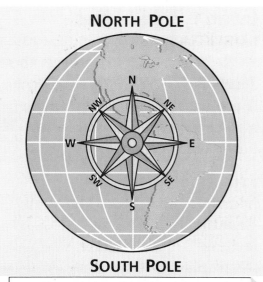

This compass rose shows the four major directions and those in between.
▶ Which direction is between north and east?

and put one finger on top of the globe and another below. He asked Gillian to slowly rotate, or turn, the globe. "My fingers are like the North and South poles," he explained. "They do not move. The earth just turns around them."

LESSON 2 REVIEW

THINK AND WRITE

A. What is a boundary?
B. What are the eight different directions that could be shown on a compass rose?
C. In what way are the North Pole and the South Pole similar to boundary lines?

SKILLS CHECK

MAP SKILL

Look at the map of the United States on page 11. For each of the following states, use a direction word to give its location in relation to Virginia: Florida, Ohio, New Jersey, and Missouri.

Using Latitude and Longitude

THINK ABOUT WHAT YOU KNOW
If you wanted to describe where a place is located on the earth, how would you do it?

STUDY THE VOCABULARY
hemisphere	Prime Meridian
Equator	grid
latitude	estimate
longitude	time zone

FOCUS YOUR READING
How can we say where a place is located on the earth?

A. The Equator

"Are you sure you really have to move?" Paul asked Lin.

"I'm sure," Lin replied. "My father is being transferred by his company. But it won't be that bad. I'll still be in Virginia!"

"I know. But with me in Newport News and you in Roanoke, it will be like we are living on opposite sides of the earth," Paul said.

Paul sometimes exaggerates. Lin is *not* moving to the other side of the earth. Let us take a look at what that would really mean. Lin would have to be moving to a different hemisphere. A hemisphere is one half of the earth. Virginia is in the Northern Hemisphere. The North-ern Hemisphere is separated from the Southern Hemisphere by an imaginary line. This line runs completely around the earth. It is called the Equator. The Equator is halfway between the North Pole and the South Pole. Find the Equator on the map on page 15. What color is the Northern Hemisphere?

B. Latitude

To find out more about Roanoke's location, the boys got out a map of Virginia like the one on page 18. They noticed lines running across the map. All lines that run across a map are lines of latitude. The Equator is a line of latitude. The lines between the Equator and the

The boys found Newport News and Roanoke on a map of Virginia.
▶ What did they learn about the latitude of the two cities?

North Pole are lines of north latitude. Those between the Equator and the South Pole are lines of south latitude.

Lin studied the map carefully. He noticed that the lines of latitude were numbered. These numbers are called degrees of latitude. The symbol for degree is °. These numbers run from 0° at the Equator to 90° at the North Pole. We use the number of degrees of latitude to tell us how far a place is from the Equator.

The two boys decided to use degrees of latitude to compare where the cities of Newport News and Roanoke are located. They noticed on the Virginia map that a line of latitude ran just above Newport News. What is its number? It is 37° north. When the boys looked at the location of Roanoke, they noticed that it was very close to that same line of latitude.

"There isn't even a whole degree of latitude between where we will be living," Paul exclaimed.

Where is your home? What is its latitude?

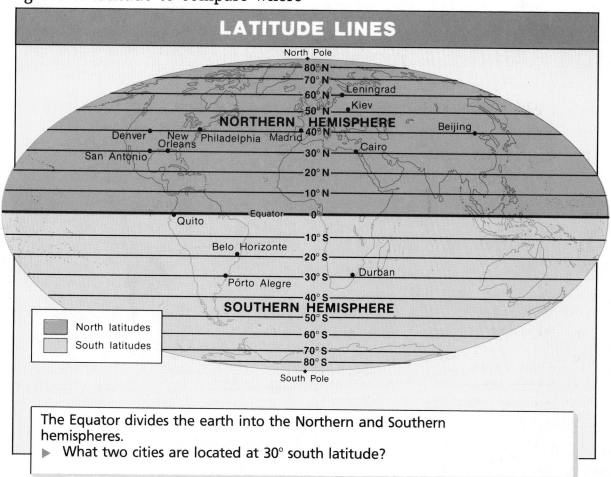

LATITUDE LINES

North latitudes

South latitudes

The Equator divides the earth into the Northern and Southern hemispheres.

▶ What two cities are located at 30° south latitude?

C. Longitude

Paul pointed out to Lin that lines were also running up and down the map. These lines run from the North Pole to the South Pole. They are called lines of **longitude.** They cross the Equator. If you look at the map below, you will notice something that is very interesting. The greatest amount of space between the lines of longitude occurs at the Equator. But the lines of longitude come together at the North and South poles. That happens because the earth is a sphere.

The Equator is the special latitude line that divides the Northern Hemisphere and the Southern Hemisphere. There is also a special line of longitude. It runs from the North Pole to the South Pole. It passes through Greenwich, England. This line of longitude is called the **Prime Meridian.** The Prime Meridian is 0° longitude. All other lines of longitude measure distances east or west of the Prime Meridian.

The half of the earth that lies west of the Prime Meridian is called the Western Hemisphere. The half

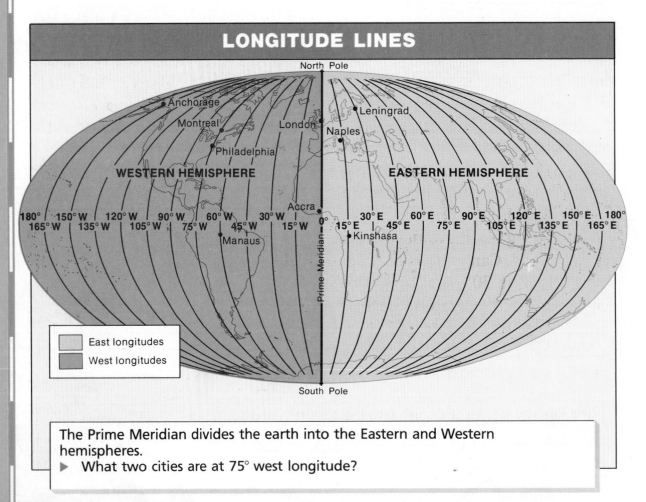

The Prime Meridian divides the earth into the Eastern and Western hemispheres.
► What two cities are at 75° west longitude?

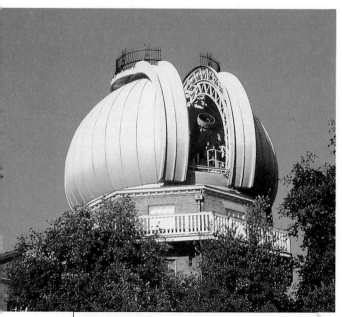

Longitude measurements are made from this observatory in Greenwich, England.
► What is longitude?

and the line of longitude of 75° west. It is most important to be able to say just where a place is on the earth.

D. Using a Grid

The lines of latitude and longitude on the map form a **grid.** A grid is a system of lines that cross and form squares or boxes. We can also use this grid to say where a place is. For example, as the boys were looking at the map of Virginia, they saw that Newport News does not lie just where the lines cross. When this happens, you have to **estimate,** or figure out *about,* where a place is.

They saw from the map that Newport News is clearly at 37° north. Yet it is almost exactly halfway between 76° west and 77° west. That made deciding between the two hard.

But this problem actually helped the boys. They discovered that there is an easier way of saying where a place is. They noticed that the boxes on their map were numbered across the top of the map from 1 to 7, just as they are on your map. They are also lettered from A to D on the side of the map. Newport News lies in the sixth box from the left in row D. It is in box D6. Where is Roanoke? Where are Charlottesville and Winchester? Grids are often used to locate a place.

that lies to the east is called the Eastern Hemisphere. Besides being in the Northern Hemisphere, Virginia is in the Western Hemisphere.

Look again at the map on page 16. Put your finger on the line marked 30°E. *E* stands for east. Move it along the line until you come to Leningrad. Can you see that Leningrad lies at 30° east longitude? Look back at the map on page 15. You will see that Leningrad also lies at 60° north latitude. You can say Leningrad is 60° north and 30° east.

Philadelphia is also shown on both maps. How would you tell someone where Philadelphia is? It is on the line of latitude of 40° north

VIRGINIA: USING A GRID

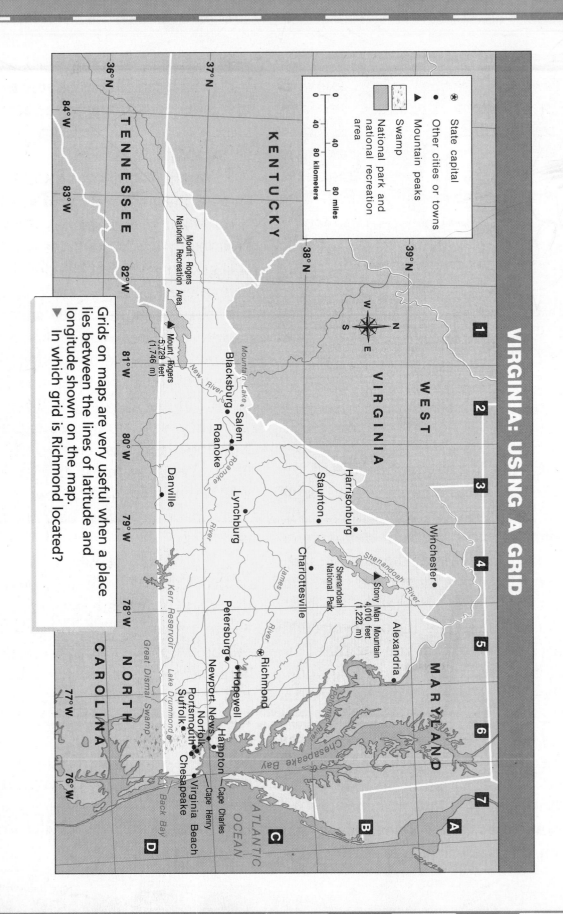

Legend:
- ⊛ State capital
- ● Other cities or towns
- ▲ Mountain peaks
- National park and national recreation area
- Swamp

Scale:
0 40 80 kilometers
0 40 80 miles

States and locations on map:
KENTUCKY, WEST VIRGINIA, VIRGINIA, MARYLAND, TENNESSEE, NORTH CAROLINA, ATLANTIC OCEAN

Cities and features: Winchester, Harrisonburg, Staunton, Alexandria, Charlottesville, Shenandoah National Park, Stony Man Mountain 4,010 feet (1,222 m), Lynchburg, Petersburg, Richmond, Hopewell, Newport News, Hampton, Norfolk, Portsmouth, Suffolk, Chesapeake, Virginia Beach, Cape Charles, Cape Henry, Danville, Roanoke, Salem, Blacksburg, Mount Rogers 5,729 feet (1,746 m), Mount Rogers National Recreation Area

Rivers and water: New River, Roanoke River, James River, Kerr Reservoir, Lake Drummond, Great Dismal Swamp, Back Bay, Chesapeake Bay, Shenandoah River, Mountain Lake

Grid labels: 1, 2, 3, 4, 5, 6, 7 (top) and A, B, C, D (right)

Latitude: 36°N, 37°N, 38°N, 39°N
Longitude: 84°W, 83°W, 82°W, 81°W, 80°W, 79°W, 78°W, 77°W, 76°W

▼ Grids on maps are very useful when a place lies between the lines of latitude and longitude shown on the map.
▼ In which grid is Richmond located?

18

E. The Time of Day

Time Differences "You know, I have a friend in Kentucky whom I sometimes call. And it's a different time there than it is here," Paul said. "I wonder, will it be a different time where you're moving? After all, Roanoke's not too far from Kentucky."

"I never heard of that," Lin said. "What do you mean?"

Have you ever traveled to a place where you had to change your watch or clock to match the local time where you were visiting? Why did that happen?

You know that the earth moves around the sun. But it looks as if the sun moves across the sky from east to west. That is why we say the sun rises in the east and sets in the west.

THE UNITED STATES: TIME ZONES

Eastern Time Zone
Central Time Zone
Mountain Time Zone
Pacific Time Zone
Other time zones

⊛ State capital
● Other cities

The United States is divided into time zones. Virginia is in the Eastern Time Zone.

▶ When it is 12 noon in Virginia, what time is it in Illinois?

At 6:30 P.M. in Virginia, evening is beginning to set in the cities and towns. However, on the country's West Coast, it is only 3:30 P.M.
▶ In what time zone is Virginia?

What time is it by your clock? Is it before noon or after noon? Noon is when the sun is highest in the sky. But the sun reaches its highest point in the sky in Virginia before it reaches its highest point in Kentucky. Kentucky is farther west, so the sun "gets there" later.

Sun Time Look again at the map of Virginia. Imagine that everyone in Virginia told time only by the sun. First it would be noon in Hampton and minutes later noon in Newport News. It would be noon in Roanoke just shortly before it was noon in Blacksburg. When you traveled east or west, you would have to adjust your watch every few miles.

About a hundred years ago, the clocks in all these places showed different times. All the times were correct by the sun. But it was awkward that the time in one city was a little bit different from the time in a neighboring city.

Time Zones Fortunately, our country has been divided into **time zones.** Within each of these large

When it is early evening in Virginia, children in California are hurrying home from school, as shown in this afternoon scene.
► What type of transportation is shown in this picture?

areas, all the clocks show the same time. Look at the time zone map on page 19. All of Virginia is in the Eastern Time Zone. To the west of the Eastern Time Zone is the Central Time Zone. Part of Kentucky is in the Central Time Zone. To the west of the Central Time Zone is the Mountain Time Zone. Beyond that is the Pacific Time Zone. When it is nine o'clock in the morning in Alexandria, Virginia, it is eight o'clock in Chicago, Illinois.

LESSON 3 REVIEW

THINK AND WRITE

A. What is the name of the imaginary line that runs around the earth midway between the North Pole and the South Pole?

B. What does it mean when someone says that a place is at a latitude of 50° north?

C. From what line do we measure longitude?

D. How do you use the grid that appears on a map to tell where a place is?

E. Is it later by the sun in a city in Virginia or in a city on the West Coast of the United States?

SKILLS CHECK

MAP SKILL

Look at the map of the United States in the Atlas on pages 354 and 355. Then estimate the latitude and longitude of each of the following places: Anchorage, Alaska; Miami Beach, Florida; Portland, Maine; Pierre, South Dakota.

21

Using Symbols and Scale

THINK ABOUT WHAT YOU KNOW
Name as many things as you can think of that are drawn on maps to stand for real things.

STUDY THE VOCABULARY
symbol **scale**
key

FOCUS YOUR READING
What do we need to know to read a map correctly?

A. Pictures and Maps

Alesia and Karyn could hardly control their excitement as they left their cabins and headed toward the recreation center at Indian Mountain Camp. It was their first day at summer camp, and they were looking forward to spending two weeks together away from home.

When they got to the recreation center, Miss Johnson, the activities director, told everyone to sit down. "Before you start exploring the camp," Miss Johnson said, "I want to tell you something about maps and how useful they can be." Then she handed each girl a photograph and a map.

She explained that the photograph had been taken from an airplane. You can see this picture on page 23. In the picture you see buildings, roads, woods, and parking lots. On the left side of the picture is the water. There are also many other things. You can see some of them clearly. Others are not so clear.

Then Miss Johnson asked the girls to look at the map. You can see the map below the photograph. She explained, "This is a map of the place seen in the photo. What differences can you find between the photo and the map?"

Alesia raised her hand to answer. "Yes, and what is your name?" asked Miss Johnson.

This woman is checking a road map. The map will show her which route to take.
► When would you use a road map?

22

FROM PHOTOGRAPH TO MAP

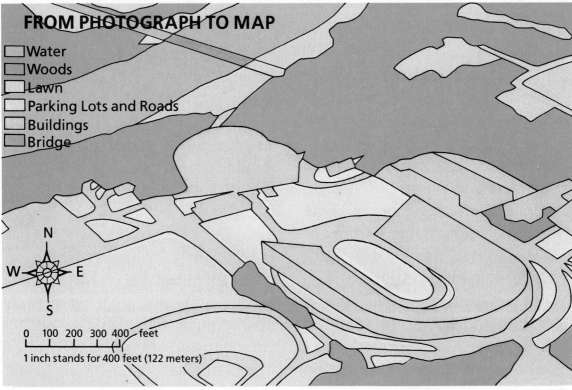

☐ Water
☐ Woods
☐ Lawn
☐ Parking Lots and Roads
☐ Buildings
☐ Bridge

N
W E
S

0 100 200 300 400 feet
1 inch stands for 400 feet (122 meters)

At the top of this page is an aerial photograph of a stadium and the surrounding area. At the bottom of the page is a map of the same place.
▶ How many things in the photograph can you find on the map?

"Alesia," she said. "One difference is that the map leaves out things that are in the picture. The map only shows some things, like roads, water, and buildings. It leaves out cars and single trees."

B. Symbols

"When you learn about maps, you also have to learn about **symbols**," said Miss Johnson. "A symbol is something that stands for the real thing. Before you can use a map, you have to find out what the symbols on it mean."

The part of the map that tells what the symbols stand for is called the **key**. It is also called a legend. A map key may contain many symbols. Look at the map on page 23. In the upper left corner is the key.

Miss Johnson explained that according to the map key, the orange symbols stand for buildings. Blue shows water, and dark green stands for woods. Roads are shown in light grey. Other symbols could be used as well.

On page 25 you can see some of these symbols. A river is shown by a wavy blue line. A railroad is a line with short lines across it. The symbol looks like a railroad track.

Miss Johnson explained that part of being a good camper is understanding these symbols.

The Metric System

On page 28 you will see that the measurement of a map is given in inches and centimeters. Later in this chapter you will find that bigger measurements are given in miles and kilometers. Centimeters and kilometers are units of measure in the metric system.

The metric system is a way of measuring area, distance, weight, capacity, and temperature. This system is used in all major countries except the United States. Plans are being made to "go metric" here also.

To prepare for this, both American and metric measurements are given in this book. Each American measurement is followed by its metric equivalent. Miles are changed to kilometers (km), inches to centimeters (cm), feet or yards to meters (m), acres to hectares (ha), pounds to kilograms (kg), and degrees Fahrenheit (°F) to degrees Celsius (°C).

SYMBOL	NAME	REAL PLACE OR THING

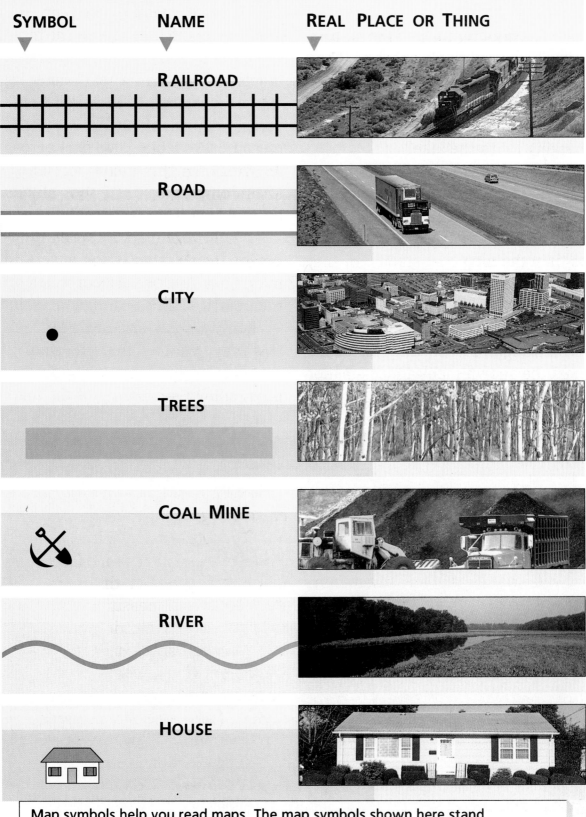

RAILROAD

ROAD

CITY

TREES

COAL MINE

RIVER

HOUSE

Map symbols help you read maps. The map symbols shown here stand for the real places or things shown at the right.
▶ In which part of a map are the symbols explained?

C. Scale

The photograph and the map on page 23 measure only about 6 inches (15 centimeters) across. But how big is the place? How far would a person have to walk to get from the parking lot to the lake?

Miss Johnson explained that to answer these questions you need to know the **scale** of the map. Scale tells how much bigger the real place is than the map.

"Maps cannot show places and things in their real sizes," she continued. "No piece of paper would be big enough. Places and distances must be shown many times smaller than they really are."

Miss Johnson picked up the model airplane that was on the table beside her. "This model airplane is much smaller than a real plane. Its wings measure 1 foot (30 cm) across. A real plane like it would measure 100 feet (3,048 cm) across its wings. In this model airplane," Miss Johnson said, "1 foot stands for 100 feet. That is its scale.

"On every map, a certain number of inches stands for a certain number of feet or yards or miles on the earth," Miss Johnson said. "When we show size or distance in this way, we say that the map is drawn to a certain scale. The scale is often shown in a corner of the map.

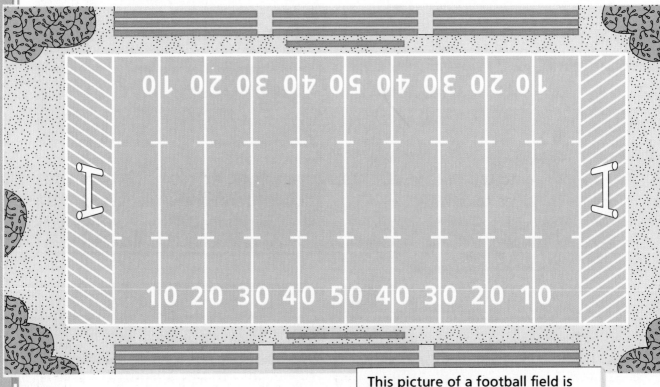

This picture of a football field is drawn to scale.
► Why could this field not be drawn to its real size?

VIRGINIA: AT TWO DIFFERENT SCALES

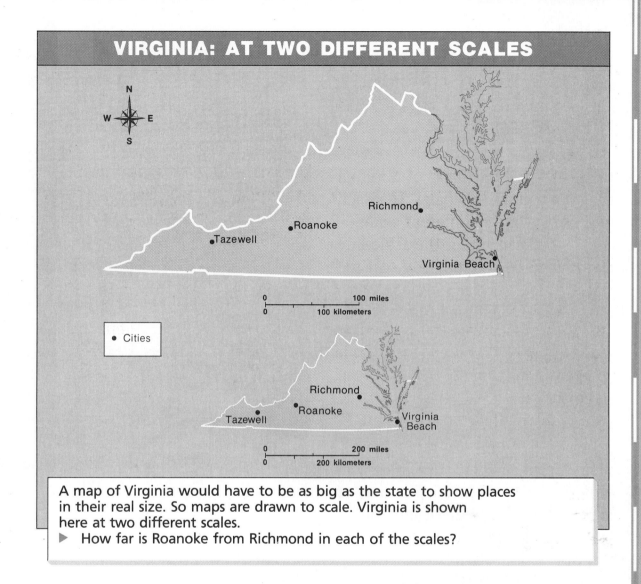

A map of Virginia would have to be as big as the state to show places in their real size. So maps are drawn to scale. Virginia is shown here at two different scales.

▶ How far is Roanoke from Richmond in each of the scales?

It allows us to tell the real distance from one place to another.

"Pretend you are high above a football field." She drew a picture on the chalkboard that looked like the drawing on page 26. This drawing was made to a scale in which 1 inch stands for 20 yards. The drawing of the field is 6 inches long. So the total length of the real football field is 120 yards, or six groups of 20 yards. Use a ruler to measure the width of the football field in inches. How many yards does this represent?

D. Virginia and Scale

The scale line on a map shows what distance an inch (or a centimeter) on the map stands for. Maps can be drawn to many different scales.

Aerial photographs let you look down on the earth.
▶ How are aerial photographs and maps alike?

Look at the two maps of Virginia that are shown on page 27. Each map is drawn to a different scale.

Put a ruler under the scale line of the map on the top. You will see that 1 inch stands for about 100 miles. (One centimeter stands for about 63 kilometers.) On this map, how many inches (centimeters) is it in a straight line from Virginia Beach to Tazewell? If you measure correctly, your answer should be about 3 inches (7¾ cm). To find out how many miles 3 inches stands for, you would multiply 3 by 100. The answer is 300 miles. To find out how many kilometers 7¾ centimeters stands for, multiply 7¾ by 63.

Do the same on the other map. Measure the distance from Virginia Beach to Tazewell. The distance on that map is 1½ inches (about 4 centimeters). Multiply 1½ by 200. The answer is 300 miles again. If you use the correct scale, you always find that the distance between two places is the same. Check this by measuring the distance between Richmond and Roanoke on the two maps and by using the two scales.

E. What a Map Shows

Miss Johnson explained that the photograph makes clear an important point about maps. The photograph lets you look down on the land. So does a map. You will be using many maps as you study the geography and history of Virginia. But each time you look at a map, you must ask what its scale is, what symbols it has, and what the symbols mean.

You will find some maps that show the whole world as well as

other maps that show only our own country or our own state of Virginia. These maps differ in scale. How much the maps can show you depends on their scale.

Look back at the map of the world on pages 352 and 353. How big would Virginia be on this map? The answer is that it would be so small that the names of Virginia's cities could not be printed or read.

Then look again at the map of Virginia on page 18. It is large enough to show the names of many cities. But how big would a map of the United States be if it was drawn on this scale? It would cover the area of a chalkboard. And a map of the world on this scale would spread across a classroom floor.

LESSON **4** *REVIEW*

THINK AND WRITE

A. What are some differences between a photograph and a map?

B. What symbol is often used on a map to show a river?

C. Why is it necessary to know a map's scale in order to measure distance correctly?

D. Imagine that 1 inch on a map equals 100 miles (161 km). A state measures 3 inches across on the map. How many miles does this represent?

E. What three things do you need to know to read a map?

SKILLS CHECK

MAP SKILL

Look at the table of map symbols on page 25. Then look at each map in Chapter 1. On a separate sheet of paper, list the names of any items that are found in the map keys but that are not in the table. Draw the symbol next to the name of each item.

MAP SKILLS HANDBOOK REVIEW

USING THE VOCABULARY

sphere   Equator
geography   longitude
boundary   time zone
ocean   symbol
compass rose   scale

On a separate sheet of paper, write the best answer to fill in the blanks in the sentences below. Choose your answers from the vocabulary words above.

1. The line on a map that separates one state from the next state is called a _____.
2. A blue line to show a river is an example of a _____ used on a map.
3. The earth is shaped like a _____.
4. Much of the earth's water is found in _____, which are the largest bodies of water on the earth.
5. The time in California is different from the time in Virginia because California is in a different _____.
6. The _____ of a map tells you how much bigger the real place is than the map.
7. _____ is the study of the earth and of how people use it.
8. To find out where north is on a map, you look at the _____.
9. The imaginary line that runs around the earth is the _____.
10. Lines that run up and down a map are called lines of _____.

REMEMBERING WHAT YOU READ

On a separate sheet of paper, answer the questions in complete sentences.

1. What is the difference between an ocean and a continent?
2. Which continent has no permanent residents?
3. What is another word that can be used for *boundary?*
4. What is the last ocean you would cross if you were to travel to the North Pole?
5. On which continent is the South Pole located?
6. Which two hemispheres are separated by the Equator?
7. On which part of the earth are lines of longitude farthest apart?
8. In which time zone is Virginia?
9. Where on a map would you look to find out what the symbols mean?
10. What does the map scale tell you?

TYING ART TO SOCIAL STUDIES

On a separate sheet of paper, draw a simple map of the neighborhood around your school. Place the school in the middle of your map. Then show the roads, buildings, parks, and any other places of interest that surround it. Be sure to include a map key.

THINKING CRITICALLY

On a separate sheet of paper, answer the following in complete sentences.

1. Why is it important to know where different places are in the world?
2. Why do you think nobody lives in Antarctica all the time?
3. In what ways do maps make people's lives easier?
4. What do you need to know to figure out what time of day it is in other parts of the United States when it is 9 A.M. in Virginia?
5. What would be a good map symbol for a school? What would be a good map symbol for a hospital?

SUMMARIZING THE CHAPTER

On a separate sheet of paper, draw a graphic organizer that is like the one shown here. Copy the information from this graphic organizer to the one you have drawn. Under the main idea for each lesson, write three statements that support it. The first one has been done for you.

CHAPTER THEME

Maps are used for many reasons.

LESSON 1

Maps and globes show where places are on the earth.

1. A map shows the earth on a flat surface.
2. A globe is a model of the earth.
3. The earth has oceans and continents.

LESSON 2

To use a map, you need to understand the lines and symbols on it.

1. _____
2. _____
3. _____

LESSON 3

Lines of longitude and latitude tell about a place's location.

1. _____
2. _____
3. _____

LESSON 4

Maps have symbols and a scale.

1. _____
2. _____
3. _____

▲ Some say that the Blue Ridge Mountain area is one of the most beautiful in the country.

Forests cover much of the state. Forests have helped Virginia's industries grow. ▶

Raising livestock is an important part of Virginia's agricultural industry. ▼

UNIT 1 VIRGINIA: OUR HOME

Virginia is a beautiful and fast-growing state. To understand Virginia today, you need to learn about the land and how Virginians use that land.

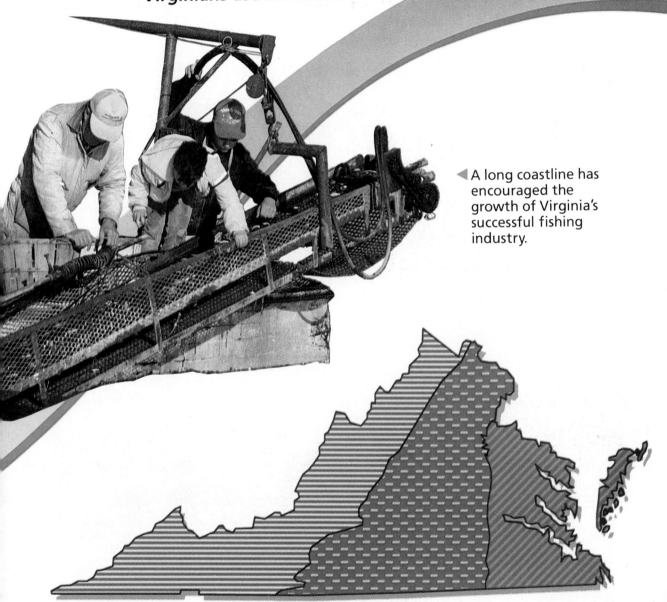

◀ A long coastline has encouraged the growth of Virginia's successful fishing industry.

CHAPTER 1 THE GEOGRAPHY OF VIRGINIA

Virginia is a rich and beautiful state. Each of its three regions has special features. The region in the east is mainly low, flat land. The central region has rolling hills. And the western-most section has spectacular mountains.

Learning About Geography

THINK ABOUT WHAT YOU KNOW

Look through the pictures of Virginia in this book. Make a list of words you would use to describe the land.

STUDY THE VOCABULARY

population
population density
county
urban
rural

relief map
elevation
contour line

FOCUS YOUR READING

What tools are needed to study the geography of Virginia?

A. Questions to Ask

In this book, you will learn many interesting things about Virginia's exciting history. But before you study what happened in the past, you need to know about Virginia's geography. Studying geography helps you understand the past. It enables you to see how the land has affected people's lives. At the same time, you will see how people have used the land.

In order to study the state of Virginia, you must be sure you know where it is located. Look at the map of the United States in the Atlas on pages 354 and 355. How would you describe Virginia's location? You might say that Virginia lies on the East Coast of the United States. You could also say that Virginia lies north of the state of North Carolina.

As you study the geography of your state, you find the answers to many questions. *Where* is this city or that river? *Why* is the location of a certain place important? *What* do people in your community do for a

Farming is important to Virginia's economy. This man is plowing the soil. He is getting ready to plant seeds.
▶ How is the boy helping?

living? *How* do people use the land in Virginia? Learning geography is an important key to understanding the state you live in.

Virginia's location on the coast makes oyster fishing an important industry in the state.
▶ What other industries might be important on the coast?

B. Virginia's People

The study of people is an important part of geography. The number of people living in a place is known as the **population** of that place. The population of Virginia is almost 6 million. Only 11 states in the United States have a higher population than Virginia.

Another term that you need to know is **population density.** Population density tells you how crowded a place is. In order to find out the population density of a place, you divide the number of people who live there by the size, or area, of the land in that place.

As you just learned, the population of Virginia is about 6 million. The size of the state is 40,767 square miles (105,587 sq km). Divide 6,000,000 by 40,767. The answer is about 147. So the population density of Virginia is about 147 people per square mile.

Compared with some other states, Virginia has a fairly high population density. For example, West Virginia's population is about 1,897,000. The land area is about 24,119 square miles (62,468 sq km). If you divide the population by the land area, you get a population density of about 79 people per square mile. So West Virginia's density is less than Virginia's density.

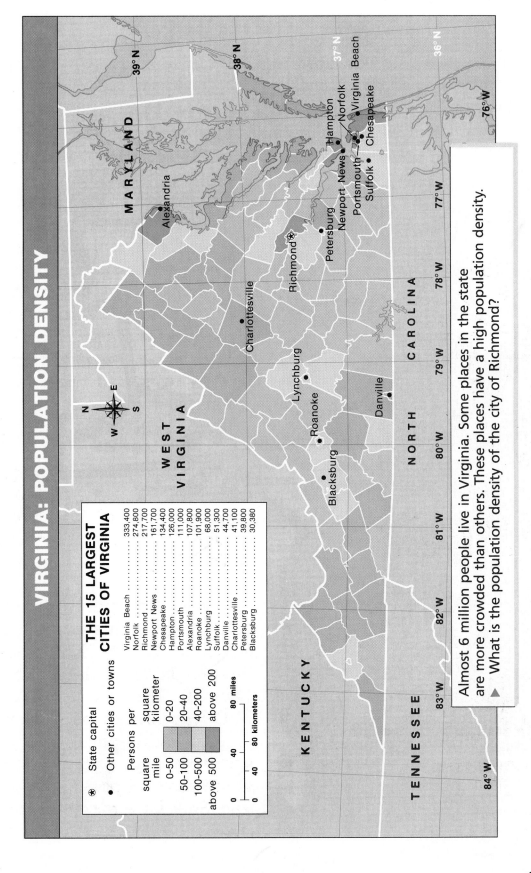

VIRGINIA: POPULATION DENSITY

THE 15 LARGEST CITIES OF VIRGINIA

Virginia Beach	333,400
Norfolk	274,800
Richmond	217,700
Newport News	161,700
Chesapeake	134,400
Hampton	126,000
Portsmouth	111,000
Alexandria	107,800
Roanoke	101,900
Lynchburg	68,000
Suffolk	51,300
Danville	44,700
Charlottesville	41,100
Petersburg	39,800
Blacksburg	30,380

⊛ State capital

• Other cities or towns

Persons per

square mile	square kilometer
0–50	0–20
50–100	20–40
100–500	40–200
above 500	above 200

0   40   80 miles

0   40   80 kilometers

Almost 6 million people live in Virginia. Some places in the state are more crowded than others. These places have a high population density.
▲ What is the population density of the city of Richmond?

35

C. Virginia's 95 Counties

What county do you live in? A county is a part of a state. Virginia is divided into 95 counties. You can find out where your county is by looking at the map below.

Below the county map is a table. A table is a list of information. The table lists each county in alphabetical order. The number next to each county shows where the county is on the map.

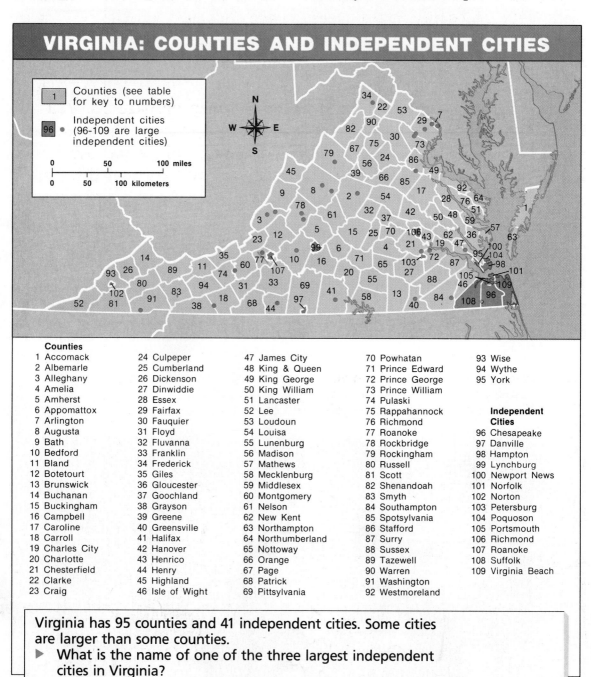

VIRGINIA: COUNTIES AND INDEPENDENT CITIES

Counties

1 Accomack	24 Culpeper	47 James City	70 Powhatan	93 Wise
2 Albemarle	25 Cumberland	48 King & Queen	71 Prince Edward	94 Wythe
3 Alleghany	26 Dickenson	49 King George	72 Prince George	95 York
4 Amelia	27 Dinwiddie	50 King William	73 Prince William	
5 Amherst	28 Essex	51 Lancaster	74 Pulaski	
6 Appomattox	29 Fairfax	52 Lee	75 Rappahannock	**Independent**
7 Arlington	30 Fauquier	53 Loudoun	76 Richmond	**Cities**
8 Augusta	31 Floyd	54 Louisa	77 Roanoke	96 Chesapeake
9 Bath	32 Fluvanna	55 Lunenburg	78 Rockbridge	97 Danville
10 Bedford	33 Franklin	56 Madison	79 Rockingham	98 Hampton
11 Bland	34 Frederick	57 Mathews	80 Russell	99 Lynchburg
12 Botetourt	35 Giles	58 Mecklenburg	81 Scott	100 Newport News
13 Brunswick	36 Gloucester	59 Middlesex	82 Shenandoah	101 Norfolk
14 Buchanan	37 Goochland	60 Montgomery	83 Smyth	102 Norton
15 Buckingham	38 Grayson	61 Nelson	84 Southampton	103 Petersburg
16 Campbell	39 Greene	62 New Kent	85 Spotsylvania	104 Poquoson
17 Caroline	40 Greensville	63 Northampton	86 Stafford	105 Portsmouth
18 Carroll	41 Halifax	64 Northumberland	87 Surry	106 Richmond
19 Charles City	42 Hanover	65 Nottoway	88 Sussex	107 Roanoke
20 Charlotte	43 Henrico	66 Orange	89 Tazewell	108 Suffolk
21 Chesterfield	44 Henry	67 Page	90 Warren	109 Virginia Beach
22 Clarke	45 Highland	68 Patrick	91 Washington	
23 Craig	46 Isle of Wight	69 Pittsylvania	92 Westmoreland	

Virginia has 95 counties and 41 independent cities. Some cities are larger than some counties.
▶ What is the name of one of the three largest independent cities in Virginia?

Now look at the table on pages 382–383. This table also lists the counties in Virginia. But it tells a great deal more about them than the list below the map did. For example, it gives the size, or area, and the population of each county. It also gives the name of the county seat. The county seat is the center of local government in your county.

Find your own county on the table and read the information about it. In the column called "Area Rank," the county that is number 1 is the largest in area. It is Pittsylvania County. Which county has the largest population? To find out, look in the column called "Population Rank." Fairfax County is number 1. That means Fairfax County has more people than any other county.

D. Virginia's Cities and Towns

The map on page 35 shows the population density for each Virginia county. Along with the map is a table listing the 15 largest cities in the state. Which of the counties have the most people per square mile? The counties that are the most crowded contain large cities.

Look again at the population density map on page 35. You will notice that much of the state has a low number of people per square mile. You will see that these areas with low density do not contain any large cities.

Knowing these facts, you can generalize. That means that you can sum up this information in a short statement. Counties that have many people per square mile have large

When more people move to a town, they bring more cars to the area. Traffic and parking in these towns can become a problem.
▶ Why are traffic and parking regulations important?

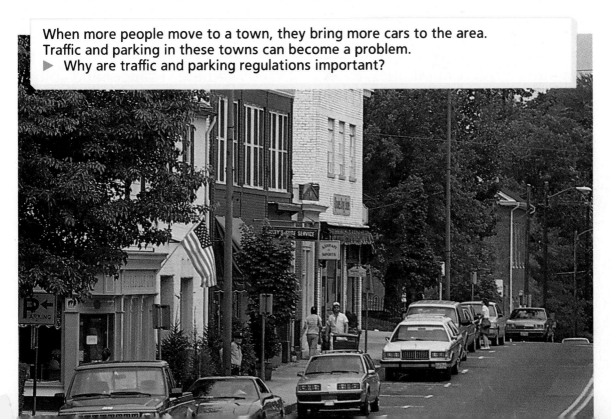

As Virginia's cities continue to grow, more roads are needed for the increased traffic.
▶ What road-building equipment do you see?

cities, or **urban** areas. The counties that have few people per square mile are **rural.** Rural areas are made up of farms and small communities. Later, you will find out why these differences occur within Virginia.

Forty-one Virginia cities are called independent cities because they are not really part of any county. Some independent cities have more people living in them than some counties do. Also, some independent cities are as large as some counties, as you can see on the map on page 36.

E. Drawings That Explain Things

Learning from Graphs Do you remember Carlos, the boy who used a map to see where his sister would be living? Carlos's mother helped him learn how to use a map to find out exactly where France and other places are located. Maps show where things are. They help you compare different places. They also help you measure distance.

But you can use many other drawings to study geography. You just used tables to find out about the places, the size, and the population of Virginia.

You can also use another tool to learn about Virginia. That tool is called a bar graph. Look at the bar graph below. This shows the size of Virginia and some nearby states. Each state has its own bar. On the left is a scale of numbers. These numbers tell you the size of states in thousands of square miles.

Comparing Populations

A bar graph can be used to compare other things. For example, in the bar graph on the right, the bars show the number of people in Virginia and its neighboring states. The scale on the left tells how many millions of people live in each state. Which state has the most people? Which state has the fewest people? Is it Virginia? The answer is no. The bar graph shows that West Virginia, Ken-

This bar graph shows the size of Virginia and nearby states.
► Which states are smaller than Virginia?

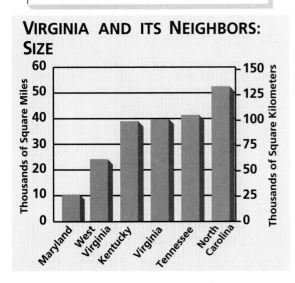

VIRGINIA AND ITS NEIGHBORS: SIZE

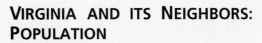

VIRGINIA AND ITS NEIGHBORS: POPULATION

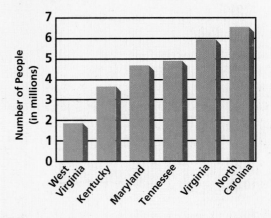

This graph shows the population of Virginia and nearby states.
► About how many people live in Virginia?

tucky, Maryland, and Tennessee have fewer people than Virginia.

You can also use pictures, lines, and circles to help explain facts about people and places and to compare different things.

For instance, since 1790 the population of Virginia has grown dramatically. How could you show this? You could show each year's population with little drawings of people. This is called a pictograph. Look at the pictograph on page 40. Each drawing stands for a half-million (500,000) people. The numbers on the left show the years. For 1850, there is a drawing of two people. They stand for 2 × 500,000, or

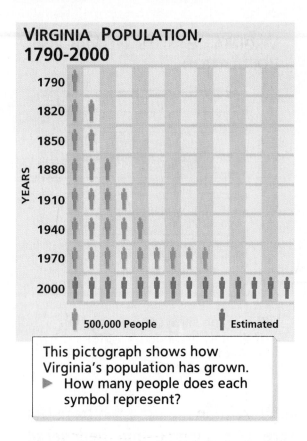

VIRGINIA POPULATION, 1790-2000

YEARS
1790
1820
1850
1880
1910
1940
1970
2000

500,000 People • Estimated

This pictograph shows how Virginia's population has grown.
▶ How many people does each symbol represent?

1,000,000, people. How many people were living in Virginia in 1940? How many people were living in Virginia in 1970?

Another way you could show this information is with a line graph. People often use line graphs to show how something changes over the years. On the right is a line graph that shows the change in Virginia's population between 1790 and 2000. The scale on the left shows the number of people in millions. Along the bottom of the graph, the years are shown. This graph can show you when the population of Virginia grew most rapidly. That would be

when the line from one year to the next year on the graph is the steepest. When does this happen? It is between 1970 and 2000.

There is one more kind of graph. Have you ever cut a pie into slices? That is how a pie graph, or circle graph, works. It shows the parts of a whole. It is a circle divided into slices of differing sizes. Look at the pie graphs on page 41. The one on the left shows where the people of Virginia live. You can see that many more people live in cities than in farming areas. The pie graph on the right shows how the land in Virginia is used. The largest slice stands for forests.

This line graph shows how much Virginia's population has grown since 1790.
▶ What is the meaning of the dotted line on the graph?

VIRGINIA POPULATION, 1790-2000

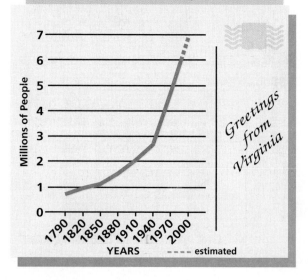

Greetings from Virginia

YEARS - - - - estimated

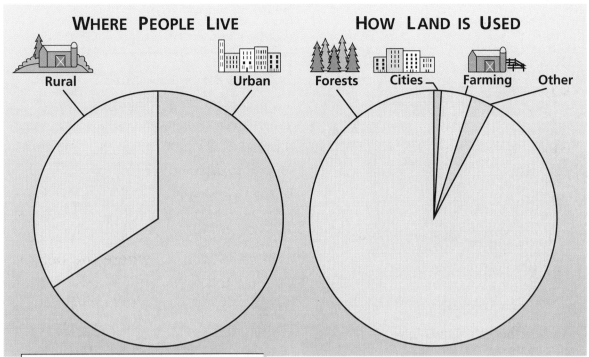

WHERE PEOPLE LIVE

Rural
Urban

HOW LAND IS USED

Forests
Cities
Farming
Other

These pie graphs show where Virginians live and how they use the land.

▶ What percent of the land of Virginia is used for farming?

F. Relief Maps

A Special Map You have already studied several types of maps in this book. Would any of these maps be able to tell you how high or low a certain place is? No. For that, you would need a special kind of map. You would need a **relief map.** Relief maps show how high or how low places are. The relief map on page 42 shows the heights of different parts of Virginia.

From what point is the height of a place measured? Every valley, hill, and mountain is measured from the same base. That base is the level of the sea. The height of a place above the level of the sea is known as its **elevation.** Sea level is 0 feet or 0 meters. We say that a place is so many feet (or meters) above sea level. For example, the highest point in Virginia is Mount Rogers. The elevation of Mount Rogers is 5,729 feet (1,746 m) above sea level.

The relief map on page 42 shows different heights by the use of different colors. The lines that separate one height from another height are called **contour lines.** A contour line is a line that is drawn through all of the places having the same height, or elevation.

VIRGINIA: RELIEF

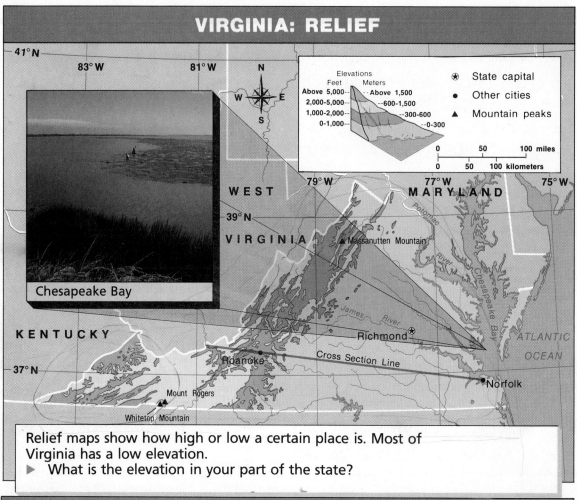

Chesapeake Bay

Relief maps show how high or low a certain place is. Most of Virginia has a low elevation.
▶ What is the elevation in your part of the state?

VIRGINIA: A CROSS SECTION FROM NORFOLK TO THE APPALACHIAN MOUNTAINS

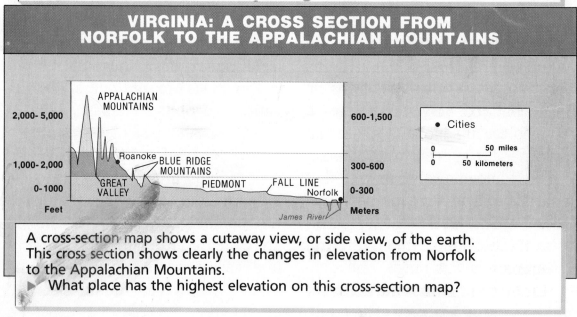

A cross-section map shows a cutaway view, or side view, of the earth. This cross section shows clearly the changes in elevation from Norfolk to the Appalachian Mountains.
▶ What place has the highest elevation on this cross-section map?

Look at the drawing of an island on this page. It rises to more than 300 feet (91 m) above sea level. The line marked "100 feet" connects all the points on the island that are 100 feet (30 m) above sea level. This line marks the 100-foot (30-m) contour. The next line marks the 200-foot (61-m) contour.

Contour Lines Below the drawing is a sketch of the contour lines as they would appear from directly overhead. This drawing also shows the different heights of individual points on the island. This type of map can be used to find the height of any place above sea level.

In the third drawing, color is used to make the contour lines clearer. All the land that is below 100 feet (30 m) is shaded green. All the land that is between 100 feet (30 m) and 200 feet (61 m) is colored orange, and so on.

Virginia's Elevation Look again at the relief map of Virginia on page 42. Where is the lowest land? What is it colored? How high above sea level is it? You will find the lowest land in east and central Virginia. It is between 0 and 1,000 feet (0 to 305 m) above sea level. Most of Virginia has an elevation in this range. The highest land lies in the mountains in the western part of the state. The cross-

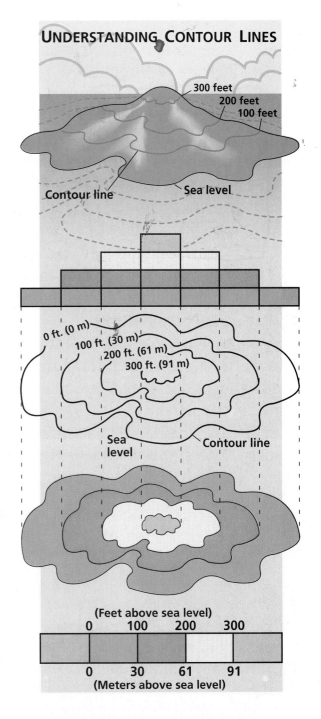

UNDERSTANDING CONTOUR LINES

300 feet
200 feet
100 feet
Contour line
Sea level

0 ft. (0 m)
100 ft. (30 m)
200 ft. (61 m)
300 ft. (91 m)
Sea level
Contour line

(Feet above sea level)
0   100   200   300

0   30   61   91
(Meters above sea level)

These drawings use contour lines to show an island's elevation.
▶ What color is used to show the land with the highest elevation?

section map on page 42 shows very clearly the range of elevations across the state of Virginia.

Suppose that you wanted to climb to the top of the island shown in the drawing on page 43. There are two possible ways to the top. One way is to go up the left side. The other way is to go up the right side. Which side will you take?

The way on the left looks shorter. You might want to take that one. But first you should look more closely at the contour lines.

When you look at the contour lines of the island as seen from overhead, you notice that the contour lines on the left lie close together. That means the land gets higher quickly. The climb would be very steep. The contour lines are much farther apart on the right. The land rises more slowly. That would make this climb a very gentle one. Which is better: a short, steep climb, or a longer and more gentle one? That depends on you!

A hiker in the Blue Ridge Mountains admires the view.
▶ What can the hiker see off in the distance?

LESSON *1* REVIEW

THINK AND WRITE

A. Why do you study geography?
B. How do you find the population density of a place?
C. How many counties are there in the state of Virginia?
D. What is the difference between urban and rural areas?
E. If you wanted to show how much coal was produced in Virginia from 1950 to 1980, what type of graph would you use?

F. Why is every valley, hill, and mountain measured from the level of the sea?

SKILLS CHECK

WRITING SKILL

Look carefully at the bar graphs on page 39. Write a sentence about the neighboring states that are larger than Virginia. Write a sentence about the neighboring states that have a population greater than Virginia.

The Tidewater Region

THINK ABOUT WHAT YOU KNOW
Have you ever been to the beach in Virginia? What is the land like near the beach?

STUDY THE VOCABULARY

landform	mainland
coastal plain	peninsula
tide	wetland
bay	peat

FOCUS YOUR READING
What is the physical geography of Virginia's Tidewater Region?

A. Virginia's Regions

Different Areas Virginia can be divided into three main regions. A region is an area that has something special about it that makes it different from other areas. Virginia's three regions are based on the different landforms that are found in the state. Landforms are kinds of land surfaces formed by nature. Steeply rising pieces of land, called mountains, and low-lying land, called valleys, are just two kinds of landforms.

The three main landform regions of Virginia are called the Tidewater Region, the Piedmont Region, and the Ridge and Valley Region. The map on page 46 shows these regions. Virginia's Tidewater Region is part of the Atlantic Coastal Plain. A coastal plain is a large area of flat or gently rolling land that is bordered by a large area of water. Look up *coastal plain* in the Geographical Dictionary on pages 370–373. This plain stretches along the East Coast of the United States. The Piedmont Region has many rolling hills. The Ridge and Valley Region is the most rugged area of the state. This region has many rocky peaks.

Changing Tides In this lesson, you will learn many important facts about the Tidewater Region. Do you

The state of Virginia has areas where elevations are low.
► Which areas of Virginia have low elevation?

45

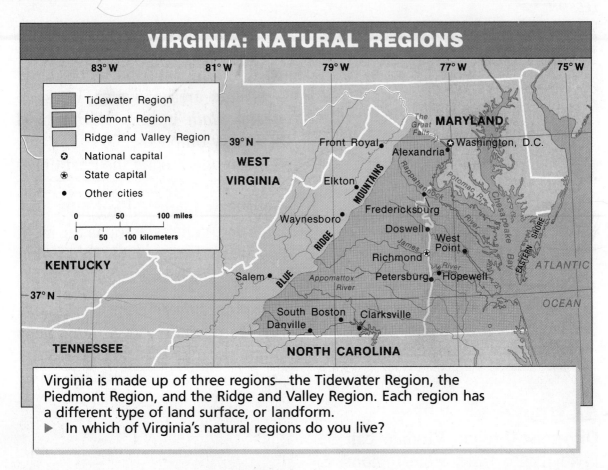

VIRGINIA: NATURAL REGIONS

Legend:
- Tidewater Region
- Piedmont Region
- Ridge and Valley Region
- ◇ National capital
- ✪ State capital
- • Other cities

0 50 100 miles
0 50 100 kilometers

Virginia is made up of three regions—the Tidewater Region, the Piedmont Region, and the Ridge and Valley Region. Each region has a different type of land surface, or landform.
▶ In which of Virginia's natural regions do you live?

know why the eastern part of Virginia is called the Tidewater Region? It is because this area is affected by the **tides.** Tides cause the ocean to rise and fall. They also cause bodies of water connected to the ocean to rise and fall.

B. Chesapeake Bay

The Bay Area The largest body of water found in the Tidewater Region is the Chesapeake (CHES uh peek) Bay. A **bay** is part of a large body of water that reaches into the land. Find the Chesapeake Bay on the map on page 47. You can see on the map that the Chesapeake Bay is part of the Atlantic Ocean.

You can also see on the map how the Chesapeake Bay separates the Tidewater Region into two parts. These parts are the Eastern Shore and the **mainland.** The mainland is the main part of Virginia. Find the mainland on the map. You can see how several rivers cut through the mainland as they flow into the bay. The Potomac (puh TOH muk), Rappahannock (rap uh HAN uk), York, and James rivers cut the mainland into **peninsulas.** A peninsula is a piece of land that has water nearly

THE TIDEWATER REGION

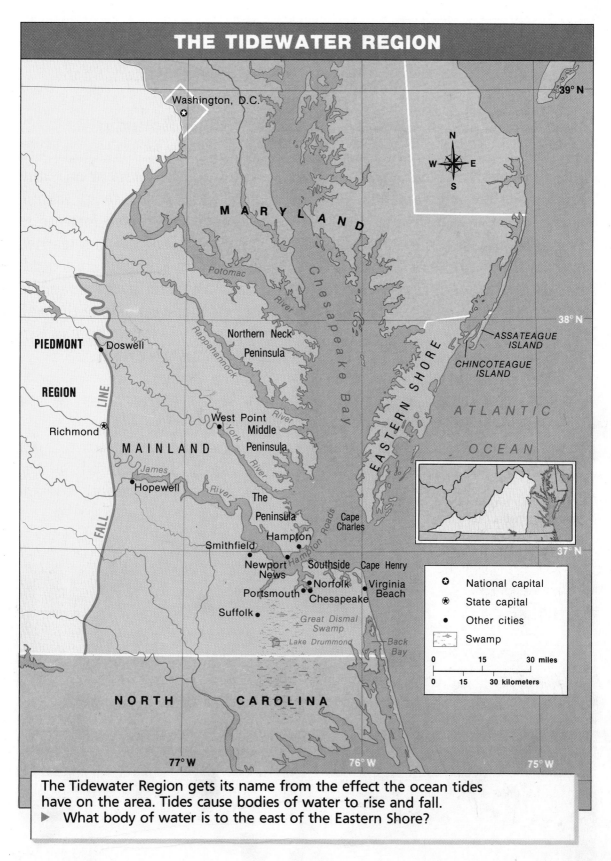

39° N

N
W E
S

MARYLAND

Potomac River

Chesapeake Bay

PIEDMONT
• Doswell

38° N

ASSATEAGUE
ISLAND

CHINCOTEAGUE
ISLAND

Northern Neck
Peninsula

Rappahannock

REGION

LINE

EASTERN SHORE

ATLANTIC

• Richmond

West Point
Middle
Peninsula

York River

MAINLAND

OCEAN

James River

• Hopewell

The
Peninsula

FALL

Cape
Charles

37° N

• Smithfield

Hampton

Newport
News

Southside   Cape Henry

Portsmouth

• Norfolk
Chesapeake

Virginia
Beach

• Suffolk

*Great Dismal
Swamp*

Lake Drummond

*Back
Bay*

✪	National capital
✪	State capital
•	Other cities
▭	Swamp

0   15   30 miles

0   15   30 kilometers

NORTH   CAROLINA

77° W

76° W

75° W

The Tidewater Region gets its name from the effect the ocean tides
have on the area. Tides cause bodies of water to rise and fall.
▶ What body of water is to the east of the Eastern Shore?

47

all the way around it. It is connected to the main part of the land.

Virginia's Peninsulas How many peninsulas can you count on Virginia's mainland? If you counted three peninsulas, you are correct. One is the Northern Neck Peninsula, between the Potomac and the Rappahannock rivers. One is the Middle Peninsula, between the Rappahannock and the York rivers. One is simply called The Peninsula, between the York and James rivers. The area that is south of the James River is called Southside.

The Eastern Shore is also a peninsula. So you might say that there are really *four* peninsulas in the Tidewater Region. There are also some islands. An island has water all the way around it. The islands are off the coast of the Eastern Shore.

C. The Pony Roundup

The sun was shining brightly as Ms. Knight parked her car on Chincoteague (SHING kuh teeg) Island. Kelly Knight had looked forward to this day for weeks. She had learned about the Pony Roundup in geography class. But she never imagined that her mother would drive them all the way to the Eastern Shore of Virginia to attend the event.

"Mom, where do we go?" Kelly's sister, Marci, asked as she got out of the car.

"Let's follow the crowd," her mother said. She pointed to the groups of people walking toward

Each July a pony roundup is held at Chincoteague Island.
▶ Why does this event draw such a large crowd of people?

the water. At the shore, hundreds of people were lined up.

"Look, Mom, there's the water," Kelly said. "The ponies will be led across the water from Assateague (AS uh teeg) Island to Chincoteague Island."

"How do the ponies get in the water?" Marci asked.

"I read that oystermen, crabbers, and fishers pull on high rubber boots and herd the ponies into the water," Ms. Knight replied.

"What happens after they swim across?" Marci asked.

"I know," Kelly shouted. "The ponies are led to an auction where they are sold to people. The ponies that aren't sold are led back to the beach and herded back to Assateague Island."

"How did the ponies get there in the first place?" Marci asked.

"Some people believe that a Spanish ship carrying a few horses sank at sea hundreds of years ago," Kelly said. "The horses that survived somehow found their way to Assateague Island."

"That's an interesting story," Marci said.

"Mom, after the Pony Roundup, can we please go to the fair?" Kelly asked.

"Yes," Ms. Knight said. "I don't want to miss any of the special entertainment that's planned for the festival here this week."

"Look," Kelly yelled, "the ponies are coming."

D. Water, Water Everywhere

For years, the only way to get from the Eastern Shore to the mainland was by ferry. A ferry is a boat that carries people and things across small bodies of water. Farmers on the Eastern Shore once used the ferries to carry their produce to cities on the mainland. Today, refrigerated trucks carry fresh fruits and vegetables across the Chesapeake Bay. They travel through tunnels and over bridges.

If you go from the Eastern Shore to Norfolk across the bay, you will cross over 17 miles (27 km) of road. Part of the road is a bridge

Two tunnels were built for the Chesapeake Bay Bridge-Tunnel.
▶ Why do you think these tunnels were built?

49

above the water. Part of it is a tunnel that goes under the water. Many people worked to build this road, called the Chesapeake Bay Bridge – Tunnel. Now, thousands of people use this great bridge – tunnel to cross the Chesapeake Bay.

A shorter bridge – tunnel in the Tidewater Region crosses Hampton Roads. Hampton Roads is a harbor. A harbor is a protected body of water. Harbors can keep boats safe from bad weather and rough water. Ships from all over the world come into Hampton Roads. Find Hampton Roads on the map on page 47.

There are also smaller harbors in the Tidewater Region. Can you find some of them on the map?

Miles and miles of shoreline are in the Tidewater Region. Shoreline is land that touches a large body of water. Some of the Tidewater shoreline has long, sandy beaches.

Much of the Tidewater shoreline is made up of marshes and swamps. Look up *swamp* in the Geographical Dictionary on pages 370 – 373. This kind of land is often called wetland. Wetland consists of low, flat land where water is always close to the surface.

E. The Great Dismal Swamp

The best example of Tidewater wetland is the Great Dismal Swamp. There are many legends of the Dismal Swamp. A legend is a story handed down through the years. It may be based on a true story, or it may come from someone's imagination. Sometimes there are several versions of the same story. The legend of the Dismal Swamp that you

One legend of the Dismal Swamp tells of two young lovers who died. It is said that their ghosts can still be seen in the swamp.
▶ What is a legend?

are about to read was started in late colonial times.

It is said that a family settled on the land near the Dismal Swamp. The daughter of the family was planning to get married. Suddenly, she got sick and died. The man who loved her missed her so much that he became sick.

The young man convinced himself that the girl he loved still lived. He thought she was waiting for him in the swamp. He went into the swamp and wandered around looking for her.

One night he came to the lake in the middle of the swamp. A firefly was shining its light somewhere over the swamp. The sad young man thought that the light was his lost love. He built a raft so that he might reach the girl.

Suddenly, the wind blew fiercely, causing the raft to break. The young man drowned in the muddy waters. It is said that the couple can be seen paddling in a canoe on the lake, guided by the light of the firefly. Do you think this legend is based on a true story?

The Dismal Swamp is in the southeastern corner of Virginia. This swamp covers about 600 square miles (1,554 sq km). It used to be twice that size, though. It was filled in with dirt so that canals could be

The Dismal Swamp covers about 600 square miles of Virginia.
▶ What does this picture show growing in the swamp?

made. A canal is a waterway that people have dug across the land. It is used for boats to travel through. It can also be used to carry water to people and places that need it.

F. A Trip Through the Great Dismal Swamp

Imagine that you are going on a boat trip with your class through the Dismal Swamp. Your guide says, "We will begin by traveling up the feeder canal that goes to Lake Drummond. The kind of wetland we are passing through is called a swamp. The water here hardly ever drains away. It provides a natural habitat, or home, for many kinds of animals and plants. There are deer, rabbits, raccoons, and muskrats. You might see foxes and bobcats, or even a bear. Many insects, especially mosquitoes, also live in the swamps. Birds, snakes, frogs, and turtles can be found here in great numbers too."

After a few questions from curious students, the guide continues. "Many kinds of wildlife can live in the swamp because there is so much rich plant life. Animals need to eat plants to survive. These wetlands even have as much plant life as fine farmlands do. Whatever you do, don't ever try to stand up in a swamp. If you did, you would sink into a black, sticky soil called **peat.** Peat is made up of partly rotted plants. In some places the peat is as much as 14 feet (4 m) deep."

G. Coastal Cities

Hampton Roads   The Tidewater Region is home to some of Virginia's most populated cities. Some important port cities, such as Norfolk,

Newport News is an important shipbuilding center. It is also a major port for shipping products.
▶ What kind of boat is pushing the barge?

Newport News, Chesapeake, and Portsmouth, are located on Hampton Roads harbor. Find these cities on the map on page 47. What large body of water are they near?

Millions of tons of products and goods are loaded into oceangoing ships in Virginia's ports. Then the ships sail to other ports in the United States and to ports all over the world. The goods and products are sold in other countries as well as in the United States.

All kinds of products also come into these ports from different parts of the world. These products include rubber, paper, and metals. From here they are sent on to other places in the United States.

Many Thousands   Thousands of people in the coastal cities work at many different kinds of shipping jobs. Thousands more people work in the cities' many factories. The nearby city of Hampton also has many factories. Jobs in the fishing and seafood business give work to many people in the coastal cities.

More people live in Virginia Beach than in any other Virginia city. It is a well-known resort, or place where people go for a vacation. Families come from all over to visit Virginia Beach. There are many reasons why Virginia Beach is such a popular vacation spot. People enjoy

Virginia Beach, on the Atlantic Ocean, is a great place for sailing and other water sports.
▶ What are some things to do at the beach?

the beautiful beaches. They like to eat the fine seafood. They like to stay in the pleasant hotels. Many people who live in Virginia Beach have jobs taking care of the visitors.

The Shipyards Norfolk is the second most populated city in Virginia. Thousands of people in Norfolk work for the United States Navy. There are important shipyards in the cities of Norfolk, Hampton, Portsmouth, and Newport News. Shipyards are places where ships are built and repaired. Many people work in these shipyards. They build ships for the United States Navy and also for commercial use. The largest shipyard in the United States is located in Newport News. In addition to shipbuilding, the cities of Norfolk and Portsmouth are major chemical manufacturing centers.

Virginia's coastal cities are very important to the state. They provide many jobs and help Virginia grow.

PLACES OF INTEREST IN THE TIDEWATER REGION

Assateague Island National Seashore	Stratford (Robert E. Lee's birthplace)
Busch Gardens	Virginia Beach
Chincoteague Wildlife Reserve	Virginia Beach Maritime Museum
Colonial Williamsburg	Yorktown Battlefield National Historical Park
Jamestown Festival Park	Chrysler Museum (Norfolk)
Mariner's Museum	Old Town, Alexandria
Pamunkey Indian Reservation	

Virginia's first settlements and early history were centered in the Tidewater Region.
▶ What are two places on this list that are historic sites?

LESSON 2 REVIEW

THINK AND WRITE

A. How are Virginia's three natural regions divided?

B. What are some of the main differences between a peninsula and an island?

C. What story do some people tell to explain the ponies' existence on Assateague Island?

D. Why was the Chesapeake Bay Bridge–Tunnel built?

E. Why do people build canals?

F. Why do many kinds of wildlife live in swamps?

G. Why are Virginia's port cities important to the state?

SKILLS CHECK

MAP SKILL

Turn to the map on page 47. What peninsula is Chincoteague Island located near?

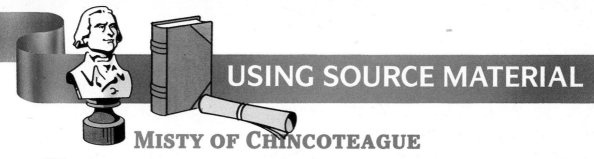

MISTY OF CHINCOTEAGUE

Fiction consists of stories that writers make up. The people in the stories usually do not exist in real life. Sometimes, however, the people take part in real events. When you read stories like this, you can learn about the event. For example, if you read *Misty of Chincoteague,* you can learn about an event that takes place every year in Virginia. That event is the roundup and sale of wild ponies in Chincoteague.

Slowly and dejectedly [sadly] the wild ponies paraded through the main streets of Chincoteague. Only the Phantom's colt seemed happy with her lot. She could smell her [mother] close by. Her stomach was stretched tight with milk. She was full of sleep. She kicked her heels sideways, dancing along, letting out little whinnies of joy. . . .

All up and down the streets the people came spilling out of their houses, shouting to one another as they recognized some mare or stallion from previous roundups. . . .

Through the shouting, elbowing crowd, the slow parade went on — past stores and restaurants, past the white frame hotel, past the red brick firehouse which the colts of other years had paid for. . . .

Understanding Source Material

On a separate sheet of paper, answer the questions in complete sentences.

1. Where were the horses being led?
2. Why did the people come out to watch the ponies parade by?
3. What was the money from the past sale of horses used to pay for?

LESSON **3**

The Piedmont Region

THINK ABOUT WHAT YOU KNOW
Have you ever traveled to Virginia's state capital or any other places in central Virginia?

STUDY THE VOCABULARY
Fall Line   **plateau**
rapids   **gap**

FOCUS YOUR READING
What is the physical geography of Virginia's Piedmont Region?

A. The Fall Line

Rushing Water The western edge of the Tidewater Region is formed by the Fall Line. The Fall Line is a line of small waterfalls and rapids. Rapids are places in rivers or streams where the water flows very quickly and roughly. The Fall Line is formed by these rivers and streams flowing from the older, harder rocks on the western side to the softer rocks on the eastern side. The flowing streams erode, or wash away, the softer rocks of the coastal plain. This erosion causes the rivers and streams to fall, or drop, 40 to 70 feet (12 to 21 m) at the Fall Line.

   The land to the west of the Fall Line is called the Piedmont Region. *Piedmont* is a French word meaning "foot of the mountain." The land of the Piedmont Region is higher than the land of the Tidewater Region.

At the Fall Line If you travel west on any of the rivers in the Tidewater Region, you will come to the waterfalls and rapids of the Fall Line. Years ago, many people traveled by boat to the Fall Line on their way to the western parts of Virginia. They were moving there to live.

There are many waterfalls and rapids at the western edge of the Tidewater Region.
▶ What is this edge called?

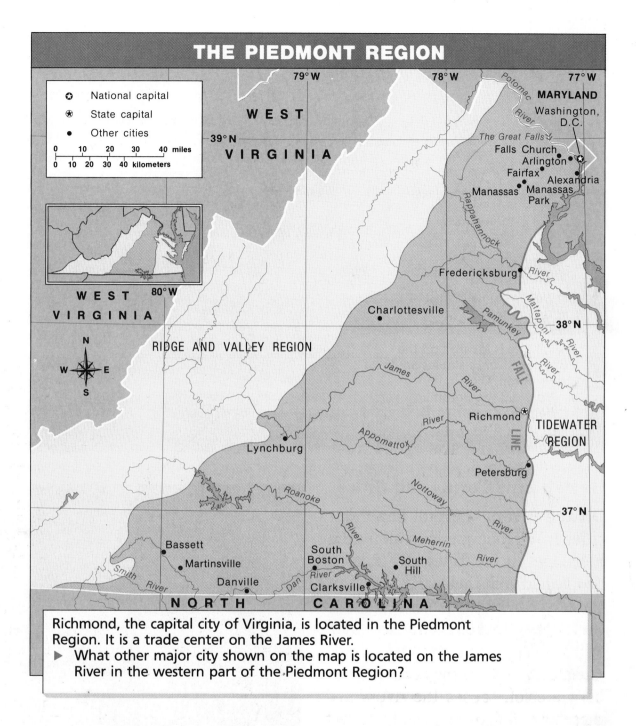

THE PIEDMONT REGION

MARYLAND

Washington, D.C.

- ☉ National capital
- ✪ State capital
- • Other cities

0 10 20 30 40 miles
0 10 20 30 40 kilometers

WEST VIRGINIA

WEST VIRGINIA

The Great Falls

Falls Church
Arlington
Fairfax
Manassas   Manassas Park
Alexandria

Fredericksburg

Charlottesville

RIDGE AND VALLEY REGION

Richmond

TIDEWATER REGION

Lynchburg

Petersburg

Bassett

Martinsville

South Boston

South Hill

Danville

Clarksville

N O R T H   C A R O L I N A

Potomac River

Rappahannock

Pamunkey

Mattaponi River

James River

Appomattox River

FALL LINE

Nottoway River

Roanoke

Meherrin River

Smith River

Dan River

Richmond, the capital city of Virginia, is located in the Piedmont Region. It is a trade center on the James River.
▶ What other major city shown on the map is located on the James River in the western part of the Piedmont Region?

When they reached the rapids and waterfalls on the rivers, they found that they could no longer use their large boats. The boats could not get through the rough waters. The people had to go around the rapids and waterfalls by land. Then, when they were past the rapids or waterfalls, they could continue their journey on the river.

Alexandria is located on the Potomac River, six miles south of Washington, D.C.
▶ How did the Potomac River help the growth of Alexandria?

B. Fall Line Towns and Cities

On the Rivers Several important cities in Virginia grew up along the Fall Line. In the Tidewater Region people had built their early towns on waterways. As they moved west, they also settled on waterways. The Fall Line cities of Alexandria, Fredericksburg, Richmond, and Petersburg are all found on rivers. Find these four Fall Line cities on the map on page 57.

Oceangoing ships could come up the rivers as far as the Fall Line. These ships brought goods from distant places. In the Fall Line towns,

the ships could trade these goods for goods made in Virginia to take back with them. Therefore, cities along the Fall Line became major transportation centers. Transportation is the moving of people and goods from one place to another. Farm products from the Piedmont Region could easily be shipped east on the rivers. Many small towns grew into large cities.

Growing Cities   Some Fall Line cities began as places where tobacco was stored in warehouses before it was shipped down the rivers. A warehouse is a building in which goods or products are stored.

Oceangoing ships could travel up the rivers to the Fall Line.
▶ How did this help the growth of towns along the Fall Line?

Near Richmond's modern skyscrapers stand old cobblestone buildings like these.
▶ How was Richmond discovered?

Another reason for the growth of cities along the Fall Line was the fast-moving rivers and streams. The power of the water could turn waterwheels, and mills could be built to grind grain or cut logs.

C. Richmond, the State Capital

Richmond has not always been the capital of Virginia. From 1699 to 1780, the state capital was located in Williamsburg.

Richmond began as a small trading town at the Fall Line on the James River. It was discovered in 1607 by an English sea captain named Christopher Newport who was exploring the river. He had traveled up the river from Jamestown and soon came to the falls of the James River. There, he saw the small island that would one day be part of Virginia's capital.

The town of Richmond grew slowly at first. In 1742 only 250 people lived there. When it became the capital, 684 people were living there. Today, Richmond is a growing city. It is a modern city with a population of over 210,000. Richmond is the center of Virginia's state government. The governor lives there. State lawmakers meet there to make laws and to govern the state.

Richmond is a center of trade, industry, and business. Many kinds of goods are made there. Richmond is also an education center.

Since the city was settled, it has been a transportation center. Oceangoing ships can go up the James River as far as Richmond. Cars, trucks, and buses move in and through Richmond on many good highways. Trains carry people and goods to and from the city. Richmond International Airport has grown rapidly to meet the needs of the capital city.

When Richmond became the capital of Virginia, only 684 people lived in that city. The state capitol was built in 1788.
► How is Richmond important to the state?

D. The Piedmont Plateau

The Piedmont Region to the west of the Fall Line is a plateau. A plateau is a large, raised, level piece of land. The Piedmont Plateau is Virginia's largest natural region. The Piedmont has an elevation of about 850 feet (259 m).

Although a plateau is usually level, much of the land in the Piedmont has beautiful rolling hills. Rivers and streams that cut across the Piedmont Plateau have helped to form those hills. Over millions of years, Piedmont rivers have carved into and washed away the land through which they flowed. Some of the rivers have caused valleys to form. A valley is a long, low area either between hills or mountains or along a river. The best way to see and feel the rolling hills of the Piedmont is to ride on the roads of the region that go up over the hills and down into the valleys.

E. Piedmont Towns and Cities

Special Reasons In the Piedmont Region, towns and cities grew up where they did for special reasons. Some towns and cities grew up as trading centers on the roads leading to the major gaps, or openings, through the Blue Ridge Mountains. Charlottesville, Lynchburg, and Martinsville are some of these

The Piedmont Plateau covers about one third of Virginia.
► How would you describe the land of the Piedmont Region of Virginia?

cities. Many roads came together at those places. People would stop there on their journey west. Traveling through the gaps was much easier and faster than going over the higher parts of the mountains.

Surrounding Washington The northern part of the Piedmont Region has a very large population. It is part of the urban area that surrounds Washington, D.C. In Virginia, the area includes the cities of Alexandria, Arlington, Fairfax, Falls Church, Manassas, Manassas Park, and Fredericksburg. That area has grown primarily because of the increase in national government jobs and government-related activities.

This aerial view shows northern Virginia and Washington, D.C.
► Where is the Potomac River in this picture?

F. A Piedmont Legend

Justin and his Uncle Evan left their cabin and headed toward the southern tip of Fairy Stone State Park. It was a beautiful Sunday morning in June. Justin and his uncle had enjoyed the week that they had spent in the foothills of the Blue Ridge Mountains.

"Uncle Evan, do you know the fairy stone legend?" Justin asked.

"I know some parts of the legend," Evan answered. "But you'll get the full story from a guide on the fairy stone walk we're going on."

After they had joined the group standing in the woods, the guide introduced herself as Belinda. She took a small, six-sided dark brown crystal out of her pocket. "This is a fairy stone," Belinda said. "These crystals were formed by the folding and crumpling of the earth's crust during the formation of the nearby mountains. The stones commonly occur in pairs, with two or more crystals growing together."

"Is it true that some people think the stones have special powers?" a young woman asked the tour guide.

"Yes," Belinda replied. "In fact, some people believe that the cross-shaped stones protect the wearer against witchcraft, accidents, and disasters of all kinds."

"Does the legend say that?" Justin asked.

"No, it doesn't. But the fairy stone legend is very mysterious," Belinda answered. "Let me tell you all about it right now."

She began, "Hundreds of years before the great Indian Chief Powhatan ruled, fairies danced near a spring. One day, a messenger arrived from a city far away. The messenger brought news of the death of Jesus Christ. When the fairies heard the sad story, they cried. As their tears fell on the ground, they crystallized into stones. Then when the fairies disappeared from the enchanted place, the land near the spring and valley was covered with these magical stones."

"Are there still fairy stones here today?" an elderly man asked the tour guide.

"You can see for yourself," Belinda said. "Because now I am going to take you to that magical spot."

There are many historic homes and battlefields in Virginia's Piedmont Region.
► Which of these have you visited?

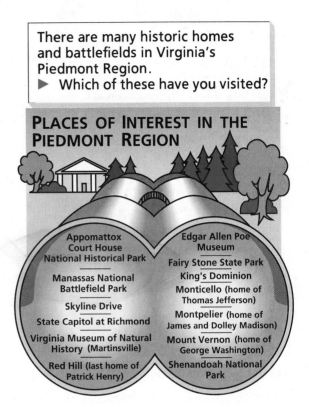

PLACES OF INTEREST IN THE PIEDMONT REGION

Appomattox Court House National Historical Park

Manassas National Battlefield Park

Skyline Drive

State Capitol at Richmond

Virginia Museum of Natural History (Martinsville)

Red Hill (last home of Patrick Henry)

Edgar Allen Poe Museum

Fairy Stone State Park

King's Dominion

Monticello (home of Thomas Jefferson)

Montpelier (home of James and Dolley Madison)

Mount Vernon (home of George Washington)

Shenandoah National Park

LESSON 3 REVIEW

THINK AND WRITE

A. How did settlers traveling west on the rivers get around the rapids and waterfalls?

B. Why did cities build up along the Fall Line?

C. What is one thing Richmond is known for?

D. How would you describe the Piedmont Plateau?

E. Why were some cities started at gaps in the Blue Ridge Mountains?

F. Do you think that the legend of the fairy stones is a true story or an imagined story?

SKILLS CHECK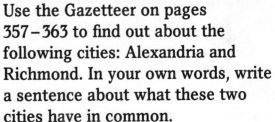

WRITING SKILL

Use the Gazetteer on pages 357–363 to find out about the following cities: Alexandria and Richmond. In your own words, write a sentence about what these two cities have in common.

The Ridge and Valley Region

THINK ABOUT WHAT YOU KNOW

Describe a mountain you have seen in person or in a picture.

STUDY THE VOCABULARY

ridge   stalactite
limestone   stalagmite

FOCUS YOUR READING

What is the physical geography of the Ridge and Valley Region in Virginia?

A. Virginia's Mountains

The Westernmost Region The land to the west of the Piedmont Region is called the Ridge and Valley Region. A ridge is a line of hills or mountains. The valleys are the land between the hills and mountains. Look up *valley* in the Geographical Dictionary on pages 370–373. Find the Ridge and Valley Region on the map on page 65. It is wide in the south and narrow in the north.

The region contains two main lines of mountains. The first high mountain ridge that you reach as you travel west is called the Blue Ridge. It stretches from Pennsylvania to Georgia. When you look at these mountains from afar, they look blue. That is how they got their name.

Blue Ridge Mountains   In Virginia, the Blue Ridge Mountains are about 3,000 to 4,500 feet (914 to 1,372 m) above sea level. A few points reach over 5,000 feet (1,524 m). The highest mountain peak in the state is in the southern part of the Blue Ridge Mountains. This peak is called Mount Rogers. Mount Rogers is found near the North Carolina border in Grayson County. Can you find Grayson County on the map on page 36? Mount Rogers is 5,729 feet (1,746 m) high.

The Blue Ridge Mountains run through Virginia, North Carolina, and Georgia.
▶ How do you think these mountains got their name?

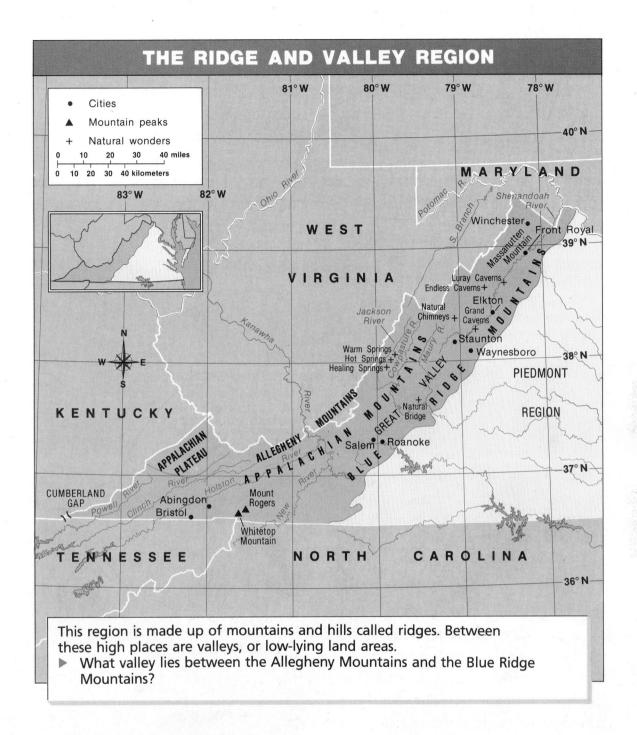

THE RIDGE AND VALLEY REGION

Cities •
Mountain peaks ▲
Natural wonders +

This region is made up of mountains and hills called ridges. Between these high places are valleys, or low-lying land areas.
▶ What valley lies between the Allegheny Mountains and the Blue Ridge Mountains?

Because the Blue Ridge is such a long ridge, people have had to find ways to travel across it. Most early roads and railroads went through the gaps in the ridge.

On top of the Blue Ridge Mountains is the Blue Ridge Parkway. This parkway was built by the United States government. It largely follows the high ridges of the Blue

Ridge Mountains. Some people say the Blue Ridge Parkway is one of the most beautiful stretches of road in the world. The land has been left as natural as possible.

The Blue Ridge Mountains are also well known for the Appalachian (ap uh LAY chun) Trail. The Appalachian Trail is a hiking trail that is about 2,000 miles (3,218 km) long. The Appalachian Trail begins in the state of Maine and follows the high mountains all the way south to the state of Georgia. Some people have hiked along the whole length of this long trail. Do you know anyone who has hiked along the Appalachian Trail in Virginia?

The Blue Ridge Parkway is at the top of the mountains. Historic farmhouses can be seen along this road.
▶ Who built the Blue Ridge Parkway?

The Appalachian Trail is the world's longest marked path. It is a fine hiking trail.
▶ Where does it begin and end?

The Appalachian Trail gets its name from the Appalachian Mountains, which stretch from Canada to Alabama. All of Virginia's mountains, including the Blue Ridge Mountains, are part of the Appalachians. The Appalachians are a large North American mountain range.

Allegheny Mountains The second main line of mountains is the Allegheny (al uh GAY nee) Mountains. They are west of the Blue Ridge Mountains. The flatter land that lies between these two mountain ranges is the location of several river valleys. This land is called the Valley of Virginia, or the Great Valley.

Shenandoah Valley Different parts of the Great Valley are called by special names. The largest of these valleys is the beautiful Shenandoah Valley. No one knows exactly how it got its name. Some people believe it is named after the lost Indian tribe, the Senedos. And no one is sure what the name means. Some believe it means "river through the spruces" or "river of high mountains." Its most popular meaning is "daughter of the stars."

Running down the middle of the Shenandoah Valley is a long mountain ridge called Massanutten (mas uh NUT un) Mountain. Massanutten Mountain lies between the two branches, or forks, of the Shenandoah River. Every winter, many people come to Massanutten Mountain to ski.

Have you ever heard the traditional folk song about the Shenandoah River? It follows here.

Oh, Shenandoah, I long to hear you,
Far away, you rolling river!
Oh, Shenandoah, I long to hear you
Away, I'm bound away
'Cross the wide Missouri. . . .

Oh, Shenandoah, I'm bound to leave you,
Far away, you rolling river!
Oh, Shenandoah, I'm bound to leave you,
Away, I'm bound away
'Cross the wide Missouri.

The Shenandoah and Potomac rivers meet at Harpers Ferry.
▶ What is blocking the view of the mountains?

B. Virginia's Underground Treasures

The Caverns "Have you ever visited any of Virginia's caves before?" Joey asked.

"No, I haven't," Darla answered. "But I've seen many pictures of them."

"The pictures aren't nearly as good as the real thing," Joey said. "I know because I've been to see all of the caves with my parents. We visited Luray, Endless, Massanutten, and Grand Caverns. I would like to be a tour guide at one of the caves when I get older."

"Tell me everything you know about them while we are on the bus," Darla said. "Why don't you pretend you are a guide?"

"Sure," Joey said. "Hello, my name is Joey Morris, and I will be your guide today. If you have any questions during the tour, please feel free to ask them. The first thing you need to know about the caves is how they were formed. All through the part of Virginia called the Ridge and Valley Region, one of the main kinds of rock is **limestone.** Limestone was formed millions of years ago from shells of tiny sea creatures. A long time ago, this region was under the ocean. Later, the land rose above the ocean and these big ridges and valleys were formed."

"But how were the caves formed?" Darla interrupted.

Dripping Limestone "I was going to get to that next," Joey said. "You see, limestone rock dissolves pretty easily when water runs over it. In many places, underground water has dissolved the limestone and created beautiful caves such as this." He used his hand to gesture to the imaginary cave. "Water keeps dripping from the walls and ceilings of these caves. This never-ending dripping has formed groups of strange shapes. These shapes are called stalactites. They hang down from the walls and ceilings. Other forms build upward from the cave floors. They are called stalagmites. It's easy to remember the differences if you memorize this: Stalactites hold tight to the ceiling, stalagmites might reach them."

"That was great," Darla said. "I bet that you are good enough to be a guide right now."

"Thanks. Now you will have your chance to compare me with a real tour guide," Joey said as their bus pulled into the parking lot at Luray Caverns.

Both stalactites and stalagmites can be seen in Virginia's caverns.
▶ What causes stalactites and stalagmites to form?

The Natural Chimneys are at Mount Salon in Virginia. These colorful towers rise 100 feet or more above the ground.
▶ How were these towers formed?

C. A Famous Natural Wonder

Other natural wonders in Virginia's Ridge and Valley Region have been formed by water wearing away rocks. Among the best known are seven tall gray stone towers in Augusta County. The towers are called Natural Chimneys. They were caused by water washing away the softer stone around them. After millions of years, the Chimneys, which are made of harder stone, were left standing alone.

An old legend says that a long time ago, in the land around Natural Chimneys, there lived two men who were both in love with the same woman. The two men decided to fight for her hand in marriage. But they did not want to fight with their fists or with guns. So the two men decided to have a joust.

You may have heard about jousting from King Arthur stories. In a joust, two horsemen ride toward each other. Each one carries a long pole called a lance. Whoever knocks the other rider off his horse with a lance is the winner of the joust.

This story began a tradition in Virginia. A tradition is something that people do that has been handed down over the years. This tradition is the oldest sporting event in the United States. Every August there is a jousting tournament at Natural Chimneys. But now the riders do not knock each other from their horses. Instead, the jousters ride toward hanging rings. They try to put their lances through the rings.

Many people come to Natural Chimneys in August for a chance to see this exciting event.

D. Other Natural Wonders

Another famous sight in the Ridge and Valley Region is Natural Bridge. Natural Bridge is a stone bridge that is 90 feet (27 m) long. Trees grow on top of this huge bridge, and a road crosses over it. A tiny stream flows under the bridge. Over millions of years, the little stream wore away tons of stone, leaving this giant bridge that stretches high above it. It is said that George Washington carved his initials 23 feet (7 m) up the wall under Natural Bridge.

Virginia is also famous for its hot springs. Streams of hot water flow under the mountains and valleys of the Ridge and Valley Region. In some places, this hot water bubbles up to form hot springs. People from all over the country come to visit them because they think that these springs heal those who bathe in them. Hot Springs, Warm Springs, and Healing Springs are all located in Bath County. They are near the West Virginia border.

The Natural Bridge crosses Cedar Creek.
▶ How was the Natural Bridge formed?

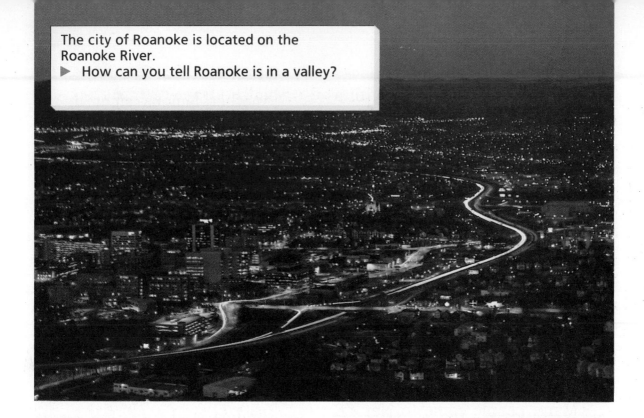

The city of Roanoke is located on the Roanoke River.
▶ How can you tell Roanoke is in a valley?

E. Valley Cities

Largest City Most cities and large towns in the Ridge and Valley Region are found in the valley land. Find the city of Roanoke on the map on page 65. Roanoke is the largest city in Virginia's Ridge and Valley Region. It grew up as a railroad center about 100 years ago. Over 100,000 people now live in the busy city of Roanoke.

Oldest City Find the city of Winchester on the map. Winchester is the oldest city in the Great Valley. It began in 1732 and became the county seat of Frederick County in 1744. Winchester has grown over the years. It is now one of Virginia's 20 most populated cities.

The Cumberland Gap was an important route for the early settlers.
▶ Why was the Cumberland Gap so important?

F. Cumberland Gap

The Cumberland Gap is important because it lets you get from one side of the high mountains to the other without climbing them. This is one of the gaps that you learned about earlier that was formed over thousands of years by running streams. The streams wore away the land. Some breaks still have streams running through them. In other openings, the water has dried up over the years. These openings are called wind gaps.

The most famous wind gap is the Cumberland Gap. Long ago, when settlers were traveling westward over the Appalachian Mountains, the Cumberland Gap was one of the most important routes they followed. About 200,000 people traveled through the Cumberland Gap between 1775 and 1800. The Cumberland Gap was also the route that was used by Union soldiers during the Civil War.

PLACES OF INTEREST IN THE RIDGE AND VALLEY REGION

Appalachian Trail
Blue Ridge Parkway
Booker T. Washington Monument
Cumberland Gap
Endless Caverns
Grand Caverns
Hot Springs
Luray Caverns

Massanutten Caverns
Natural Bridge
Natural Chimneys
Shenandoah National Park
Skyline Drive
Mount Rogers National Recreation Area

The Ridge and Valley Region has many natural wonders that visitors come to see.
▶ Which of these are underground?

LESSON 4 REVIEW

THINK AND WRITE

A. What are the two main lines of mountains in the Ridge and Valley Region?

B. What are the similarities and differences between stalactites and stalagmites?

C. How were the towers at Natural Chimneys formed?

D. Why do many people visit Virginia's hot springs?

E. Why was Roanoke important about 100 years ago?

F. What is the Cumberland Gap?

SKILLS CHECK

THINKING SKILL

Describe the natural region in which you live. What are some of the advantages of living in that region? What are some of the disadvantages of living there?

USING THE VOCABULARY

elevation   peninsula
contour line   rapids
coastal plain   plateau
tide   ridge
bay   stalagmite

On a separate sheet of paper, write the best ending for each sentence below. Choose your answers from the vocabulary words above.

1. A line of hills or mountains is called a _____.
2. A rocky shape formed from dripping limestone in a cave, and growing up from the floor is called a _____.
3. The height of a place above the level of sea is its _____.
4. The parts of rivers where the waters flow very quickly and roughly are the _____.
5. A _____ separates one height from another on a relief map.
6. The oceans rise and fall because of the _____.
7. A piece of land that has water nearly all around it is a _____.
8. A large area of flat land that is bordered by water is a _____.
9. A large, raised level piece of land is a _____.
10. Part of a large body of water that reaches into the land is a _____.

REMEMBERING WHAT YOU READ

Write your answers in complete sentences on a separate sheet of paper.

1. What is Virginia's population?
2. How does a person generalize?
3. Why are some Virginia cities called independent cities?
4. What is the largest body of water in the Tidewater Region?
5. Which two islands are part of the yearly pony roundup?
6. What is the most populated city in the state of Virginia?
7. Who was the person who discovered the city of Richmond?
8. Why has the northern part of the Piedmont Region grown?
9. What is the Appalachian Trail?
10. What are wind gaps?

TYING LANGUAGE ARTS TO SOCIAL STUDIES: WRITING TO LEARN

Think about the three regions of Virginia. Choose one region. Imagine that you are going on a trip to that region. Write a paragraph in which you tell what you would like to see. Tell what kinds of things you would like to do while you are there.

THINKING CRITICALLY

Write your answers in complete sentences on a separate sheet of paper.

1. How do relief maps differ from other maps you have studied so far?
2. How did Virginia's Tidewater Region get its name?
3. Why is the Tidewater Region so heavily populated?
4. How have rivers affected settlement in the Tidewater and Piedmont regions of Virginia?
5. How do the Ridge and Valley Region and the Piedmont differ?

SUMMARIZING THE CHAPTER

On a separate sheet of paper, draw a graphic organizer that is like the one shown here. Copy the information from this graphic organizer to the one you have drawn. Under the main idea for each lesson, write three statements that support it. The first one has been done for you.

CHAPTER THEME

To study the geography of Virginia and its many landforms, certain tools are needed.

LESSON 1

People who study geography use certain tools.

1. Ask many questions
2. Use many words
3. Learn about place names

LESSON 2

The Tidewater Region is a coastal plain.

1.
2.
3.

LESSON 3

The Piedmont Region has many rolling hills.

1.
2.
3.

LESSON 4

The Ridge and Valley Region has many mountains and valleys.

1.
2.
3.

CHAPTER 2

VIRGINIA'S NATURAL RESOURCES

$\mathcal{V}$irginians use natural resources in many ways. A lot of people have jobs such as farming, fishing, and mining in which they work with these resources. Some people use these resources for recreational activities.

1

Nature and Virginia

THINK ABOUT WHAT YOU KNOW

For how many different things do you use water?

STUDY THE VOCABULARY

natural resource	mineral
agriculture	fossil
fertile	fuel
dam	
hydroelectric power	

FOCUS YOUR READING

How are soil, water, and minerals useful to people?

A. Nature's Resources

Virginia has many different **natural resources.** A natural resource is something found in nature that is useful to people.

Soil, water, coal, and forests are some of the natural resources found in Virginia. They were not made by people, but people can use them for many purposes. For example, the trees in the forests might be used to build houses or make furniture. Coal can be burned to heat buildings or make electricity.

Virginians use their natural resources to make many things for themselves, their state, their country, and the world. Nature's resources have provided for the needs of Virginians for many years.

The sandy soil of the Tidewater Region is ideally suited to peanut farming.
▶ What farm machine, do you think, is behind the farmer?

Virginia's forests are home to many different kinds of wildlife, including deer.
▶ What are two other kinds of wildlife that live in Virginia's forests?

Soil is one of the most valuable natural resources. Without the soil, agriculture would not be possible. *Agriculture* is another word for "farming." Farming means growing crops such as wheat and corn. It also involves raising farm animals such as cows, pigs, and chickens.

Farming is important work for many Virginians. All three regions of the state have fertile, or good, soil. Virginia also has a mild climate and a good annual rainfall. Plants in the state get the sunshine, warmth, water, and fine soil they need to grow well.

Livestock and poultry provide more than half of Virginia's farm income.
▶ What are some products we get from hogs?

B. Water Resources

Water is also a very important natural resource. People, plants, and animals all need to drink water to live. People need water to bathe and brush their teeth. They use it to wash their clothes.

Water can also be used as a highway, just as a road is. Oceans, rivers, and lakes can be used for transportation. Water provides fish and other seafood for people to eat.

Water can make power too. The rushing of rivers over falls provides power, or energy. This power can run mills and other small factories.

People build **dams** to control the flow of water. A dam is a wall that holds back water. The water is trapped behind the dam. When the gates of the dam are opened, the water rushes down. The falling water makes wheels turn. As the wheels turn, they drive machines that make electric power.

Electric power made by falling water is called **hydroelectric** (hye droh ee LEK trihk) **power.** This power is sent through lines to many parts of Virginia. It is used to light buildings, run machines, heat homes, and do many other things.

> This diagram shows how water is used to make electricity.
> ▶ Why is the power station located below the dam?

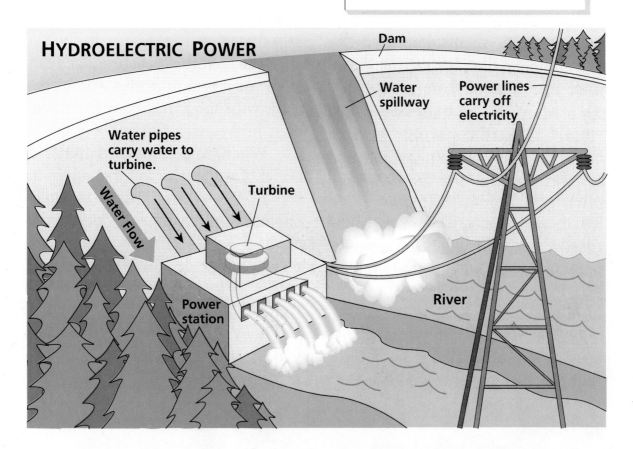

HYDROELECTRIC POWER

Dam

Water spillway

Power lines carry off electricity

Water pipes carry water to turbine.

Water Flow

Turbine

Power station

River

C. Mineral Resources

Most Important Mineral Virginia has many valuable minerals. Minerals are natural resources found in the earth. Minerals can be dug out of the earth and used in many ways.

Coal is Virginia's most important mineral resource. Its production provides more income than any other mineral product in the entire state. Virginia is the seventh largest producer of coal in the United States. Most of Virginia's coal deposits are located in the southwestern part of the state.

Trapped Energy Coal is sometimes called "buried sunshine" because of the way it was formed. Many years ago, before people lived on the earth, plants captured the sun's energy that fell on the earth. Coal was formed from plants that decayed. When we burn coal today, we are using the energy that was captured from the sun long ago.

If you look at pieces of coal, you often see what looks like plant leaves and stems. These are called fossils. A fossil is what remains of a plant or animal that lived a long time ago. Fossils are often found in rocks or minerals.

Coal, like oil and natural gas, is used as a fuel. A fuel is something that can be burned to make heat or

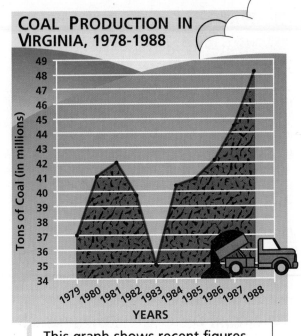

COAL PRODUCTION IN VIRGINIA, 1978-1988

Tons of Coal (in millions)

YEARS

This graph shows recent figures for coal production in Virginia.
▶ When did coal production have its largest one-year increase?

power. It can be used to heat buildings. It can be used to run machines.

The heat that coal produces can keep you warm in winter. It can also cook your food. But heat from coal does many other things.

When coal is burned under a boiler of water, the water changes to steam. The steam is used to make engines and machines work. As the engines and machines turn, they make energy, or power. Almost one half of all the electrical power in the United States is made from coal in this way. Electricity keeps homes and factories warm during the winter months.

Another very important use of coal is for making steel. When coal is baked in large ovens, it changes into something called coke. Coke is then burned with iron ore in huge furnaces. The burning coke changes the iron ore into pure iron. Then steel can be made from the iron by adding other minerals.

Making Steel About two thirds of a ton of coal is used to make one ton of steel. A very large pile of coal was used to make your family's car. The pile of coal weighed almost as much as the car itself!

Coal can also be used to make other products. For example, you may be surprised to learn that some medicines, dyes, and fertilizers can be made from coal.

Stone ranks second in importance among mineral resources in Virginia. There is stone in almost every part of Virginia. Granite, slate, and sandstone are some of the kinds of stone found throughout the state. Stone has many uses. It can be used in building. It can be crushed and used to make roads. Some of the stone can be used to make bricks.

The amount of stone mined in Virginia is second only to that of coal mined in the state.
▶ What stone makes up blackboards?

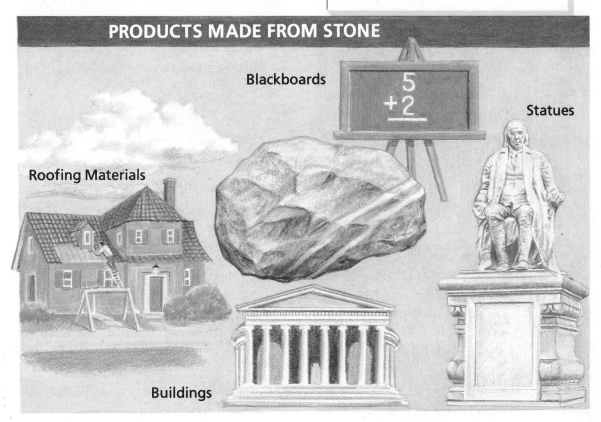

PRODUCTS MADE FROM STONE

Blackboards

Statues

Roofing Materials

Buildings

Limestone, which is softer than most stone, has many uses. It can be cut into blocks to make walls for buildings. It can also be crushed to make lime. Lime is used to help make cement, glass, and iron. Lime is also used to make medicines. Many farmers use lime on their fields to help their crops grow. Much of Virginia's limestone is found in the Great Valley of the Ridge and Valley Region.

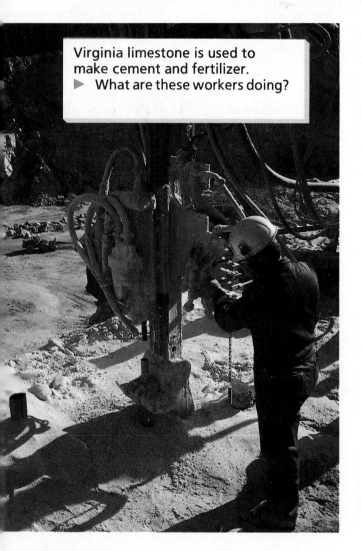

Virginia limestone is used to make cement and fertilizer.
▶ What are these workers doing?

The forestry, farming, and fishing industries depend on the state's natural resources.
▶ To which industry does soybean growing belong?

D. Human Resources

People must have natural resources to live. But people themselves are resources. They are human resources. They have the skills needed to use natural resources wisely. People farm the soil, mine the coal, and take care of the trees. They also make things from these resources. In Virginia they make clothing, steel, chemicals, furniture, and other products.

People use their talents and skills to make life better for themselves and for others. In Virginia, people work to provide many valuable services to the state and the local community.

LESSON *1* REVIEW

THINK AND WRITE

A. What is a natural resource?
B. What are three important ways in which people use water?
C. Why is coal a fuel?
D. How are people a resource?

SKILLS CHECK

WRITING SKILL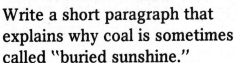

Write a short paragraph that explains why coal is sometimes called "buried sunshine."

2 Forests, Wildlife, Rivers, and Lakes

THINK ABOUT WHAT YOU KNOW

Do you have any forests, rivers, or lakes in your community? If so, do you visit them for fun?

STUDY THE VOCABULARY

coniferous   reservoir
deciduous   irrigation
artificial lake

FOCUS YOUR READING

In what ways are forests, wildlife, rivers, and lakes important natural resources?

A. Virginia's Forests

Mostly Forests Forests are an important natural resource in Virginia. More than 60 percent of Virginia's land is made up of forests. Virginia's beautiful forests are alive with trees and bushes. They also have colorful wildflowers. Ferns and many other plants are plentiful too. Soil, sun, and rain make the plants grow strong and healthy. The plants provide food for many of the animals that live in the forests.

Forests are important to people too. The forests' soil soaks up the rain. It keeps heavy rains from flooding farms and other land. The water goes under the ground. It flows into lakes and streams. Then people can have fresh, clean water.

People have fun exploring Virginia's forests. They can hike and camp. They can hunt and fish. Many visitors can just enjoy the beauty around them.

Types of Trees Not all of Virginia's forests are alike. In some regions, where the soil is very sandy or rocky, or where temperatures get cold, the forests have mainly coniferous (koh NIHF ur us), or cone-bearing, trees. Coniferous trees are also called evergreens because they usually remain green year-round. The wood from these trees is called softwood. Examples of softwood trees are pine, spruce, and fir. Coniferous forests

Virginia's forests provide homes for animals and are places that people enjoy year round.
► In what ways do people use the forests for recreation?

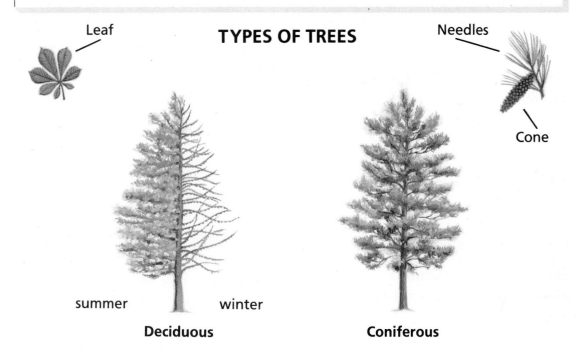

Coniferous trees remain green throughout the year. Deciduous trees lose their leaves in the autumn.

▶ Which type of tree provides hardwood?

TYPES OF TREES

Leaf

Needles

Cone

summer   winter

Deciduous

Coniferous

are found in Virginia's Ridge and Valley Region and in the sandy parts of the Tidewater Region.

Some forests in Virginia have mainly **deciduous** (dee SIHJ oo us) trees. Deciduous trees shed their leaves in the fall. The wood from these trees is called hardwood. Hardwood trees are oak, maple, hickory, and beech. Many forests in the Piedmont Region and the mountain valleys are deciduous forests.

B. Virginia's Wildlife

Virginia has many kinds of wildlife, such as deer, foxes, squirrels, rabbits, wild turkeys, and beaver. Birds, fish, and insects are

also wildlife. All of these animals are important natural resources.

Each kind of animal has its own special type of home. Gray squirrels, for example, need trees that grow the nuts and buds the squirrels eat. They need the trees for nests too. Some birds live only in hollow trees. Others make their home in open fields. Wild animals and fish are found in every forest, swamp, stream, and lake in Virginia. All natural areas are homes for wildlife.

C. Virginia's Rivers

Rivers in the East As you can see from the map on page 87, many rivers flow through Virginia. Some

85

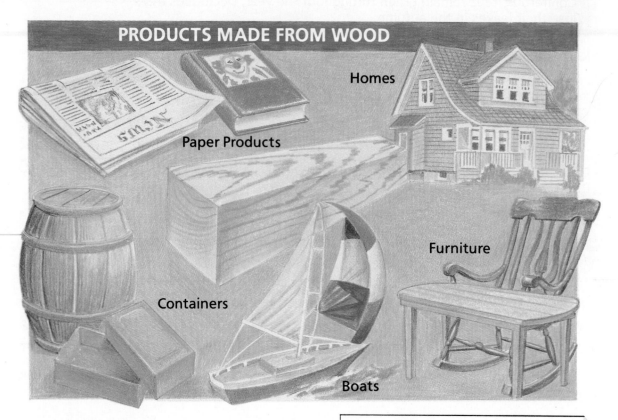

PRODUCTS MADE FROM WOOD

Paper Products

Homes

Containers

Boats

Furniture

Many goods are made from wood harvested in Virginia's forests.
▶ What other wood products can you think of?

rivers start in the mountains of western Virginia. Others start in the mountains of other states.

Find the rivers that flow into Chesapeake Bay. These rivers are the Potomac, the Rappahannock, the James, and the York. You can see from the map that two small rivers flow together into the York. What are their names?

The Potomac, Rappahannock, York, and James rivers are deep and wide and slow-moving as they cross the Tidewater Region. Because of this, the rivers are easy to travel on. Long ago, settlers sailed these rivers

as they explored Virginia. All of these rivers are still important for transportation today.

Can you find a river on the map that flows through all three regions of the state? If you said the James River, you were right. Find the three rivers that flow into the James River. They are the Jackson, Cowpasture, and Maury (MAR ee) rivers.

Naming Rivers Sometimes a river gives its name to the valley through which it flows. One of the most beautiful valleys in the state is the Shenandoah Valley. Find the Shenandoah River on the map on this page. Two other rivers that have given their names to the valleys through which they flow are the Clinch and the Holston rivers. They both flow southwest into the Tennessee River.

The New River flows north through Virginia. It continues into West Virginia. Then it flows into another river, which empties into the Ohio River. The Roanoke River flows southeast through Virginia and North Carolina. It empties into Albemarle (AL buh mahrl) Sound in the Atlantic Ocean.

D. Virginia's Lakes

Lakes are another important part of Virginia. Lake Drummond is the largest natural lake in the state. It is in the Great Dismal Swamp. Mountain Lake is another natural lake. Many people like to visit and enjoy Mountain Lake.

Most of Virginia's lakes, however, are not natural lakes. Instead, they are **artificial lakes.** This means that they have been made by people, not by nature. These artificial lakes have been formed by building dams across rivers. The water in the river backs up behind the dam, and this creates a lake.

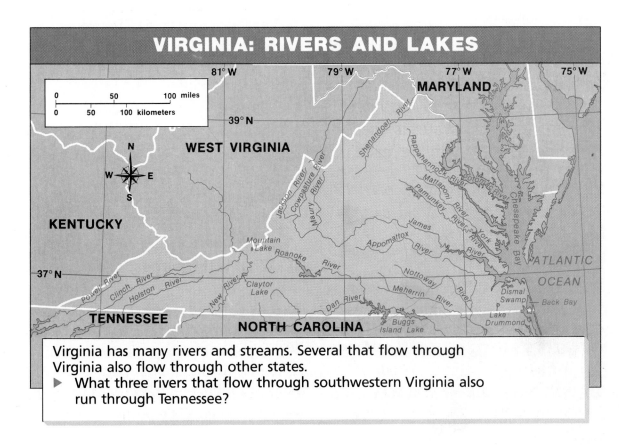

Virginia has many rivers and streams. Several that flow through Virginia also flow through other states.
► What three rivers that flow through southwestern Virginia also run through Tennessee?

Water is stored in Kerr Reservoir until it is needed for drinking or irrigation.
▶ Which part of the reservoir was made by people?

Sometimes artificial lakes are made to form a **reservoir** (REZ ur vwahr). A reservoir is a place where water can be stored until it is needed. Often the water is used for drinking. Or it might be used for **irrigation.** Irrigation is the bringing of water to crops or other plants where it is needed. The largest artificial lake in Virginia is called Buggs Island Lake. Find this lake on the map on page 87.

LESSON 2 REVIEW

THINK AND WRITE

A. What is the difference between coniferous and deciduous trees?

B. What are three places where wildlife can be found in the state of Virginia?

C. What type of river is easy to travel on?

D. What is the purpose of reservoirs?

SKILLS CHECK

WRITING SKILL
Write a short paragraph to explain how people use many natural resources, such as forests, rivers, and lakes, to make a living.

Virginia's Climate

THINK ABOUT WHAT YOU KNOW

What kind of weather do you like? Why do you like it?

STUDY THE VOCABULARY

climate   thermometer
temperature   precipitation

FOCUS YOUR READING

What are the weather and climate of Virginia?

A. Weather and Climate

Have you ever had to change your plans because it was colder than you had expected? Was there ever a time when it was too cloudy to go swimming? Has your school ever closed because of a snowstorm?

Rain, snow, wind, heat, and cold are all part of weather. Weather is also the way the air is at a certain time. The weather may change from day to day or even from hour to hour. For instance, it might be sunny in the morning and then become cloudy in the afternoon.

The kind of weather a place has over a long period of time is called its climate. The climate of Virginia is called humid subtropical. It is humid because the air contains a lot of moisture. It is subtropical because it is warm and mild most of the year.

Climate is very important. It affects the way people make their living. For example, climate affects the number of days a year that farmers have to grow their crops. Climate also affects the things that people do for recreation.

Lightning storms are common in Virginia's climate.
▶ What do the lines of lightning look like?

89

B. Temperature

Temperature is how hot or cold the air is. **Thermometers** tell what the temperature of the air is. In most parts of Virginia, the air is neither too hot nor too cold. The climate is mild. The coldest places in the state are in the mountains. That is because the higher you go, the colder the air becomes.

Look at the temperature graphs on page 379. The letters along the bottoms of the graphs stand for the months of the year. In Roanoke the average temperature of the air in December is 38°F (3°C). Is the average December temperature in Norfolk

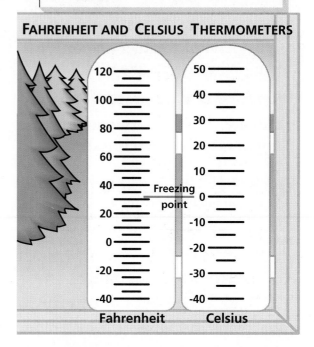

These thermometers show the temperature of the air.
▶ Which is warmer, 40°F or 40°C?

FAHRENHEIT AND CELSIUS THERMOMETERS

Fahrenheit

Celsius

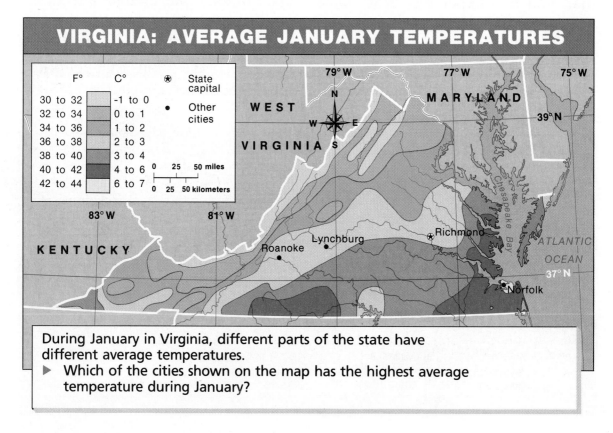

VIRGINIA: AVERAGE JANUARY TEMPERATURES

F°	C°
30 to 32	-1 to 0
32 to 34	0 to 1
34 to 36	1 to 2
36 to 38	2 to 3
38 to 40	3 to 4
40 to 42	4 to 6
42 to 44	6 to 7

⊛ State capital
• Other cities

During January in Virginia, different parts of the state have different average temperatures.
▶ Which of the cities shown on the map has the highest average temperature during January?

higher or lower than it is in Roanoke? By looking at the graph, you can see that it is higher in Norfolk.

Look at the map labeled "Average July Temperatures" below. What is the average July temperature of the air in the part of the state where you live?

C. Precipitation

Raindrops and Snowfall To understand the climate of a particular place, you must know about the temperatures of its air. You must also know about its precipitation (pree sihp uh TAY shun). Rain, snow, hail, and all the other forms of water that fall to the earth are called precipitation.

Look at the precipitation graphs on page 378. They show how much precipitation falls in each month of the year in Richmond, Norfolk, Lynchburg, and Roanoke. In Lynchburg the average precipitation in July is 4 inches (10 cm). What is the average July precipitation in Richmond?

Now look at the precipitation map of Virginia on page 92. How much precipitation falls in your part of the state each year?

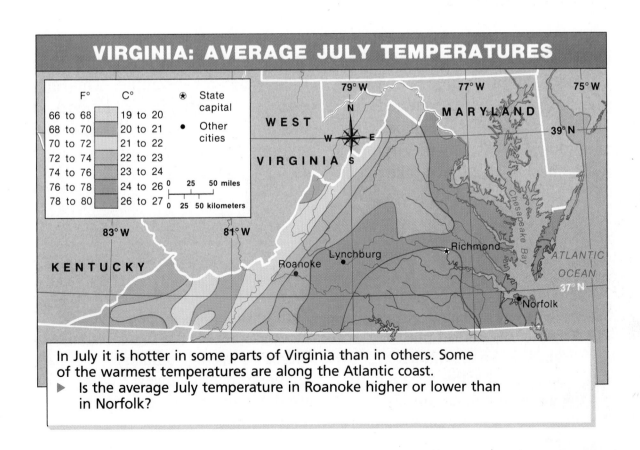

VIRGINIA: AVERAGE JULY TEMPERATURES

F°	C°
66 to 68	19 to 20
68 to 70	20 to 21
70 to 72	21 to 22
72 to 74	22 to 23
74 to 76	23 to 24
76 to 78	24 to 26
78 to 80	26 to 27

✹ State capital
• Other cities

0   25   50 miles
0   25   50 kilometers

In July it is hotter in some parts of Virginia than in others. Some of the warmest temperatures are along the Atlantic coast.
▶ Is the average July temperature in Roanoke higher or lower than in Norfolk?

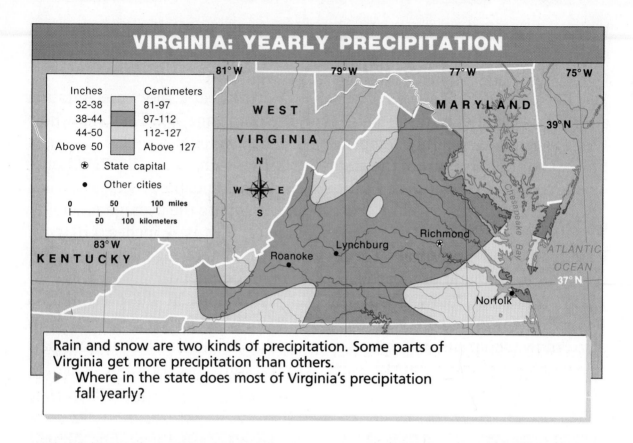

VIRGINIA: YEARLY PRECIPITATION

Inches	Centimeters
32-38	81-97
38-44	97-112
44-50	112-127
Above 50	Above 127

✴ State capital
• Other cities

Rain and snow are two kinds of precipitation. Some parts of Virginia get more precipitation than others.
▶ Where in the state does most of Virginia's precipitation fall yearly?

Mild Climate Climate affects the precipitation of an area. For example, most of the temperatures in Virginia are mild. Therefore, most of the precipitation that falls in Virginia is in the form of rain. Let's take a look at the amount of precipitation in Richmond, for example. This city gets about 44 inches (112 cm) of precipitation each year. Of this total amount, snow accounts for only about 1 inch (3 cm).

LESSON 3 REVIEW

THINK AND WRITE

A. What is the difference between weather and climate?

B. Why are the coldest places in Virginia in the mountains?

C. What form of water accounts for the greatest amount of precipitation in Virginia?

SKILLS CHECK

MAP SKILL

Turn to the maps on pages 90 and 91. Along what state border are Virginia's average January temperatures the lowest? What are the highest average temperatures in July?

92

4

Protecting Virginia's Resources

THINK ABOUT WHAT YOU KNOW

Have you ever cleaned up something that was dirty? How do you think it got dirty?

STUDY THE VOCABULARY

pollution	conservation
erosion	extinct
cover crop	refuge

FOCUS YOUR READING

How are Virginians protecting their natural resources?

A. Air Pollution

Some people are careless with natural resources. They act in ways that harm the air, water, or land and make it dirty. When they do that, they cause **pollution.**

Many years ago the air was very clean. It was safe for people, plants, and animals to breathe. Now, smoke and gases from cars, factories, and fires pollute the air and make it dirty. Unclean air can make people sick and even kill them.

Many countries, such as the United States, have passed laws to protect the clean air from becoming polluted. People and factories are working together to get rid of pollution by improving air filters. Filters are cleaners that companies put on their chimneys and smokestacks.

B. Water Pollution

Water is another important natural resource that can become dirty. People pollute water by dumping factory and human wastes into rivers, lakes, and oceans. You cannot eat fish or other seafood from dirty waters. You may become very sick. Sometimes the polluted water kills the fish.

Some companies bury chemical wastes in the ground. As rainwater passes through the ground, it mixes with the buried chemicals. That can pollute the water supply, which often comes from the ground. When

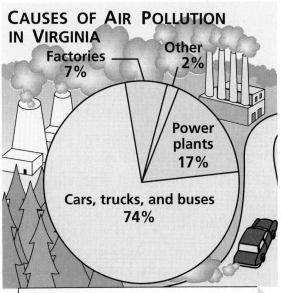

CAUSES OF AIR POLLUTION IN VIRGINIA

Factories 7%

Other 2%

Power plants 17%

Cars, trucks, and buses 74%

Air pollution has become a very serious problem in Virginia.
► What causes the most pollution in Virginia?

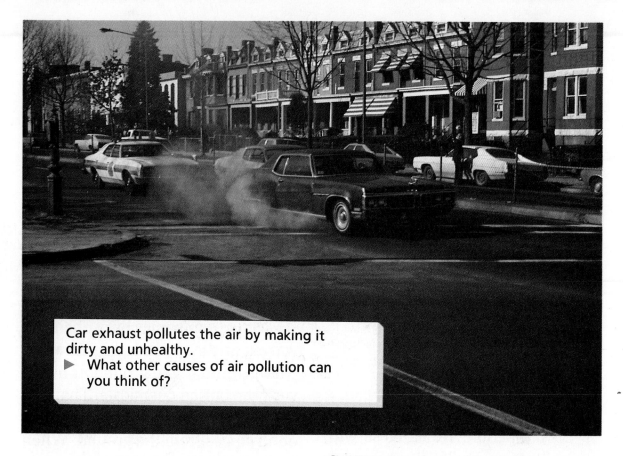

Car exhaust pollutes the air by making it dirty and unhealthy.
► What other causes of air pollution can you think of?

that happens, people can become very sick from drinking the water.

Water is a renewable resource, or a resource that can be replaced. The earth keeps getting more water through rain and snow that falls to the ground. Sometimes, though, as the rain or snow falls through polluted air, it becomes dirty also.

It is possible to clean water that has been polluted, but the process is very expensive. Several laws have been made to help keep water clean. Many factories are no longer pouring chemicals into the lakes, rivers, and oceans.

C. Protecting the Soil

Wearing Away Erosion is the wearing away of the soil by rain or wind. Erosion is a natural process that occurs even when people do not use the land. But when people use the soil to plant crops, they increase the chances of erosion. Ever since people began farming, they have had to battle soil erosion.

Plowing the Hills Farmers can take many steps to lessen the amount of soil that is lost to erosion. In hilly land, the farmer might plow across the slopes in rows rather than up and down. Plowing this way helps

Contour plowing can help decrease soil erosion.
▶ How does contour plowing differ from regular plowing?

prevent the soil from being washed away. This method of plowing is called contour plowing.

Farmers also protect the soil by growing a **cover crop.** This crop is a tree, grass, or special plant that is planted so that the roots of the trees or plant drink most of the rain and hold the soil in place. In this way, the soil cannot be washed away or blown away.

D. Protecting the Forests

Conserving Resources Trees are an important natural resource. Each year, as the number of people in Virginia and in the rest of the world increases, more trees are cut down to meet people's need for wood and wood products. Because of this, people everywhere should use trees wisely. Using natural resources wisely is called **conservation.**

How can people conserve forest resources? One thing they can do is stop wasting the things that come from trees. Paper is one major product that comes from trees.

Another important thing is to help protect Virginia's forests from fire. Forest fires destroy much of the forest lands. Many fires are started by careless people.

Trees are a renewable resource. New trees can be planted. They take the place of the ones that are cut

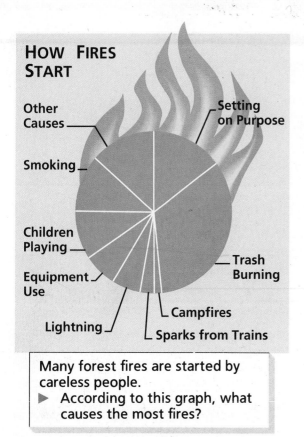

HOW FIRES START

Other Causes

Setting on Purpose

Smoking

Children Playing

Trash Burning

Equipment Use

Campfires

Lightning

Sparks from Trains

Many forest fires are started by careless people.
▶ According to this graph, what causes the most fires?

down. Many people and companies in Virginia are working hard to protect the forests. They are careful about how many trees are cut for lumber. They hire workers called foresters to plant new trees and to care for these trees.

Help from the Government Much of Virginia's forest land is being protected in national forests and state forests. These are forests that are cared for by the government of the United States and the government of Virginia. These forests belong to all the people.

The George Washington National Forest, the Jefferson National Forest, and the Shenandoah National Park are three large areas of public forest land. The Lee State Forest and the Cumberland State Forest are two more. There are many smaller state forests and parks in Virginia too. Have you ever visited one of them?

E. Protecting Wildlife

Report on Conservation "Shelly, would you please give your science report now," Mr. Taylor said.

Shelly walked to the front of the classroom. She was glad that Mr. Taylor had called on her first. She gets nervous when she has to wait.

"My science report is on wildlife conservation," Shelly began. "People have changed the land so much that many animals have a hard time finding the right place to live. They cannot always find food or clean water. A few kinds of animals have died and are gone forever. Those animals are extinct."

Obeying the Laws "People can keep this from happening to other animals by practicing wildlife conservation," Shelly continued. "There are many ways to do this: by being careful with fire, by getting rid of wastes so wild animals aren't harmed, and by obeying all hunting and fishing laws.

"The Virginia government has set up special parks and public lands where wild animals can live in safety," Shelly stated. "These places are called **refuges.** But not all wildlife in Virginia lives on these protected lands. Wildlife is found almost everywhere. Wild birds and animals are in this schoolyard. They are around our homes. They are on farms. And they are in the forests. So wildlife conservation is everyone's job. Just think how bad you would feel if you could no longer look at a beautiful red cardinal or hear a bluejay squawking to its young."

Shelly waited a minute. Then she walked back to her desk.

"Thank you very much, Shelly," Mr. Taylor said. "That was very good, and it gives us all something to think about."

Wildlife conservation will save the lives of many animals.
► How do forest rangers help wild animals?

LESSON 4 REVIEW

THINK AND WRITE

A. What has caused air pollution?
B. In what ways can dirty water make people sick?
C. What can farmers do to lessen the amount of soil that is lost from erosion?
D. Why do people need to conserve forest resources?
E. How can you practice wildlife conservation?

SKILLS CHECK

THINKING SKILL

Choose one of the following important issues from this lesson: air pollution, water pollution, soil erosion, forest conservation, or wildlife conservation. List at least three things that are not mentioned in the lesson that you can do to help with the problem.

2 PUTTING IT ALL TOGETHER

USING THE VOCABULARY

agriculture
fertile
dam
hydroelectric
  power
mineral

reservoir
precipitation
pollution
erosion
conservation

On a separate sheet of paper, write the best ending for each sentence below. Choose your answers from the vocabulary words above.

1. Electric power made by falling water is called _____.
2. A type of natural resource that can be dug out of the earth is known as a _____.
3. Rain, snow, and sleet are examples of _____.
4. Harmful substances that are present in the air and water are usually caused by _____.
5. If you care about using our natural resources wisely, then you care about _____.

REMEMBERING WHAT YOU READ

Write your answers in complete sentences on a separate sheet of paper.

1. What does the job of farming in Virginia involve?

2. What is Virginia's most important mineral resource?
3. About how much of the land area in the state of Virginia is made up of forests?
4. Which four rivers flow into the Chesapeake Bay?
5. How were the artificial lakes in Virginia formed?
6. What kind of climate does the state of Virginia have?
7. What is Virginia's most common form of precipitation?
8. What are some things that cause water to become polluted?
9. Why is soil erosion said to be a natural process?
10. Why has the Virginia government set up refuges?

TYING SCIENCE TO SOCIAL STUDIES

Collect at least eight different leaves and needles from trees near your home or school. Use encyclopedias or other library books to identify the tree from which each sample came. Use your samples to make a chart. You may either draw the leaves and needles or paste them on your chart. Your chart should show the samples that came from deciduous trees and the samples that came from coniferous trees.

THINKING CRITICALLY

Write your answers in complete sentences on a separate sheet of paper.

1. In what ways does Virginia's good soil help people?
2. Why are forests important?
3. In what ways does climate affect how people live?
4. What are some of the reasons why air pollution is so dangerous?
5. How can buried chemical wastes cause pollution?

SUMMARIZING THE CHAPTER

On a separate sheet of paper, draw a graphic organizer that is like the one shown here. Copy the information from this graphic organizer to the one you have drawn. Under the main idea for each lesson, write three statements that support it. The first one has been done for you.

CHAPTER THEME

Virginia is rich in natural resources that people use for many purposes.

LESSON 1

People in Virginia use soil, water, and minerals for many purposes.

1. Soil to grow crops
2. Water to make power
3. Coal to make heat

LESSON 2

Forests, rivers, and lakes are important for many reasons.

1. Rivers run
2. Forests are pretty
3. Lakes sits still

LESSON 3

Virginia's climate is mild.

1. _____
2. _____
3. _____

LESSON 4

Virginians can protect their natural resources in many ways.

1. _____
2. _____
3. _____

THE PROBLEM OF WATER POLLUTION

In some parts of the world, there is not enough water to meet the needs of the people. In the United States, we are fortunate to have plenty of water. Our problem, however, is to keep that water clean and safe.

Water becomes unsafe, or polluted, for several reasons. Some industrial plants dump chemicals or other harmful substances into our streams and rivers. This poisons the water and kills the fish and plants that live there. Some factories burn coal or oil and release dangerous chemicals into the air. These chemicals combine with the moisture in the air and fall to the ground as acid rain. Acid rain pollutes the streams, rivers, and lakes.

Agriculture is another major source of water pollution. Farmers use fertilizers and pesticides on their crops. Rain washes many of these chemicals into streams, rivers, and lakes. The result is polluted water.

Many steps have been taken to clean up polluted waters and to prevent water pollution in the future. The United States Congress passed the Safe Drinking Water Act. This law set standards for drinking water throughout the country. In Virginia, state lawmakers passed a law banning oil drilling in the Chesapeake Bay. This was done to prevent oil spills in the bay. A slick coating of oil on the bay would kill the plants and fish in the water. It would also harm birds and animals on the shore. Water pollution is a serious problem that needs an immediate solution.

Thinking for Yourself

On a separate sheet of paper, answer the questions in complete sentences.

1. Why do you think it is important to keep our rivers and lakes clean?
2. What are some ways in which individuals can help stop water pollution?
3. What do you think should happen to polluters?

3

INDUSTRY IN VIRGINIA

Most industries in Virginia depend on natural resources. Fishing, farming, mining, oystering, and lumbering are Virginia's main industries. Manufacturing is another important industry in the state.

102

Natural Resources and Industry

THINK ABOUT WHAT YOU KNOW

Name three ways that people can use natural resources to make money.

STUDY THE VOCABULARY

industry	timber
surface mining	lumbering
reclaim	tourism

FOCUS YOUR READING

What industries depend on Virginia's natural resources?

A. Mining

Burning Rocks   We learned in Chapter 2 that coal is a valuable mineral resource in Virginia. The first humans to find coal in Virginia were Native Americans living long ago. Imagine the Indians' surprise when they discovered that these strange black rocks could burn!

Today, getting these black rocks out of the earth has become one of Virginia's leading **industries.** An industry is a business or trade, such as fishing, farming, or printing.

The places where coal is found are known as coal seams, or coal beds. In Virginia, the first of these beds was found in Chesterfield County, outside of Richmond.

But how do humans get the coal out of the earth? They dig holes or tunnels called mines. The job of the people who do this digging is mining. The first major coal mining business in the United States began in Virginia in 1750.

Surface Mining   Sometimes pockets of coal are found just below the earth's surface. In these cases a type of mining called **surface mining** is used. In surface mining, huge power shovels scoop out dirt and rock. As the shovel scrapes deeper, small mountains are formed from the scooped-out soil. Once the coal is reached, smaller shovels are brought in to lift it from its bed.

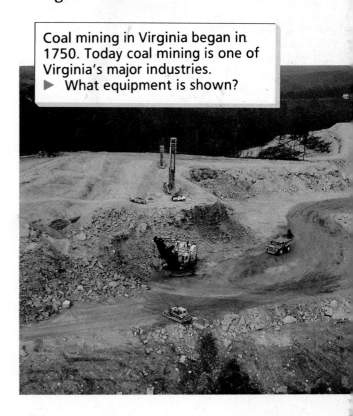

Coal mining in Virginia began in 1750. Today coal mining is one of Virginia's major industries.
▶ What equipment is shown?

The government has passed laws to protect land used for surface mining. Once the coal is dug out, the soil must be reclaimed. This means that it must be put back the way it was before the mine was dug. When this is done, the land is useful again.

Underground Mining Frequently, the coal beds are not close to the earth's surface. They are hidden deep within the earth. To get to these beds, miners must carve out long, dark tunnels. This type of mining is called underground mining. It is very hard and dirty work.

Today, mining coal is different from what it used to be. Most of the work is done by machines. Machines remove the coal from the walls, load it in cars or on conveyor belts, and do other steps that were once done by hand. A conveyor belt is a mechanical belt that is used to transport objects short distances. Today, one miner operating a machine can get the same amount of coal in the same amount of time that it took many miners of the past, working with picks and shovels.

Dangerous Work Over the years, many coal miners have been killed or badly hurt in accidents in the underground tunnels. There is always the danger that tunnel roofs or walls may fall. Deadly gases sometimes

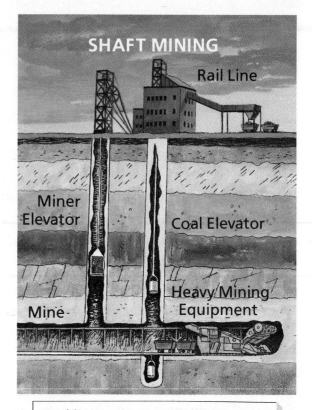

SHAFT MINING

Rail Line

Miner Elevator

Coal Elevator

Heavy Mining Equipment

Mine

Coal lines are generally deep under the ground. This causes dangerous working conditions.
► What are some of the dangers of shaft mining?

gather in the tunnels, so air has to be blown into the mine from the surface. Sometimes water collects in the tunnels. It must be pumped away. Coal dust can sometimes cause an explosion. When miners breathe in the dust, it can cause damage to their lungs.

Coal mine owners have taken many steps to make the workers and workplace as safe as possible. But getting coal from the earth is still hard and dangerous work.

From: IN COAL COUNTRY

By: Judith Hendershot

Setting: A coal mining town in the 1930s

Judith Hendershot grew up in a coal mining town. Her father as well as both of her grandfathers were coal miners. Her own memories and those of her relatives were the basis for her first book, *In Coal Country*. In the following passage, a daughter is describing the life of her father, who mines coal.

Papa dug coal from deep in the earth to earn a living. He dressed for work when everyone else went to bed. He wore faded denims [blue-jeans] and steel-toed shoes and he walked a mile to his job at the mine every night. . . .

In the morning I listened for the whistle that signaled the end of the hoot-owl shift. Sometimes I walked up the run [path] to meet Papa. He was always covered with grime and dirt, but I could see the whites of his eyes smiling at me. . . .

When we got home, Mama took the number three [large] tub from where it hung on the back porch and filled it with water heated on the huge iron stove. She draped [hung] a blanket across one corner of the kitchen, and Papa washed off the coal dust. . . .

PRODUCTS MADE FROM COAL

Batteries

Aspirin

Medicine

Steel

Pencils

Film

PAINT

Radio Parts

In the 1820s, the area around Richmond provided most American coal. Now, most of Virginia's coal comes from the southwestern part of the state.
▶ What are some products made from coal and coal chemicals?

B. Lumbering

You may recall from Chapter 2 that Virginia's forests are an important natural resource. Have you ever thought about all the things for which wood is used? Wood is used to make houses and furniture. The page you are reading right now began as wood. Wood goes into some medicines. It even becomes the film for cameras. Many goods we use every day are made of wood. And many people in Virginia have jobs making these goods.

All wood comes from trees growing in the forest. Trees that are cut and used for wood are called **timber.** Cutting the trees down and cutting the wood into pieces is called **lumbering.** The pieces of wood are called lumber. Many people in many parts of Virginia have jobs in lumbering.

Like mining, lumbering is a key industry in Virginia. It is carried out in all three parts of the state. In the Piedmont Region and in the mountain valleys of the Ridge and Valley Region, deciduous trees are important for lumbering. In the Tidewater Region, coniferous trees are the most important.

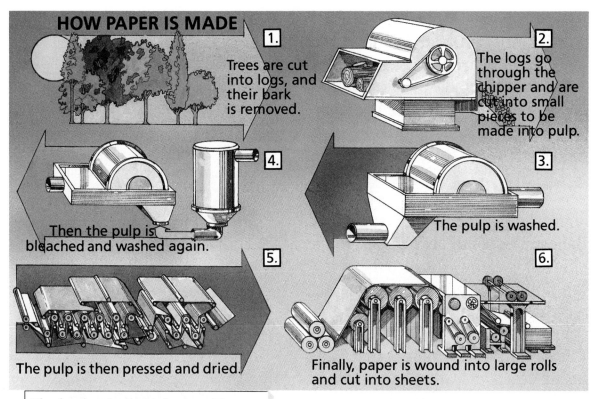

HOW PAPER IS MADE

1. Trees are cut into logs, and their bark is removed.

2. The logs go through the chipper and are cut into small pieces to be made into pulp.

3. The pulp is washed.

4. Then the pulp is bleached and washed again.

5. The pulp is then pressed and dried.

6. Finally, paper is wound into large rolls and cut into sheets.

The lumber industry is the oldest industry in the country. Lumbering is an important industry in Virginia.
▶ How is paper made from trees?

Paul Bunyan and his ox friend, Babe, had many adventures.
▶ What are people who work at lumbering called?

C. A Famous Lumbering Legend

People who work at lumbering are called lumberjacks. Many tales were told about the life of lumberjacks who lived in other parts of North America. One popular story was about a man named Paul Bunyan. He became famous for his great strength and daring actions.

For the ordinary lumberjack, lumbering was hard and dangerous work. For Paul, the supposed inventor of lumbering, it was just a sport.

According to the legend, Paul was 20 feet (6m) tall when he was one month old. At that age, he left home with his cradle on his shoulder and began to work as a lumberjack. With the help of an enormous blue ox named Babe, Paul cleared entire forests in a day.

Many stories about Paul tell about Babe. The legend says that Babe measured 42 ax handles and a plug of chewing tobacco between the horns. The ox ate tremendous amounts of hay and potato peels and could haul a whole forest of logs. Babe's thirst was so great that Paul had to create the Great Lakes as reservoirs for Babe's drinking water. Every time Babe needed new shoes, the blacksmith had to open a new iron mine in the state of Minnesota.

D. Fishing and Oystering

An Ideal Location Virginia's location on the Atlantic Ocean makes it an ideal place for another major industry. That industry is fishing. About 8,000 Virginians make a living by selling the fish and shellfish they catch. Another 5,600 Virginians have jobs getting these fish ready for market.

Do you like clams, oysters, or crabs? Those are just a few of the many kinds of shellfish found in Virginia's coastal waters. Virginia is es-

TOP FIVE FISHING STATES

States

MISSISSIPPI

CALIFORNIA

VIRGINIA

ALASKA

LOUISIANA

0 200 400 600 800 1,000 1,200 1,400 1,600 1,800 2,000

Quantity of Catch (in millions of pounds)

Virginia and other coastal states catch millions of pounds of fish each year.
► How many pounds of fish did the top state catch?

pecially famous for its oysters. The following story describes the business of gathering oysters.

In another few weeks, summer would be over. Jeff's visit with Uncle Ray and Aunt Joan would end. He would have to start school again.

The Oysterman Jeff's favorite part of his Virginia vacation had been going out on his uncle's boat. Uncle Ray was an oysterman. Each day they had sailed far out into the Chesapeake Bay. Jeff's uncle was getting ready for another oyster season.

"Please Uncle Ray," Jeff said as the boat skipped over the waves, "would you explain again about the *R* months?"

"Sure, Jeff," he said. "It's really easy. The law says we can take oysters from the water only in months spelled with the letter *R*. Right now we're in August. There's no *R* in the spelling of August. So the law says we can't take oysters."

"I think I understand now," Jeff said. "So next month it will be okay for you to take oysters, because there's an *R* in September."

"That's right!" Uncle Ray said.

"But why does the law say it is okay to take oysters only in *R* months?" Jeff asked his uncle.

"That's so the oysters will have a chance to grow and multiply," Uncle Ray said.

Virginia is famous for its oysters. The man in this picture is using tongs to pick up oysters from the beds where they live.
▶ What do these tongs look like?

The first oystermen of the Chesapeake Bay were the Native Americans who lived long ago. Today, oystermen use a tool called tongs. Tongs look like wooden scissors that are about 25 feet (8 m) long. They open and close like scissors. The oystermen use tongs to lift oysters from the beds where they grow.

Catching Oysters On a good day an oysterman might gather enough oysters to fill six to ten bushel baskets. Oystermen have to practice for many hours before they are trained well enough to catch that much. They also need good weather to have a good day. The wind or the tide can make the water too choppy for the oystermen to work.

Pollution is another problem for oystermen. The law says that oysters cannot be gathered from waters that are polluted.

Other Water Creatures Oysters and other shellfish are not the only creatures fished from Virginia's waters. Menhaden (men HAYD UN), shad, and sea bass are all very important to the fishing industry.

People who fish for sport also enjoy the many kinds of fish that abound in Virginia's coastal and inland waters. Some of the popular sport fish include flounder, shad, herring, striped bass, and sea trout.

E. Tourism in Virginia

Sport fishers are one group of people who contribute to another industry in Virginia. That industry is **tourism.** Tourism is providing services for people who travel for pleasure. Each year tourists spend $6 billion while visiting places in Virginia. Many Virginians have jobs taking care of tourists.

What is there to do and see in Virginia? The list is nearly endless. There are beautiful sandy beaches. There are parks in the green forests and blue-colored mountains. There are theme parks and natural wonders. There are colorful festivals and lively sporting events. Every year

Tourism has become big business in Virginia.
▶ How much money did tourists spend in Virginia in 1987?

DOLLARS SPENT ON TOURISM IN VIRGINIA 1980-1988

Billions of Dollars

Years   .... estimated

The Powhatan Village shows how Native Americans lived long ago.
▶ What are some things that tourists might learn here?

thousands of tourists visit Virginia to enjoy these things.

Tourists also come to learn about Virginia's rich history. Many important events in the first 200 years of the United States took place in Virginia. Battles of the War for Independence and the Civil War were fought in Virginia. Many Presidents, explorers, inventors, and other important people were born or have lived in Virginia.

LESSON *1* REVIEW

THINK AND WRITE

A. How does surface mining differ from underground mining?
B. What are some products that wood is used to make?
C. What is Paul Bunyan known for?
D. Why are oystermen allowed to take oysters only in months spelled with *R*?
E. What are some attractions that bring tourists to Virginia each year?

SKILLS CHECK

MAP SKILL

The Great Lakes mentioned in Paul Bunyan's legend are five large lakes located on the border between Canada and the United States. Turn to the map of the United States in the Atlas on pages 354–355. Name the five Great Lakes.

Farming in Virginia

THINK ABOUT WHAT YOU KNOW
Why do different people have different jobs?

STUDY THE VOCABULARY
specialized farming   **orchard**
fertilizer   **livestock**

FOCUS YOUR READING
What kind of farming is done in each of Virginia's three regions?

A. Specialized Farming

Farming Then   Farming is another industry that depends on natural resources. Over the years, Virginia farmers have learned how to make the best use of the resources in their part of the state.

Imagine that you were a Virginia farmer living long ago. Your farm would be like your own little world. You might grow potatoes, corn, and beans for your table. Your cows would supply you with fresh milk and with sweet cream for butter. When you needed eggs, you would visit your henhouse. Almost everything your family needed would come from your own land.

Farming Now   Today, Virginia farming is totally different. Farmers practice specialized farming. Specialized farming is the growing or raising of only one thing.

The move toward specialized farming began in the early 1800s. During that time, machines were invented to make the farmer's work easier. With the use of machines, farmers could grow more crops. Suddenly, they were growing and raising much more than their own families could use.

Farming has always been important in Virginia. This farmer is harvesting potatoes.
▶ How are they being harvested?

Farming has changed over the years. Modern farmers use machines to make farming easier.
▶ In what ways have machines made farming easier?

When farmers practice specialized farming, they give full attention to the one thing that grows best in their soil. Each farmer needs to use only those machines that are useful for farming that crop.

Specialized farming has made people depend on one another. Farmers buy the things they no longer grow or raise themselves. For example, a farmer whose special crop is potatoes will sell most of those potatoes. Then he will buy the other food he needs with the money he made from selling his potatoes.

B. Tidewater Farming

Sandy Soil Each of the three regions of Virginia is known for some special crops. In most cases, the region's soil determines which crops will grow best.

Much of the soil in the Tidewater Region is sandy and light-colored. This type of soil has little plant food, or chemicals on which plants live. For that reason, farmers in that region often give their crops help in growing. They do this by using **fertilizer**. Fertilizer is a substance, such as manure or special chemicals, spread over the soil to help plants grow much bigger and stronger.

113

When spring arrives, the light, sandy soil warms up quickly. Because of this, farmers can plant early in the year. Having a long season allows many Tidewater farmers to grow two or three shifts of crops a year. Within days of picking one crop, the farmers are out plowing their fields again. After this, they fertilize the soil and plant another crop.

Tidewater Crops Many farmers in the southeastern section of the Tidewater Region grow soybeans and peanuts. Virginia peanuts are famous for their large size. They are shipped all over the world.

Plants are checked to make sure insects are not damaging them.
▶ Why is this work done by hand?

When the peanuts are ready they are pulled out of the ground and left to dry in the sun.
▶ How are peanuts used?

Peanuts are not only good to eat. They are also good for you. Oil pressed from peanuts is a healthful product used for frying foods. This oil is also used in salad dressings and margarine. And when roasted peanuts are crushed into a thick paste, they become a delicious spread — peanut butter.

Tidewater peanuts are connected to another well-known Tidewater product — Smithfield hams. People in many parts of the world enjoy Smithfield hams from the southeastern Tidewater Region. Sometimes the pigs that provide these hams eat Tidewater peanuts. That is one reason why Virginia's Smithfield hams taste so good.

Truck farmers take their crops to nearby cities in just a few hours. These farmers have grown pumpkins.
► What season do you think it is?

Another reason is that they are still cured, or prepared, by the method that the Indians in Virginia taught to the first English settlers.

Truck Farming Many farms in the Tidewater Region are called truck farms. Read the following story to see why.

The Cohen family from Pennsylvania had spent a great week in Virginia Beach. Now they were driving back home after their vacation.

They were just outside of Portsmouth when ten-year-old Mark yelled, "Look!" He was pointing out the back window of the car. On the side of the road was a truck. It was piled high with a rainbow of fruits and vegetables. There were huge melons surrounded by cucumbers, tomatoes, and green beans. Mounds of sweet and white potatoes lay next to a pile of ears of corn. On the side of the truck were painted the words *Gilby's Truck Farm.*

"Those fruits and vegetables look good," Mark's mother said.

Mark's father pulled off the road. "Hi," he said stepping out of the family car.

"Hello," said the truck driver.

"Are those vegetables for sale?" asked Mark's mother.

"No, I'm afraid they're not," the driver said. "I'm on my way to market with these. I just stopped to let my truck's engine cool."

"How many kinds of fruits and vegetables do you grow altogether?" Mark asked.

"I grow about 30 different kinds of fruits and vegetables," the farmer replied. "Some other truck farmers grow even more."

Over 60 kinds of fruits and vegetables are grown each year on the Eastern Shore, a part of the Tidewater Region. They are delivered to nearby cities just a few hours after they are picked. This is why the Eastern Shore is often called Virginia's Market Basket.

115

C. Piedmont Farming

Good for Grains Unlike the sandy Tidewater soil, soil in the Piedmont Region contains a great deal of clay. Small amounts of iron give the soil a reddish color.

The Piedmont is good for growing corn. Much of the corn is sold to be eaten straight off the cob. Other corn is ground into cornmeal, a grain used in cooking. Some corn is used as food for farm animals.

The soil in the northern Piedmont is well suited to growing another grain. That grain is wheat. Mills grind this important crop into flour. Are you fond of bread, cakes, crackers, or noodles? All of these tasty foods and many others are made from flour.

The northern counties of the Piedmont are also known for their dairy farms. These are homes to cattle that give rich milk. Some of the top cream from this milk is churned into creamy butter. Other products, such as cheeses, are also made from the milk.

Raising Horses The northern Piedmont is well known for the horses raised there. Many horse farms are located in the area around Fauquier (FAW kihr) and Loudoun (LOUD un) counties. The area is sometimes called Virginia's Horse Country.

The Piedmont is also noted for peaches. Trees heavy with the fruit can be seen on the lower hills of the Blue Ridge Mountains.

Farther south in the Piedmont is tobacco country. For a long time, tobacco has been the top money-making crop in Virginia. Very long ago in Virginia, people used the tobacco leaves as money.

Soil in the Piedmont Region is good for growing corn.
▶ What other crops are grown in the Piedmont Region?

PRODUCTS MADE FROM PEANUTS

Peanut Butter

Cooking Oil

Artificial Logs

Soaps and Shampoos

Paints

Animal Feed and Fertilizer

Peanuts are grown in the southeastern part of Virginia. In this country, most peanuts are used for food rather than for oil.
▶ What products made from peanuts do you use?

Though Virginians still make more money from tobacco than any other crop, that is changing. Tobacco sales have fallen because of the dangers of using tobacco. Fewer people are using tobacco, and farmers are earning less from their tobacco crops.

D. Farming in the Ridge and Valley Region

Many Types of Land There are many kinds of land in the Ridge and Valley Region. There are broad green valleys. There are plateaus. There is hilly land dotted with rocks. What can grow well in such different types of land? Many things can!

Rocky hills and mountains may not be the best land for running large farm machines. And rocky soil may not be good for growing many crops. But neither fact has stopped Ridge and Valley farmers from growing much of Virginia's corn and wheat crop. And these are just two of the many farm products for which the Ridge and Valley Region is known.

Famous for Apples The Great Valley is most famous for its apple **orchards.** Orchards are fields of fruit trees. In the spring, the apple trees are full of beautiful white blossoms.

Each year in early May, the Shenandoah Apple Blossom Festival is held in Winchester. The joyous sounds of music from a brass band fill the warm spring air. Colorful floats from

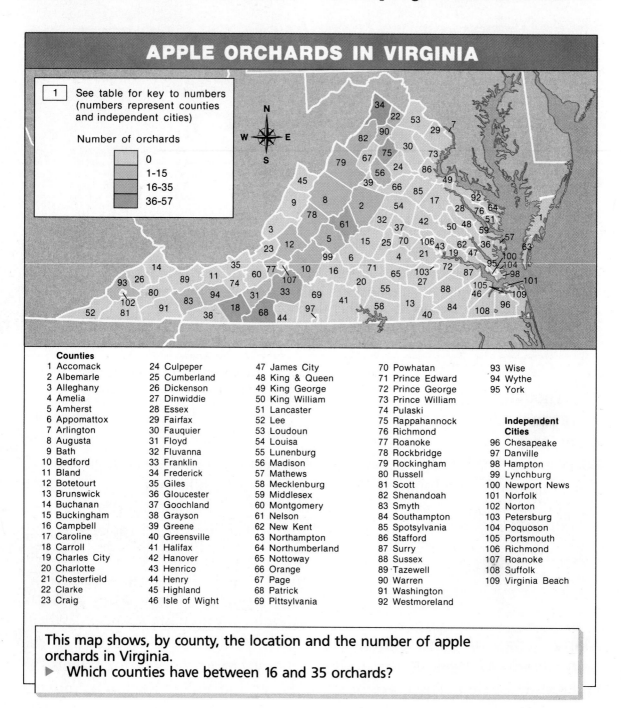

APPLE ORCHARDS IN VIRGINIA

1 See table for key to numbers (numbers represent counties and independent cities)

Number of orchards

	0
	1-15
	16-35
	36-57

Counties

1 Accomack	24 Culpeper	47 James City	70 Powhatan	93 Wise
2 Albemarle	25 Cumberland	48 King & Queen	71 Prince Edward	94 Wythe
3 Alleghany	26 Dickenson	49 King George	72 Prince George	95 York
4 Amelia	27 Dinwiddie	50 King William	73 Prince William	
5 Amherst	28 Essex	51 Lancaster	74 Pulaski	
6 Appomattox	29 Fairfax	52 Lee	75 Rappahannock	**Independent**
7 Arlington	30 Fauquier	53 Loudoun	76 Richmond	**Cities**
8 Augusta	31 Floyd	54 Louisa	77 Roanoke	96 Chesapeake
9 Bath	32 Fluvanna	55 Lunenburg	78 Rockbridge	97 Danville
10 Bedford	33 Franklin	56 Madison	79 Rockingham	98 Hampton
11 Bland	34 Frederick	57 Mathews	80 Russell	99 Lynchburg
12 Botetourt	35 Giles	58 Mecklenburg	81 Scott	100 Newport News
13 Brunswick	36 Gloucester	59 Middlesex	82 Shenandoah	101 Norfolk
14 Buchanan	37 Goochland	60 Montgomery	83 Smyth	102 Norton
15 Buckingham	38 Grayson	61 Nelson	84 Southampton	103 Petersburg
16 Campbell	39 Greene	62 New Kent	85 Spotsylvania	104 Poquoson
17 Caroline	40 Greensville	63 Northampton	86 Stafford	105 Portsmouth
18 Carroll	41 Halifax	64 Northumberland	87 Surry	106 Richmond
19 Charles City	42 Hanover	65 Nottoway	88 Sussex	107 Roanoke
20 Charlotte	43 Henrico	66 Orange	89 Tazewell	108 Suffolk
21 Chesterfield	44 Henry	67 Page	90 Warren	109 Virginia Beach
22 Clarke	45 Highland	68 Patrick	91 Washington	
23 Craig	46 Isle of Wight	69 Pittsylvania	92 Westmoreland	

This map shows, by county, the location and the number of apple orchards in Virginia.
▶ Which counties have between 16 and 35 orchards?

all across the state drift along the town's main street. But the important fruits of the Great Valley's apple trees come out in fall. That is when the apples are ready for picking.

Raising Livestock The Ridge and Valley Region is also known for the raising of livestock. *Livestock* is the name given to farm animals, such as cattle, sheep, and pigs. In 1987 Virginia farmers earned more money from raising livestock than from any other area of farming.

Raising cattle for milk or meat is an especially important part of Ridge and Valley farming. Rockingham County leads all Virginia counties in the number of cattle raised. Many sheep are also raised in the Ridge and Valley Region. Chickens and turkeys are raised there too. Farmers who raise these birds are called poultry farmers.

There are many turkey farms in the Valley Region.
▶ What do we call people who raise turkeys and chickens?

LESSON 2 *REVIEW*

THINK AND WRITE

A. How did farming change after farm machines were invented?
B. How do Tidewater farmers improve the sandy soil?
C. Why have tobacco sales in the southern Piedmont fallen?
D. In what ways is the Ridge and Valley Region different from Virginia's other two regions?

SKILLS CHECK

THINKING SKILL

What is the natural region of Virginia in which you live? Think about the things that are grown there. If you were a farmer, which agricultural products would you raise?

SHIPS THROUGH THE TIMES

1 Egyptian vessel, 2,500 B.C.

Viking ship, 1100 **2**

The Godspeed, 1607 **3**

Fulton's Steamboat, 1807 **4**

Modern Cruise Ship, 1990 **5**

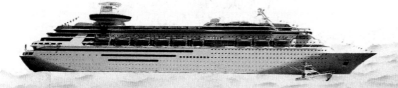

Travel by water is one of the earliest forms of transportation. More than 4,000 years ago the Egyptians showed great skill at building and sailing ships. Shipbuilding has always been an important manufacturing industry in Virginia. The Hampton Roads area is a major center for building and repairing ships.

▶ How does Virginia's location make it a good place for shipbuilding?

Manufacturing in Virginia

THINK ABOUT WHAT YOU KNOW

What things can you name that are made in factories?

STUDY THE VOCABULARY

manufacturing   food
synthetic fiber   processing
textile   electronics

FOCUS YOUR READING

What are Virginia's most important manufacturing industries today?

A. Growth in Manufacturing

Mining, fishing, and farming are all important industries in Virginia. But Virginia makes even more money from manufacturing. Manufacturing is the making of goods by people. Today, most goods in Virginia are made in factories where people use machines.

Many different manufacturing industries are in Virginia. Over 400,000 Virginians work at making goods. In the past 20 years, almost every manufacturing industry in Virginia has grown. Because of this growth, more and more Virginians hold jobs in factories and plants. Manufactured goods are sold to people both inside and outside the state.

Manufacturing brings money to Virginia. It provides many Virginians with different kinds of jobs.

B. Major Manufacturing Industries

Products from Chemicals The chemical industry is among the most important in Virginia. Chemical factories in both the Tidewater and Piedmont regions manufacture fertilizers. Another thing made by the chemical industry is medicines. Lynchburg, Elkton, Hopewell, and Richmond all have chemical plants that produce medicines.

The chemical industry also makes synthetic fibers. These are fibers, such as nylon and rayon, that

Manufacturing in Virginia became important in the 1900s.
► Which manufacturing industry employs the most people?

MANUFACTURING INDUSTRIES IN VIRGINIA EMPLOYING THE MOST PEOPLE

Type of Industry:	Number of People Employed in Virginia
Textiles	43,000
Transportation equipment	43,000
Food processing	40,000
Electronics	39,000
Chemicals	33,000
Printing	31,500
Apparel	29,000
Furniture	24,500
Lumber and wood products	24,000
Metal products	18,000

121

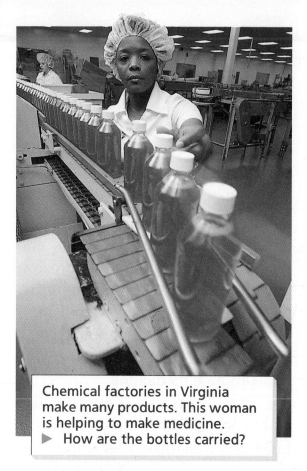

Chemical factories in Virginia make many products. This woman is helping to make medicine.
▶ How are the bottles carried?

Food processing is preparing farm products for sale. Many of the foods that you eat are prepared by the 40,000 people who work in Virginia's food processing factories.

Fruits and vegetables are just two of the products made ready to eat in this way. Some of the fruits and vegetables prepared in factories arrive frozen at the market. Some arrive in cans and jars.

Seafood is also processed in factories near the Chesapeake Bay. Crabs, oysters, and other shellfish are canned or frozen there. People can then enjoy these foods all year long.

are not found in nature. Synthetic fibers are made in Hopewell and in Chesterfield County. These synthetic fibers are then made into cloth by the **textile** (TEKS tyl) industry. Textiles are cloths and fabrics.

Virginia Tobacco The tobacco industry is also important. Cigarettes and pipe tobacco are produced in Virginia factories. Most large tobacco factories are located in Richmond, Danville, and Petersburg.

Food Industries Another industry that makes a large amount of money for Virginia is **food processing.**

These women are working in a food processing plant.
▶ What are they wearing to help keep the food clean?

FISH PROCESSING

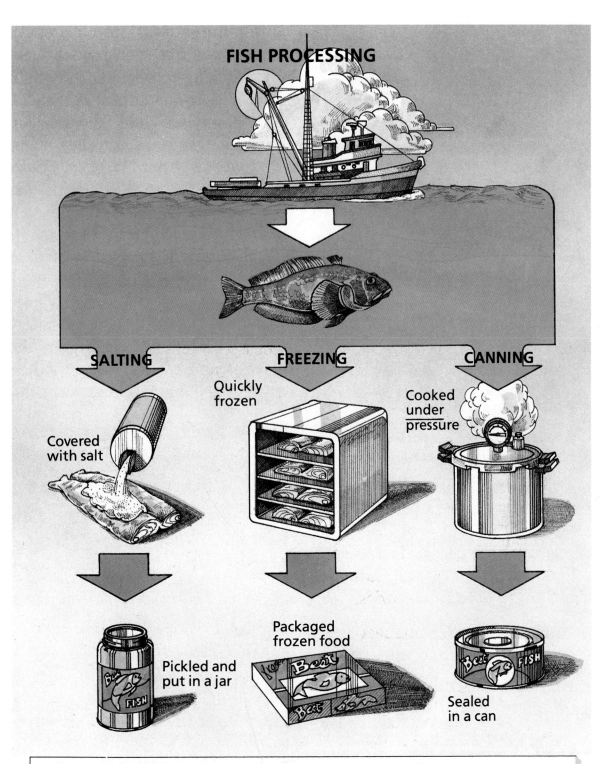

SALTING

Covered with salt

Pickled and put in a jar

FREEZING

Quickly frozen

Packaged frozen food

CANNING

Cooked under pressure

Sealed in a can

As you can see, Virginia seafood is processed in several different ways. Many processing plants are located close to the Chesapeake Bay.
► Why is the location of processing plants close to the Chesapeake Bay important to the fish-processing industry?

Electronic products are being made at this workplace.
► What are two types of electronic products?

Other Industries If you are like most Americans, you probably enjoy watching television. You might also like to listen to the radio. You may never think about where those things are made. They might have come from Virginia. **Electronics** (ee lek TRAHN ihks) is Virginia's fourth most important manufacturing industry. Electronics is the use of electricity to give us many products.

Radios and televisions are only two of the goods made by the nearly 39,000 Virginians working in the electronics industry. Toasters, hair dryers, and many other electrical

Making transportation equipment is an important industry in Virginia.
► By what means does the bus get from one work station to the next during construction?

Some factories in Virginia make bakery goods such as cakes, cookies, bread, and rolls. Other factories prepare dairy foods such as milk, cheese, yogurt, and butter. Some factories process meat products such as Smithfield hams. Factories around Winchester prepare apple juice and applesauce.

goods are made in Virginia. There are electronics plants in Charlottesville, Lynchburg, Salem, Suffolk, and Waynesboro.

The industry that makes transportation equipment is also very important in Virginia. That industry manufactures goods that are used in travel. Airplane tires, for example, are transportation equipment. Virginia has the world's biggest airplane tire plant.

Another important industry in Virginia is the printing and publishing industry. This industry gives you the books that you read. It also provides you with a variety of magazines and newspapers.

The textile industry is another major industry. It employs the largest number of people of any industry in Virginia. Textile mills are located in the cities of Danville, South Boston, and Martinsville and in Halifax County. Virginia also has the largest textile mill under one roof in the world. It is the Dan River Mill, and it is located in Danville.

The textile industry is a major industry in Virginia. Textile mills are found in several cities throughout the state.
▶ What are some products that textile workers make?

LEADING TEXTILE-PRODUCING STATES, 1988

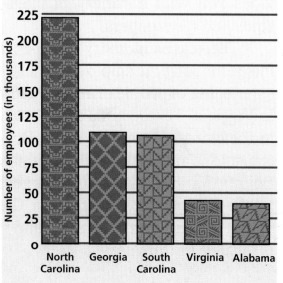

The top five textile producers in the United States are shown here.
► How many Virginians work in the textile industry?

C. Manufacturing and Natural Resources

If we did not have natural resources, there could be no manufacturing. Trees and minerals are necessary for many of the goods you have read about. Many of the machines that are used to make these goods need coal or water to run.

Manufacturing depends on nature. But it is also true that nature can be improved by manufacturing. Fertilizers made in Virginia's factories can help worn-out soil to become fertile again. Chemicals made in Virginia's factories can be used to destroy harmful insects.

Virginia's state government is aware that its industries depend on natural resources. It also knows that industries can damage or destroy the natural resources they need.

That is why the government makes laws to control how industries use natural resources. Most of these laws are concerned with pollution. Some are designed to control the amounts of chemicals that are dumped into Virginia's waters. Other laws control the amount of pollutants that factories are allowed to release into the air.

LESSON *3* REVIEW

THINK AND WRITE

A. Why are manufacturing industries important to Virginia and to the people who live in the state?

B. What are three of the leading manufacturing industries that are found in Virginia?

C. Why are natural resources important to manufacturing?

SKILLS CHECK

WRITING SKILL

Write a sentence to describe Virginia's position on the graph above.

USING THE VOCABULARY

industry	livestock
reclaim	manufacturing
timber	synthetic fiber
fertilizer	textile
orchard	food processing

On a separate sheet of paper, write the word that best matches each definition below. Choose your answers from the vocabulary words above.

1. farm animals, such as cattle, sheep, and pigs
2. any kind of business or trade
3. industry that manufactures cloths and fabrics
4. trees that are cut into pieces and used for wood
5. the making of goods by people
6. a field of fruit trees
7. a substance that helps plants grow bigger and stronger
8. a fiber not found in nature
9. preparing farm products for sale
10. to put something back the way it was before

REMEMBERING WHAT YOU READ

Write your answers in complete sentences on a separate sheet of paper.

1. What two names are given to the places where coal is found?
2. In which regions of Virginia is lumbering done?
3. How many Virginians make a living selling the fish and shellfish they catch?
4. Who were the first oystermen of the Chesapeake Bay?
5. When did the move toward specialized farming begin?
6. Why can Tidewater farmers plant early in the year?
7. Which fruit is the Piedmont Region noted for?
8. What area of Virginia is most famous for its apple orchards?
9. Which industry in Virginia manufactures fertilizer?
10. Which industry in Virginia employs the most people?

TYING LITERATURE TO SOCIAL STUDIES

Peanuts are an important crop in Virginia. George Washington Carver was a famous scientist who found many uses for peanuts. Find a biography of George Washington Carver in your school library. A biography is an account of the life of a person. Look through the biography you have chosen to find some unusual ways that George Washington Carver used peanuts. Take notes as you read. Then report what you have learned to the class.

THINKING CRITICALLY

Write your answers in complete sentences on a separate sheet of paper.

1. What are some reasons why coal mining is a dangerous job?
2. Why is fishing an important industry in Virginia?
3. How does specialized farming compare with the farming done during the early days of Virginia?
4. Why can Tidewater farmers grow more shifts of crops per year than other farmers?
5. What is a Virginia industry that helps people in other states?

SUMMARIZING THE CHAPTER

On a separate sheet of paper, draw a graphic organizer that is like the one shown here. Copy the information from this graphic organizer to the one you have drawn. Under the main idea for each lesson, write three statements that support it. The first one has been done for you.

CHAPTER THEME

Virginia has many different kinds of industry, many of which involve natural resources.

LESSON 1

Many industries in Virginia depend on natural resources.

1. Coal mining
2. Lumbering
3. Fishing and oystering

LESSON 2

Each region is known for special kinds of farming.

1. _____
2. _____
3. _____

LESSON 3

Virginia has many important manufacturing industries.

1. _____
2. _____
3. _____

COOPERATIVE LEARNING

One way to understand history is by putting on skits. A skit is a very short play. It shows how something may have happened or the way things might have been.

REMEMBER TO:
- Give your ideas.
- Listen to others' ideas.
- Plan your work with the group.
- Present your project.
- Discuss how your group worked.

PROJECT

- Working in groups of four or five, choose some kind of work that Virginians do for the subject of your skit. You might want your skit to take place in a coal mine or at a lumber camp. Other places might be aboard a fishing boat, on a farm, or in a factory. You may use one of these places or choose one of your own. The important thing is to show people working and talking about their work.

- As a group, write parts for each person in your skit. One member of the group should be the director. This person tells the actors what to do, where to move, and how to say their parts. Be sure that there is a part for each member of the group.

- Practice what you are going to say and do two or three times. This will help all the people in the group feel more comfortable with their part.

PRESENTATION AND REVIEW

- Present the skit to your class.

- Ask your classmates what they liked most about your skit. Did they learn anything from it? Did the talking sound real? Was there enough action?

- Talk about the skit with your own group. How might you have improved the skit?

Reading SKILLBUILDER to Learn

A. WHY DO I NEED THIS SKILL?

Some books we read for fun. Other books we read to learn. Textbooks, such as this one, contain many ideas to learn and remember. You will do better if you have a plan of action when you study. SQR is a study-reading plan that will help you understand and remember the ideas in this book and in other textbooks, too. The letters *SQR* stand for **Survey, Question, Read.**

B. LEARNING THE SKILL

There are three easy steps in the SQR plan. Each step is described below.

The first step is to survey the lesson. To do this, look at the headings, questions, and vocabulary words. Also look at any photographs, maps, and other visuals in the lesson. This will give you a general idea of what the lesson is about. Then think about what you already know about the topic. Make some guesses about the ideas you think will be in this lesson.

The second step is to think of questions you may have about this topic. If questions do not come to mind, use the words *where, when, how,* and *why* to get you started. Look at the questions at the beginning and at the end of the lesson. Then look at the question that goes with each picture. Make a list of questions about the lesson and plan to find answers for them.

The third step is to read the lesson. As you read, find the answers to the questions on your list. If you think of other questions as you read, answer them as well.

C. PRACTICING THE SKILL

Turn to page 84. Practice the SQR study-reading plan on Lesson 2 of Chapter 2. The lesson is called "Forests, Wildlife, Rivers, and Lakes."

Start by surveying the lesson. Follow the directions given above. Think about what you already know about Virginia's forests, wildlife, rivers, and lakes. What guesses can you make about the ideas in this lesson? Look at the questions in this lesson. Prepare your own list of questions. Read the lesson carefully. Find the answers to your questions. If you cannot answer all your questions, try reading the lesson once again.

D. APPLYING THE SKILL

The SQR strategy is important to use whenever you are reading to learn. Try this strategy when you read your next science lesson.

USING SQR

Survey	Look at the questions, vocabulary words, and visuals in the lesson. Think about some things that you already know about the topic. Make predictions about the lesson content.
Question	Note questions already in the lesson. Use vocabulary words and headings to prepare other questions. Write your questions or at least make a mental note of them.
Read	Read the text to answer your questions. Write out answers or say them to yourself. Ask and answer other questions that come to mind as you read.

The USING SQR chart on this page will help you remember the steps. Make a copy of the chart and use it when you are studying.

A. WHY DO I NEED THIS SKILL?

Maps use symbols to stand for real places and things. Map symbols are explained in the map key. Learning what the symbols stand for will help you get the most information from the map.

B. LEARNING THE SKILL

Every map has symbols. The symbols may be letters, numbers, lines, colors, or a small drawing of an object. For example, a small circle can stand for a town or city. A small drawing of a picnic table can stand for a picnic area. The symbols are placed on the map to show where the places or things are located.

Map symbols can stand for many things. They can stand for roads, cities, or rivers. And they can stand for airports, railroads, or parks. Map symbols are listed and explained in the map key.

Look at the map on the facing page. This is a map of an imaginary place called Buck's Island. The map shows places and things on the island and the surrounding area.

Look at the symbols on the map. You can probably guess what some of the symbols mean just by looking at them. Find the small airplane on the map. You may have figured out that it stands for the airport.

Other symbols are not as easy to figure out. Look at the small triangles on the map. A triangle can stand for many different things. To find out what it means on this map, you must look at the map key.

Find the triangle symbol in the map key. Read the word across from the triangle. Now you know that this symbol stands for a beach. When you look back at the map, you can tell how many beaches there are on the island and where they are located.

Look at all the map symbols shown in the key. Find each one of them on the map. The symbols help you read the map. And they help you learn about Buck's Island.

C. PRACTICING THE SKILL

Use the map of Buck's Island to answer the following questions.

1. How many towns are there on Buck's Island?
2. What does a small square on the map stand for?
3. What does a large square on the map stand for?

4. Where can people do their shopping on Buck's Island?
5. What is the highway that runs between two mountains?
6. Where is the airport located?
7. What towns on Buck's Island have ferry service?
8. What towns does the railroad link?
9. Where is the school located?
10. Where can people go fishing on Buck's Island?

D. APPLYING THE SKILL

Prepare a map of your school and the surrounding area. Begin by listing all the things you want to show on your map, such as the school building, the parking lot, and the playground. Then draw a symbol to stand for each item on your list. Draw the map using your symbols for the real places and things. Be sure that you include a map key to explain your symbols.

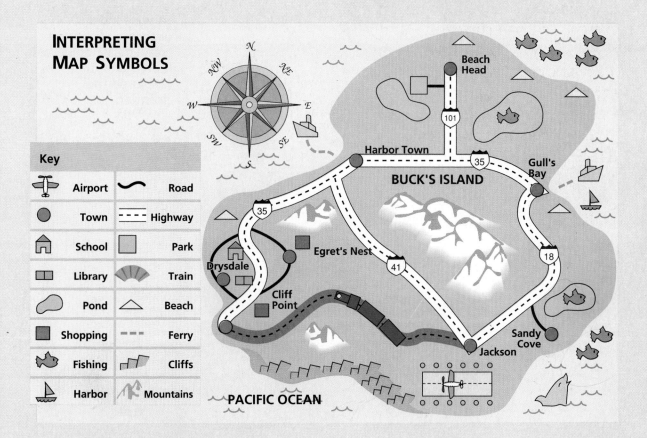

INTERPRETING MAP SYMBOLS

Key

Airport		Road	
Town		Highway	
School		Park	
Library		Train	
Pond		Beach	
Shopping		Ferry	
Fishing		Cliffs	
Harbor		Mountains	

Beach Head

101

Harbor Town

35

BUCK'S ISLAND

Gull's Bay

35

Egret's Nest

41

Drysdale

18

Cliff Point

Jackson

Sandy Cove

PACIFIC OCEAN

In 1607 three sailing ships made their way up the Chesapeake Bay looking for the best place to build a settlement.

A wise Indian woman, Sacagawea, served as a guide as Lewis and Clark explored the frontier.

134

McCormick's reaper revolutionized farming in Virginia and in the entire nation. ▶

◀ General George Washington, a Virginian, addressed the Continental Congress.

2 VIRGINIA'S HISTORY TO 1850

Some of the most important events in our country's history occurred in Virginia. From the founding of the colony at Jamestown to the founding of the United States of America, Virginians led the way. Virginia is the birthplace of eight Presidents.

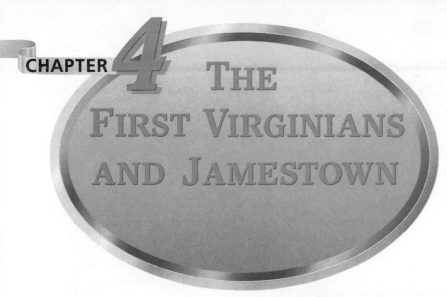

CHAPTER 4

THE FIRST VIRGINIANS AND JAMESTOWN

In 1607 the English made their first permanent settlement in the New World. They called it Jamestown. The settlers faced many hardships, but their lives improved after they learned how to make a living from the land.

Native Americans

THINK ABOUT WHAT YOU KNOW

Make a list of places you know about that have Indian names. Have you ever seen any of these places in person?

STUDY THE VOCABULARY

tribe   **wigwam**
longhouse

FOCUS YOUR READING

What was life like for the Indians living in Virginia at the time of the first English settlement?

A. Virginia's Many Tribes

The First People   Long before any European set foot on Virginia soil, people were making their homes there. The blue smoke from their campfires rose in the forests. The glassy surface of the calm lakes and rivers was stirred by the strokes of their paddles. These early people of Virginia were Native Americans. The European explorers later gave these people the name *Indians*.

The Indians of early Virginia lived together in groups called tribes. Hundreds of such tribes were spread across the continent of North America. And there were many different kinds of Indian tribes living here in Virginia.

The Indians had no written history, so they relied on legends to explain many things. The following legend was told to explain why there were so many Indian tribes.

An Indian Legend   In the beginning (the story goes) all Indians lived together beneath the earth. Their animals lived there with them. One day a curious mole crawled far away and found a hole in the ground. Scrambling through, the creature discovered a lovely sunlit world. When the Indians learned of this exciting new place, they all wanted to see it. Many Indians decided they wanted to live in this beautiful world. Some Indians, though, decided to stay in the underground home they were used to. They remained behind. There were now two groups of Indians—those underground and those above the ground.

The Story Continues   Those Indians who had reached the sunlight moved on. They came, after a time, to a river. There, a splendid bird beat its wings, causing the waters of the river to part. The Indians began to walk across the dry river bed. But soon the beautiful bird flew away. The swirling waters closed, leaving some of the Indians on the near bank of the river. Now there were three groups of Indians.

Indians roasted fish and other food over open fires. They cooked much like people today who cook their food outdoors.
► How did Indians carry the fish they caught back to their village?

Those who had crossed the river came next to a very high mountain. Some deer showed them a path through the jagged rocks. But before all could follow, some eagles chased the deer away. Now there were four groups of Indians.

Those who journeyed on found themselves at last in a thick forest. The trees made it difficult for the Indians to see one another. Small bands wandered off in different directions. Now there were many groups of Indians.

And that (the story ends) is why the Indian tribes live in many different places.

B. How the Tribes Lived

Indian Homes   Imagine that you were a European on an early voyage to Virginia. As your ship nears land, you see groups of long, low buildings scattered along the shore. You find similar buildings set in clearings in the woods. These **longhouses,** as they were called, were used by some Indians as homes.

Using Skins and Bark   The longhouses were set up in villages. Each longhouse was covered on the sides with ropelike grass and tree bark. Its roof was made of bark strengthened with animal skins. If you peeled away the skins and bark, you would discover a frame of bent young trees. Stepping inside, you would find a crackling fire. A hole was cut in the roof of the longhouse to allow the smoke from the fire to escape.

Sometimes the Indians built smaller houses in much the same way. They called these smaller houses **wigwams.**

C. What the Tribes Ate

Indian Food The land and waters of early Virginia offered many possibilities for daily living and especially

This picture of a 1587 Indian village, near Chesapeake Bay, shows Indian homes.
▶ What else does this village picture show?

SECOTON.

for good eating. The local trees produced nuts and juicy berries. Squirrels, rabbits, wild turkeys, and deer all roamed the forest. The cold, salty waters of Chesapeake Bay were full of meaty crabs, oysters, and other tasty seafood. (The name *Chesapeake* is an Indian word meaning "great salt water.")

Gathering Food The Indians knew many ways of gathering this food. They took careful aim with bows and arrows to hunt the turkeys, deer, and other animals in the forest. They used sticks and sturdy vines to make traps for raccoons and opossums. They sharpened bones into fishing hooks and spear tips. They wove grasses and weeds into nets.

A day of hunting and fishing was followed by an evening of great feasting. One evening the Indians may have turned a side of meat over a blazing fire to cook it on all sides. Or they may have roasted whole fish on sticks above glowing coals.

Growing Food But the Indians not only gathered food. They also grew crops. In the rich soil, they raised ears of sweet corn. They planted different types of beans.

The Indians made use of all they could. Skins taken from animals were used to make warm clothing. Animal fur provided bed covers that were used during long winter nights. Animal bones served as tools and many other useful things.

D. Chief Powhatan's Tribes

The first English settlers to reach Virginia may have expected to meet a loose scattering of savages. Instead, they found a tightly knit group united under a fearless chief. The chief's name was Powhatan (POU uh tan). He was the leader of about 30 tribes.

The Indians honored Powhatan. He lived in the finest longhouse in the most important village. Leaders from each village gave food to the chief and his loyal braves. For his part, Powhatan was like a watchful father to the people of his tribes. He kept them safe from the attacks of outsiders. He also protected them from evil spirits.

The dress of this Indian warrior is probably similar to the way Chief Powhatan dressed.
▶ What weapon is this Indian brave carrying?

LESSON **1** REVIEW

THINK AND WRITE

A. What do you think the Indian legend tells the reader about how the Indians felt toward nature and animals?

B. How would you describe the homes the Indians lived in?

C. How did the Indians get the food they ate?

D. Why did the Indians honor Powhatan as a leader?

SKILLS CHECK

THINKING SKILL

What do you think might be some of the good points and some of the bad points of living under a fearless and powerful leader?

LESSON 2

The Village of Jamestown

THINK ABOUT WHAT YOU KNOW

Think of a place where no one lives, such as Mars or the North Pole. What fears might you have about being one of the first persons to live in such a place?

STUDY THE VOCABULARY

colony   planter
plantation

FOCUS YOUR READING

What problems faced the English on their voyage to Jamestown and after they arrived?

A. The Arrival of the English

A Letter to Home Like all early arrivals to the New World, the first group to come to Virginia from England had a very long, hard trip. A letter such as the following might have been written by one of these brave voyagers.

26 April, 1607

My Dearest Wife,

Over four months have passed since I saw you. It seems like forever!

Some days ago our ship met with a terribly fierce storm. So badly were we tossed about that Captain Ratcliffe nearly headed back toward England. The captain claims that we will reach Virginia any day now.

Of the three ships, ours, the *Discovery*, is the smallest. The *Godspeed,* at 40 tons, is twice as large. And the *Susan Constant,* the main vessel, is five times the size of ours. That great ship is under the command of Captain Christopher Newport. I hear that Captain Newport is a brave man and a fine sailor.

So much has happened since we set sail in December. Soon after we left port, we lost our wind. Our three ships stood still for six weeks before the breeze returned! We used up much of our food and water. This left little to eat during the long Atlantic crossing. All we had were some stale crackers.

This early map shows the James Fort and the surrounding area.
▶ Why did the mapmaker draw Chief Powhatan so large?

141

The *Susan Constant,* the *Godspeed,* and the *Discovery* brought the early settlers to Virginia.
▶ How did these big ships move across the ocean?

The ocean crossing was like a bad dream. We suffered through four weeks of bone-wearying storms. Many of the men became sick. Soon after we reached the West Indies, one man died. But now, as I have mentioned, our voyage is nearly ended.

I long for the day when I can see you again. But now, dearest, I must end this letter. The captain has asked all men to be present on deck. I believe the crew has just sighted land!

As Always
Your Loving Husband,
Edmund

The three ships mentioned in this letter were not the first to have come this way. The sea trail to Virginia had been blazed years earlier by a Spanish fleet. However, after 1570, the country of Spain decided to give up its plan to settle Virginia.

The English trip was backed by a group of businesspeople from London. These people took the name *Virginia Company of London*. The owners of the company dreamed of finding gold in Virginia. They also planned to use the soil to test new crops. Finally, they hoped to plant Christianity in the hearts and minds of the Indians.

Reaching Land The first place where English feet touched Virginia soil was called Cape Henry. The adventurers did not settle there. Instead, they decided to explore more of the Chesapeake. Eventually, they reached the mouth of a wide river. To honor King James, their ruler, they called it the James River. The voyagers honored the king again on May 13, 1607, when they chose the area they would settle. They called their settlement Jamestown.

The place the settlers chose had water on three sides. This shielded the spot from attack by enemies on land. The dark blue waters around Jamestown were deep. This allowed the ships to draw close to the shore.

Building a Fort As soon as the men left their ships, they began building a fort from logs. Great trees were chopped down and carved into thick posts. Planted in the ground, these posts became the walls of James Fort. This three-sided fort had a cannon at each corner to protect the fort from attacks by the Spanish.

The settlers built walls around their settlement to protect it from enemy attacks.
▶ How many walls does this fort have?

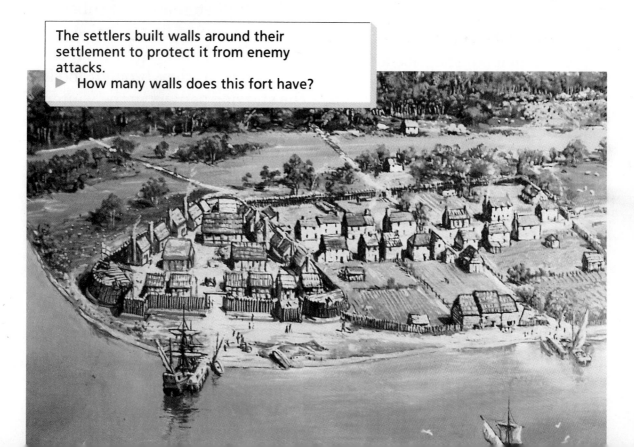

The early settlers had to build their own furniture and containers in which to store food.
▶ What are the men in this picture making?

As Jamestown's leader, John Smith guided the settlers through the first hard months. Of the 104 people who landed, fewer than half lived through the first year. Indian attacks claimed some lives. Other people died from fever and sickness. Sickness was often caused by having too little food and water. Many settlers had been "gentlepeople" in England. They knew little about farming or hunting for food. They did not realize they should dig a well to provide clean, fresh water.

Unfriendly Indians were another threat to the early British settlers. Before the settlers finished the fort, one boy died in an Indian raid.

Once the walls were up, the men gathered more lumber for buildings inside. They needed places to store their food. They needed huts in which to live.

B. The Leader of Jamestown

Strong Leadership The new colony needed a strong leader. A colony is land that is settled far from the country that governs it. Captain Christopher Newport, who commanded the *Susan Constant,* decided to place Captain John Smith in charge of building James Fort. Under Smith's leadership, the fort was built almost overnight.

Forming a Friendship Once in command, John Smith took action. He ordered the settlers to clear land and plant food crops. He had them dig a well. He made friends with Chief Powhatan and his tribes. He gave presents of beads, knives, and axes to the Indians who lived close by. In return, they brought food to the starving settlers in the winter of 1608. Captain Smith helped his remaining men stay alive until ships arrived from England with more settlers, food, and supplies.

Keeping Records In his short time as Jamestown's leader, John Smith explored much of Virginia. He went by boat on Virginia's rivers. He made maps of the new land that he explored. He wrote a book about what he saw and did on his journeys.

Captain John Smith was in charge of the Jamestown settlement. He also explored the land and rivers of Virginia.
▶ Who saved John Smith's life?

John Smith also looked for gold and silver. But no treasure was found.

C. John Smith and Pocahontas

Indian Princess Chief Powhatan had a beautiful daughter with dark eyes and dark flowing hair. Her name was Pocahontas (poh kuh HAHNT us). Pocahontas had a very happy childhood. She loved life. She loved and honored her father. She, in turn, was Chief Powhatan's favorite daughter.

Pocahontas was 11 years old when the English ships arrived. Like most Indians, Pocahontas knew little about the "strangers from far off." She had heard that they wore coats on their backs and had hair on their faces. She knew they were willing to make trades for corn.

Her first sight of a stranger was of one who was brought to her father's camp. She had known for several weeks that the stranger was coming. Talk of the stranger was on the lips of everyone in her village. He was a chief among his people. His name was John Smith.

Taken Prisoner Weeks earlier John Smith had been out exploring. Suddenly, he and his Indian guide were surrounded by Indians of the Pamunkey tribe. They ordered Smith to drop his gun. He refused. John Smith was taken prisoner and marched from village to village. Each chief asked him the same questions. What were the strangers doing here? And how long did they plan to stay here?

Saving a Life At last John Smith was taken to Powhatan's village. There he might be killed. Fortunately for him, Pocahontas saved his life. That story is told on page 146. After Pocahontas's brave action, John Smith became a member of the tribe. The Indians and the "strangers" could now live in peace.

From: POCAHONTAS

By: Ingri and Edgar Parin d'Aulaire

Setting: Jamestown, Virginia, 1608

Ingri and Edgar Parin d'Aulaire are a husband and wife writing and illustrating team. In their book *Pocahontas,* they tell the story of the daughter of Powhatan and her rescue of John Smith. The following passage tells what happened.

*I*n Powhatan's longhouse John Smith faced the chief bravely. With words and with signs he answered all questions outright. Powhatan looked pleased with what he heard. . . . But the medicine men were scowling as they danced and shouted. . . .

At last they spoke to Powhatan, and said that the spirits had told them . . . the prisoner must die. But as the medicine men made ready to kill John Smith, Pocahontas suddenly rushed forward. She took his head in her arms . . . to save him from death.

. . . Powhatan said the prisoner should live. For there was a custom among the Indians that a maiden could save a prisoner from death if she had taken a liking to him. . . .

Eventually Pocahontas married another Englishman, John Rolfe. Her son, Thomas Rolfe, later became a leading citizen in Virginia.

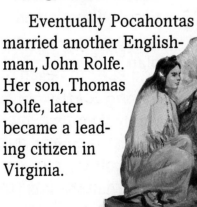

Ships from England brought supplies to Jamestown in 1610.
▶ How did the supplies save the settlement?

D. More Struggles and Victories

Lack of Food John Smith had to return to England in 1609. He had helped Jamestown to flourish. By the time he left, there were about 500 people living there. But the settlers still had a hard time.

Few of the men knew how to raise crops or catch fish or hunt animals. Rats and insects ate what little grain the settlers stored away. The winter after John Smith left, the people ran out of food. By the end of that winter, only about 60 settlers were still alive. This terrible winter became known as the "starving time."

The remaining settlers decided to leave Jamestown. Sailing down the James River toward the coast, they met an unexpected sight. In the distance, they saw sails moving toward them. The sails turned out to belong to English ships on their way to Jamestown. The ships carried more people and food for the settlement. Virginia had been saved!

Getting Better Now slowly, life in Jamestown began to get better. The Native Americans shared what they knew about living off the land. They taught the settlers how to get corn and other crops to grow. They taught them how to hunt and trap animals and how to catch fish. The "starving time" was at an end.

Most settlers now felt it was safe to leave James Fort. They

VIRGINIA: SOME HISTORIC SITES

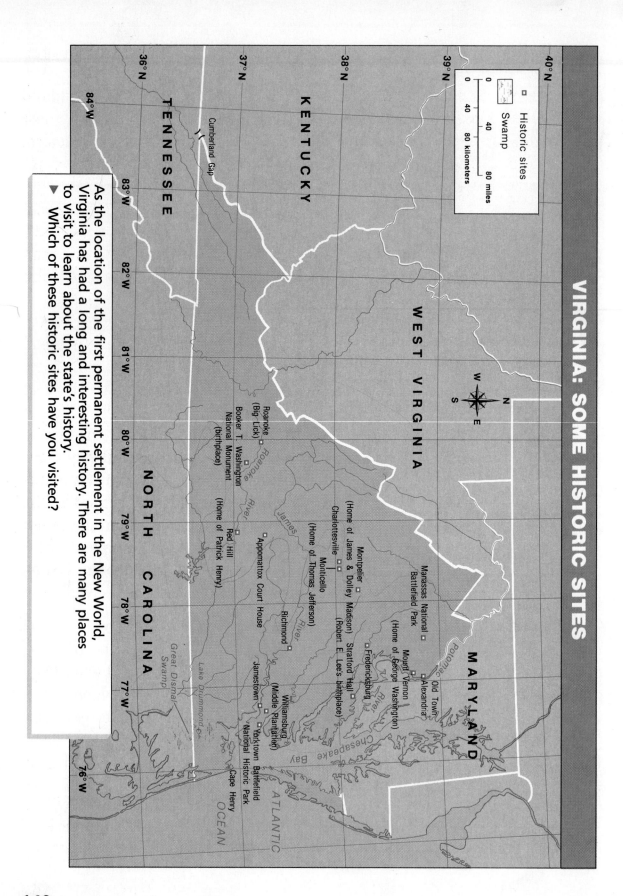

As the location of the first permanent settlement in the New World, Virginia has had a long and interesting history. There are many places to visit to learn about the state's history.

▼ Which of these historic sites have you visited?

cleared the lands around Jamestown and built small farmhouses. More people came from England. Still other shiploads were due to arrive. This led to the building of larger farms called **plantations.** The people in charge were known as **planters.**

Beginning to Grow The settlers found new ways to earn money. Some of them cut trees and shipped the trunks to England. There, the wood was carved into masts for ships. Other settlers melted the sand from Jamestown's beaches to make glass. This glass was used to make bottles and windows. At last Jamestown was starting to grow.

E. John Rolfe

John Rolfe was the first English settler to grow tobacco. The Native Americans had taught him how to grow it. In 1614 Rolfe shipped his first tobacco to England. He traded it for things such as farm animals, furniture, and clothes.

Many people in England wanted tobacco. They did not know that tobacco can hurt your health. Many settlers began growing tobacco to send to England.

At Jamestown, Rolfe met Pocahontas. She had grown into a beautiful young woman. And she had become a Christian. She and John Rolfe were married in 1614.

In 1616 Rolfe and Pocahontas sailed to England. By then they had a son, Thomas. In England, Pocahontas met the queen. She also met her old friend John Smith. While she was in England, Pocahontas died.

John Rolfe was deeply saddened by the death of Pocahontas and returned alone to his Virginia farm. Thomas followed his father some years later. By that time Thomas was a young man and ready to start his own family.

LESSON **2** *REVIEW*

THINK AND WRITE

A. What were some of the struggles and rewards of the early settlers?

B. What was one quality that made John Smith a good leader?

C. In what way did Pocahontas help John Smith?

D. What were three hardships faced by the settlers?

E. How did John Rolfe help make the Jamestown settlement stronger than ever?

SKILLS CHECK

WRITING SKILL

Write a paragraph suggesting ways in which Jamestown's settlers could have made their lives easier.

New Settlers and New Lawmakers

THINK ABOUT WHAT YOU KNOW

How do we get laws, and why do we have them?

STUDY THE VOCABULARY

indentured servant	capital
governor	House of Burgesses
burgess	reservation

FOCUS YOUR READING

As Jamestown grew, what changes took place in the people and in the colony?

A. Land of Promise

The First Colony As time passed, Virginia started to change. Life in the colony was still not easy. However, the settlers felt that the terrible days of sickness and hunger were now behind them.

The rulers of England watched the growing colony with great interest. Virginia was England's first colony, and the rulers had high hopes for it. They hoped to see the colony spread until it covered all of North America. As the colony grew, England's power as a nation also grew. The rulers were eager to have more and more English people settle in Virginia. But how would they be able to make this happen?

Free Land One of the king's helpers had an idea for getting people to settle in Virginia. The English government would offer free land in Virginia to all people who would go there! The government printed booklets that painted word pictures of a "promised land." The booklets offered hopes of great wealth to new settlers in Virginia.

The plan worked very well! Most English people did not own land in their own small country. But many of them wanted to be land-

This needlepoint picture shows colonial Virginia in the 1700s.
▶ What kind of work are the people in the picture doing?

owners and live the good life. And so they made the long journey to Virginia. By 1618, instead of only 1 settlement along the James River, there were 11 settlements.

B. The Indentured Servant

Servant and Master   Roger Higgins was polishing a pair of boots on the deck of the sailing ship.

Roger thought about his new home in a place called Virginia as he pulled a scrap of paper from his vest pocket. The paper had the name *Ernest Talbot* on it. Roger wondered what his new master would be like.

Like many people in England, Roger Higgins had wanted to come to Virginia. But, like many people, he had been too poor to pay for the ship passage. So Roger had agreed to become an **indentured servant** to Ernest Talbot. Under the plan, Ernest Talbot would pay the cost of Roger's ship passage. In return, Roger would have to work for Ernest Talbot for four years.

A Fair Exchange   Roger thought that the plan sounded fair. Some indentured servants, he knew, had to work as long as seven years. He had to work for only four years. At the end of that time, Roger would be free. He could then own his own land. He could work for himself. He might even become rich!

The English government printed booklets like this to get people to go to Virginia.
▶ Why did the government want people to move to Virginia?

C. The First Women in the Colony

Women were not on the first ships to arrive in Virginia from England. The first English women to reach Jamestown came one year later, in 1608. One of the women, Mrs. Forrest, brought her maid, Anne Burras, with her. The maid married John Laydon. The Laydons' daughter Virginia was the first English child to be born in Jamestown.

The first women to come to Jamestown arrived in 1608, one year after the settlement was started.
▶ Why did women come to Jamestown?

After Mrs. Forrest and her maid came to Virginia, other women also came. At first, only small numbers of them came to settle in the new land with their families. Then, in 1619, the Virginia Company sent a shipload of 90 young girls to the new land. The girls were sent there to marry Virginians. The girls were expected to set up housekeeping and raise families in Virginia.

From then on, more and more women came to Virginia. The women worked very hard on farms and at other jobs. They helped the colony to grow strong.

D. The First Blacks in the Colony

A Slave Ship   Another important ship reached the shores of Virginia in 1619. The ship was owned by the Dutch. Among its cargo were 20 black people who had been captured in the country of Africa.

Slavery was nothing new in Africa. For hundreds of years African tribe members had been selling captives into slavery. The blacks who were newcomers to Virginia, however, were not treated as slaves right away. The Dutch traded them to Virginia settlers for food. And the settlers treated the black people as indentured servants. Like many indentured servants, some of them earned their freedom after a time.

Then, in 1661, slavery became legal in Virginia. The law said that any non-Christians brought in by ships were slaves for life. The law said children born to slaves would be slaves too. African blacks were the target of these laws.

Unpaid Labor   In Jamestown, black slaves worked hard on planters' tobacco farms. They planted, harvested, dried, and packed the tobacco into big barrels. Then they rolled these heavy barrels onto ships headed for England. The blacks were not paid for their labor. Their white masters thought of them as property. For blacks, life in early Virginia was very difficult.

E. House of Burgesses

Sir George Yeardley looked important walking through the streets of Jamestown. A large feather stuck out of his hat. A sword clanked at his side. The year was 1618. Sir George Yeardley had just been named **governor** of Virginia by King James. In those days a governor was the top leader of a colony. Now a governor is the top leader of a state.

As new governor, Sir George had orders from the king to allow the Virginians to make their own laws. The people in Virginia were very pleased. Up until that time, laws for Virginia had been handed down from England. Virginians believed this was unfair. They felt that they better understood their colony's needs. They felt that Virginia's laws should be created by Virginians.

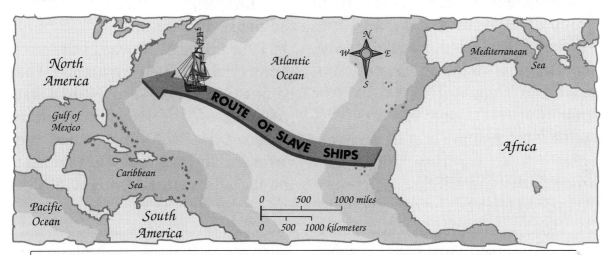

The ships that brought slaves from Africa to North America generally traveled by the route shown here. It was a long and terrible trip.
▶ Many slaves became ill and died before reaching North America. In which direction did these slave ships travel?

But now they had to figure out how to put their new power into action. To start, they picked two men from each of the 11 settlements. These men were called **burgesses.** The burgesses were to make the new laws for all the people of Virginia.

The next step was to pick a place where the burgesses would be able to meet. Jamestown seemed to be a wise choice. It was already Virginia's first **capital.** A capital is a city where government leaders get together to make laws.

Once Jamestown was agreed upon as the burgesses' meeting place, the 22 men began their journeys there. Some of them came by boat. Others came on horseback. Still others arrived on foot.

The first meeting of the burgesses took place on July 30, 1619, in Jamestown's church. The new group of lawmakers was called the **House of Burgesses.** Another name for the group was the General Assembly of Virginia. This was the beginning of government by the people in the New World.

F. A Fight for Land

Attack at Night The day of March 21, 1622, was a quiet Thursday in Jamestown. Governor Francis Wyatt had a pleasant dinner that evening and went to bed.

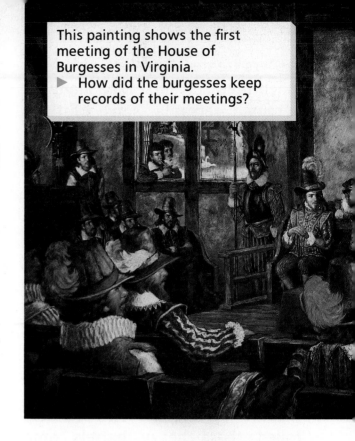

This painting shows the first meeting of the House of Burgesses in Virginia.
▶ How did the burgesses keep records of their meetings?

But the governor's night was not to be peaceful after all. He was awakened in the middle of the night by his housekeeper. A farmer needed to see the governor at once, the housekeeper said.

The farmer who was at the governor's door looked frightened. His name was Richard Pace. He had just rowed across the James River from his farm. He had come to tell the governor about a raid. He said that the Indians were planning to attack the settlements in the morning.

The governor was surprised. Since the early days, the Indians and settlers had been living in peace. Feelings of trust had led the settlers

to lend the Indians boats. The two groups had worked side by side. Some Indian children had even gone to live with settler families. (An Indian boy who was living with Richard Pace's family had even warned Richard of the attack.)

The governor should not have been surprised. He should have noticed an important change. As more and more settlers had arrived, the Indians had less and less. Their cornfields and hunting grounds were being taken over. The Indians were being crowded out of their own homes. They wanted to keep what little they had left. Sadly, attack seemed to them to be their only hope.

Sounding the Alarm   Still, the governor knew he needed to take action. He sounded the alarm. A warning was also sent out to settlers who lived close by. When the Indians arrived the next morning, the people of Jamestown were waiting for them. Armed with guns, the settlers drove back the Indians and saved their settlement.

But in settlements farther out of town, the story was different. There had not been enough time to warn those settlers about the attack. Shortly after the Indian attack began, 357 colonists lay dead. The Indians had burned their farms and houses and had destroyed their factories and plantations. The attack on the colonists was a great setback to the settlement of Virginia.

Sad Results   After the Indian attack, the settlers punished the Indians. Many Indians were forced to move to the forests beyond the Fall Line. Years later, small pieces of land were returned to the Indians. The state government set up tribal villages, or reservations, for the Indians on these lands.

Two tribes, the Mattaponi (mat uh puh NIH) and the Pamunkey (puh MUNG kee), still have reservations in King William County, Virginia. Each of these tribes has about 100 people in it. The Mattaponi

Today, many of Virginia's Native Americans have responsible jobs in high-technology industries.
▶ About how many Native Americans live in Virginia today?

on the reservation live in modern houses. The days of longhouses and wigwams are behind them. Their pride as a people, however, remains.

Five other Indian tribes are officially recognized in Virginia. None of these tribes have reservations. Approximately two thirds of the state's nearly 10,000 Indians live in or near cities. Many Indians have moved to the cities in the hope of making more money.

LESSON 3 REVIEW

THINK AND WRITE

A. Why were the English rulers so eager for the colony to grow?

B. What do you think were some of the good and bad points of being an indentured servant?

C. How did bringing in women for Virginians to marry help the colony grow?

D. In what ways was life in early Virginia difficult for blacks?

E. What was the job of the burgesses?

F. Why did the Indians attack the settlers in 1622?

SKILLS CHECK

MAP SKILL

Turn to the map of the Piedmont Region on page 57. Find the Fall Line. What importance did this line have for the Indians after their attack on the settlements?

New Ideas

THINK ABOUT WHAT YOU KNOW

School is one place where you learn things. What are some other places where a person can learn new things?

STUDY THE VOCABULARY

frontier   **hornbook**
rebellion   **time line**
dissenter

FOCUS YOUR READING

How did the beliefs and feelings of the colonists change as Virginia grew?

A. Bacon's Rebellion

Demand for Land   Imagine that you are a settler arriving in Virginia in 1670. You have heard reports about the Tidewater lowlands. You have made plans to become a farmer. You will use the rich brown lowland soil to raise crops.

Settlers with such ideas often found that things were not as they imagined. The best farmland, they discovered, had already been snatched up. The wave of new settlers was moving west of the Fall Line and into the Piedmont. Land in Virginia, once plentiful, was now in great demand. Before long, even the new wilderness, the Piedmont, had many settlers.

The Frontier   How was life different for Piedmont farmers? For one thing, they lived close to land belonging to the Indians. This was **frontier** country. A frontier is land on the edge of unsettled country. Sometimes, late at night, the Piedmont farmer would be awakened by an Indian war cry echoing in the woods! And the next morning the farmer would find that the neighbors had been attacked.

The English governor of Virginia at this time was William Berkeley. The frontier farmers demanded help in fighting the Indians. When Governor Berkeley did not send help, the farmers were angry.

Angry at the governor, Bacon and his followers set fire to Jamestown.
► Why was Nathaniel Bacon angry?

The Farmer Rebel One of these farmers was Nathaniel Bacon. In 1676 he got his own men together to fight the Indians. He defeated the Indians. Then he fought Governor Berkeley's soldiers. The fighting between Bacon and Governor Berkeley was called Bacon's Rebellion. A **rebellion** (rih BEL yun) is a fight against the ruling government.

Bacon did not win the fight. He died of a disease during the fighting, and the rebellion ended. But Nathaniel Bacon showed the English rulers that Virginians would fight for themselves against an unfair government. This was an important new idea in the colony.

B. Churches

Church played a big part in the lives of the settlers. The Church of England was the official religion of England. It was the only religion that English people were supposed to follow. That was the law. Most English settlers in Virginia were members of the Church of England.

Most settlements had more churches than ministers. So the different churches shared a minister. Some of these ministers traveled from church to church on horseback. Others came by boat.

Each church looked after the poor people who lived nearby. Wed-

St. Luke's Church in Smithfield is a historic site. Built in 1632, it is open to visitors.
▶ Why were churches important to the early settlers?

dings and funerals were held in the churches. In this new country, a church was one of the few places where people could get together with their neighbors.

Not all of the people in Virginia went to Church of England services. Some people had different religious beliefs. These people were called **dissenters.** In Virginia, the English laws against following different religions became less and less strict over the years. So these new groups grew and spread new ideas and beliefs throughout Virginia.

C. Schooling

Going to School It was a bright, sunny day as Joshua and his younger sister rounded the bend before the schoolhouse. A few years earlier, Joshua's parents and a group of other parents from the settlement had built the small schoolhouse for their children. On the steps of the building was Preacher Ames. A school bell was in his hand. On Sundays Preacher Ames was their minister. But on other days he was their teacher. It was often this way in schools in early Virginia.

Joshua and his sister were in the same class. There were 44 other children in their class as well. Some children came from distant parts of the settlement because there were not enough of these "free schools" to go around. In fact, there were almost no free schools. Free schools were for children whose families could not pay for their schooling.

Paying for Education Most parents had to pay for their children's education. Wealthy families often hired private teachers for their children. Some families sent their children to boarding schools in England. Other parents taught their own children at home.

Joshua took his place on the long bench. A piece of board hung from a cord around his neck. This was Joshua's **hornbook.** All the children had one. The hornbook was an early schoolbook. It was covered with paper on both sides. On the paper were numbers and letters. The children learned how to read and write and do arithmetic. On one side of the hornbook was the Lord's Prayer. A thin sheet of animal horn covered the paper. The horn kept the paper clean. The children were able to read right through the horn.

The hornbook around this boy's neck was an early textbook. It had paper on both sides, covered by a thin sheet of animal horn.
► What was written on it?

D. The First Virginia College

Higher Education A few students were fortunate enough to go to the first college in Virginia. It was called the College of William and Mary. The college was located in the small village of Middle Plantation. Founded, or set up, in 1693, the college was named for King William and Queen Mary. They were on the throne in England at the time. Before the college was started, sons of the wealthier planters had to go all the way to England to study.

Training for the Ministry Students who attended the College of William and Mary trained to be ministers. It was hoped that they would spread Christianity to the Indians. Students at the college also studied history and science. Many of those who went to the school became leaders in Virginia.

For Boys Only Think about how different conditions were then. Only boys were allowed to attend college. Girls were expected to stay home. There, their mothers taught them to cook, sew, and store food. They also were trained to plan for the expenses of the household. Whether the family ate well and had warm

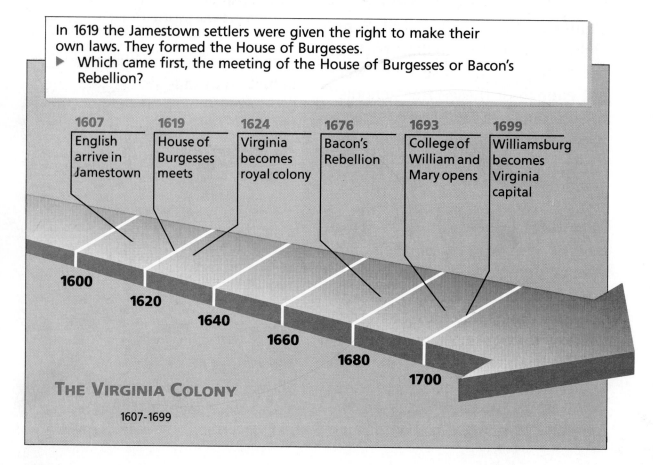

In 1619 the Jamestown settlers were given the right to make their own laws. They formed the House of Burgesses.
▶ Which came first, the meeting of the House of Burgesses or Bacon's Rebellion?

1607 English arrive in Jamestown

1619 House of Burgesses meets

1624 Virginia becomes royal colony

1676 Bacon's Rebellion

1693 College of William and Mary opens

1699 Williamsburg becomes Virginia capital

1600
1620
1640
1660
1680
1700

THE VIRGINIA COLONY
1607-1699

Founded in 1693, the College of William and Mary is the second oldest college in America.
► What did the early students at William and Mary study?

clothes depended on how well the women planned.

The time line on page 160 helps you see the changes in Virginia. A time line is a tool. It shows you when certain things happened. It shows you the order in which they happened. This time line shows important events that occurred in the Virginia colony between 1607 and 1699. In what year did the English arrive in Jamestown?

LESSON 4 REVIEW

THINK AND WRITE

A. Why did settlers begin to move into the Piedmont Region?

B. What were some of the purposes that the church served in the lives of the settlers?

C. In what ways were the schools in early Virginia different from schools today?

D. How did the education of girls in the colony differ from the education of boys?

SKILLS CHECK

THINKING SKILL

Why do you think Governor Berkeley did not send help to Nathaniel Bacon and the other frontier farmers?

USING THE VOCABULARY

tribe	burgess
wigwam	capital
colony	reservation
plantation	frontier
governor	rebellion

On a separate sheet of paper, write the best ending for each sentence below. Choose your answers from the vocabulary words above.

1. A large farm started by English settlers was called a ___p___ .
2. Another name for a group of Indians is a ___t___ .
3. A city where government leaders get together to make decisions about laws is called a ___c___ .
4. Land on the edge of unsettled country is a ___f___ .
5. A man who made new laws for all the people who lived in Virginia was called a ___b___ .

REMEMBERING WHAT YOU READ

Write your answers in complete sentences on a separate sheet of paper.

1. How were longhouses made?
2. What foods did Indians get from the bays and from the forests?

3. How did Indians use the bones and skins of animals?
4. What were the names of the three English ships that sailed to Virginia in 1607?
5. What plans did the owners of the Virginia Company of London have for the colony?
6. How did the new settlers honor their king?
7. What did the English government offer to the English who settled in the colony?
8. Which two Indian tribes still have reservations in Virginia's King William County?
9. Why did Nathaniel Bacon lead a rebellion against the governor?
10. What subjects did the first students at the College of William and Mary study?

TYING LANGUAGE ARTS TO SOCIAL STUDIES: WRITING TO LEARN

Pretend that you are either a Native American or a settler in the Jamestown colony. If you are a Native American, write a paragraph describing your reactions to the new settlers. If you are a settler, write a paragraph describing your reactions to the people you found in the new land.

THINKING CRITICALLY

Write your answers in complete sentences on a separate sheet of paper.

1. Why do you think people develop and repeat legends?
2. In what ways did the Native Americans help the early settlers?
3. In what way was the life of an indentured servant different from the life of a slave?
4. Why did Virginians want to have their own government?
5. Why was life often difficult for Piedmont farmers?

SUMMARIZING THE CHAPTER

On a separate sheet of paper, draw a graphic organizer that is like the one shown here. Copy the information from this graphic organizer to the one you have drawn. Under the main idea for each lesson, write three statements that support it. The first one has been done for you.

CHAPTER THEME

The settlers who came to Jamestown had many adventures and faced many hardships.

LESSON 1

Native Americans lived in Virginia before the English came.

1. Lived in tribes
2. Lived in longhouses
   and wigwams
3. Ate nuts, berries,
   seafood, and meat from
   wild animals

LESSON 2

The English faced many problems.

1. _____
2. _____
3. _____

LESSON 3

Many changes took place at Jamestown.

1. _____
2. _____
3. _____

LESSON 4

As the Virginia colony grew, the life of the settlers changed.

1. _____
2. _____
3. _____

INDIANS AND SETTLERS WORKING TOGETHER

Sometimes when we think of the Indians during the early history of the United States, we think of bad feelings and wars. In fact, the Indians were protecting their land and defending their way of life. Some settlers ignored the needs of the Indians and broke promises made to them. Yet the relationships between the Indians and the settlers were usually friendly at first. Without help from the Indians, the early settlements would surely not have survived.

In the spring of 1621, the Pilgrims who settled in Massachusetts met two Indians named Samoset and Squanto. Both men had learned to speak English. Squanto stayed with the Pilgrims. He showed them where to fish and taught them how to plant corn. Squanto also served as a guide and peacemaker.

Samoset brought his tribal chief and the Pilgrims together. They agreed to live next to each other in peace. When the Pilgrims decided to have a celebration to thank God for good crops during the first year, they asked the Indians to join them. The Indians brought turkey and deer to the feast.

Jamestown was the first permanent English settlement in Virginia. Although there were disagreements between the Indians and the colonists, there was also much cooperation and goodwill. John Rolfe, one of the leaders of the colony, even married an Indian princess. His marriage to Pocahontas, daughter of Chief Powhatan, helped to keep peace between the Indians and the colonists for many years.

A careful look at history will show that where there was cooperation between the Indians and the settlers, there was friendship. And where there was friendship, there was peace.

Thinking for Yourself

On a separate sheet of paper, answer the questions in complete sentences.

1. Why do you think cooperation between different groups of people is important?
2. In your opinion, could more of the conflicts between the Indians and the European colonists have been settled peacefully? Explain your answer.
3. How do you think cooperation and friendship help keep peace?

CHAPTER 5

A COLONY GROWS AND EXPANDS

When part of Jamestown burned in 1699, Williamsburg became the new capital. This small village grew into a fine town.

As farms expanded into plantations and more settlers arrived, people moved west.

Building a New Capital

THINK ABOUT WHAT YOU KNOW
Have you ever visited the capital of a state? How are capital cities different from other cities?

STUDY THE VOCABULARY
**capitol   restore
stable**

FOCUS YOUR READING
How was Virginia's new capital different from its old one?

A. A New Capital for Virginia

Planning Williamsburg   As Virginia grew, the needs of the people changed. They needed a new capital. People felt that Virginia's capital should be a fine town. Its streets should be wide and straight, unlike the narrow paths of Jamestown.

In 1699 a fire in Jamestown destroyed part of the State House where the House of Burgesses met. After the fire, the burgesses needed a new place to meet. They chose the College of William and Mary. Once there, they decided that the village near the college should be the new capital. They called it Williamsburg, after their king, William.

Francis Nicholson, the governor of Virginia, became very interested in the new capital. He had had experience before in planning a state capital. When he was governor of Maryland, he had successfully planned that colony's new capital. So he began to work, sketching the plans for Williamsburg.

The main street in the capital was Duke of Gloucester (GLAHS tur) Street. It was nearly 1 mile (2 km) long and 99 feet (30 m) wide. At one end of the street stood the College of William and Mary. At the other end

Williamsburg, Virginia's new capital, was planned by Governor Francis Nicholson.
▶ Who was Williamsburg named after?

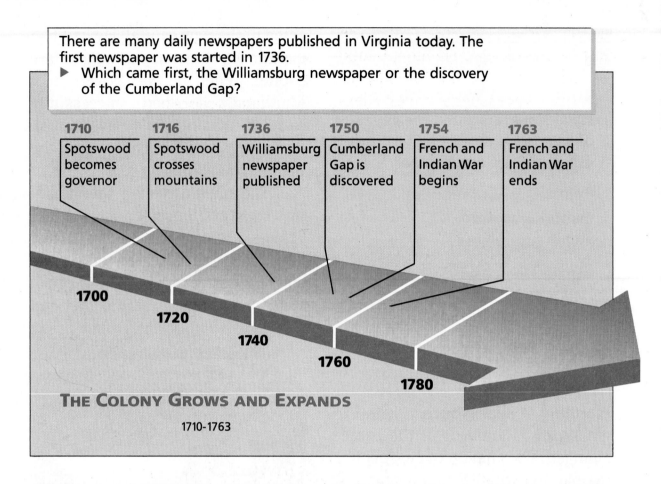

There are many daily newspapers published in Virginia today. The first newspaper was started in 1736.
▶ Which came first, the Williamsburg newspaper or the discovery of the Cumberland Gap?

1710	1716	1736	1750	1754	1763
Spotswood becomes governor	Spotswood crosses mountains	Williamsburg newspaper published	Cumberland Gap is discovered	French and Indian War begins	French and Indian War ends

1700
1720
1740
1760
1780

THE COLONY GROWS AND EXPANDS

1710–1763

was Virginia's **capitol.** A capitol is a building where lawmakers meet to conduct government business.

More Like a City Along Duke of Gloucester Street there were many small shops and pleasant inns. People could buy fine clothes, linens, and household goods in the shops. They could meet and talk with their friends at the inns.

The homes here were different from the small huts of Jamestown. The Williamsburg settlers, who were quite wealthy, built handsome houses of wood and brick. Each

settler's house stood on a large lot. There was room for a garden. Each lot also had a **stable.** A stable is a building for the owner's horses. In 1661 the Virginia Assembly had ruled that people in the colony could own slaves. Therefore, a house owner in Williamsburg might also have a cottage for a family of slaves.

B. The Governor's Palace

The people and other leaders of the colony were unhappy with the leadership of Governor Francis Nicholson. They had a hard time dealing with his temper. After the king heard about their complaints, he sent a new governor to Virginia.

That new governor was Alexander Spotswood. When he arrived in Williamsburg in 1710, he found that many buildings, including the capitol building, had been completed. One building that still needed to be finished, however, was the house he was to live in.

The former governor had planned a fine house for himself. The brick mansion was on Duke of Gloucester Street. It sat halfway between the capitol and the college. It had brick walls with iron gates and a great circle of green lawn out front.

When Governor Spotswood arrived, he immediately began the work of finishing his home. He spent much of his own money on the work. When it was done, it was such a grand house that people called it the Governor's Palace.

C. Lively Times

John Selkirk was having lunch with his family when the bell over the front door of his inn jingled. "More guests have arrived," said John to his wife.

John was used to having his lunch disturbed these days. During Public Times, the stream of guests to John's inn was endless.

Governor Alexander Spotswood used his own money to complete work on the Governor's Palace.
▶ Why do you think it was called a palace?

Public Times were when the House of Burgesses met. The meetings were held in the new capitol building. They took place twice a year and lasted several weeks. At these meetings, the burgesses made laws for Virginia.

John went to help the new guests. He came through a door behind the desk. He saw a man, a woman, and two children waiting.

"Hello," the man said. "I'm Thomas Burton. This is my wife, Sara. And these are our children, Tom junior and Missy."

The colonists often gathered to celebrate important occasions, such as weddings.
▶ How did the guests arrive?

"Welcome to the Bull and Finch," said John. "I guess you're in need of a place to stay."

During Public Times, Williamsburg buzzed with activity. Planters came from their plantations, bringing their families. Many other people crowded into the new capital. There were horse races, games, fairs, and dances. People bought and sold land. They visited and exchanged news. They went to the theater.

Williamsburg was a lively and interesting place. You can see how the early town might have looked by visiting Williamsburg today. When you are there, it is easy to imagine what life was like in the old capital. Part of old Williamsburg has been **restored** and rebuilt. When something is restored, it is brought back to a former state or condition. This process, which began in 1927 and took seven years to complete, cost almost $80 million. Thirty-seven buildings, with 230 exhibition rooms, were restored. Even today, buildings are being restored and opened to the public. Would you like to visit Williamsburg?

LESSON **1** *REVIEW*

THINK AND WRITE

A. What does the early Virginians' desire to build a new capital tell you about their feelings toward the colony?

B. What caused Alexander Spotswood to become the new governor of Virginia?

C. What events took place during Public Times?

SKILLS CHECK

WRITING SKILL

Write a paragraph describing Williamsburg during the time that it was the capital of the colony.

170

PACKING FOR THE JOURNEY

Careful planning can be the key to success. With careful planning, people often find that they are prepared for new, and sometimes dangerous, experiences. The first settlers in Virginia faced serious problems in the new land. To help future settlers avoid these same problems, the London Company printed this list of necessary items to take on the journey to Virginia.

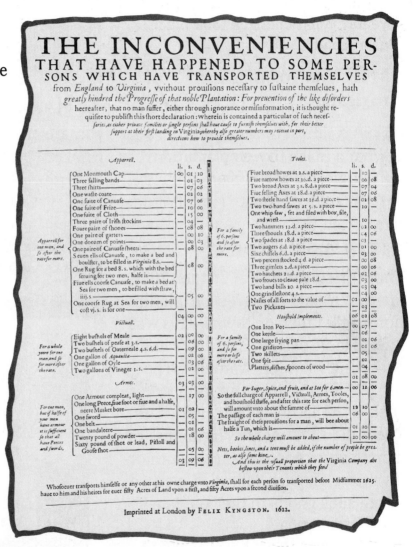

Understanding Source Material

On a separate sheet of paper, answer the questions in complete sentences.

1. What are four items on this list that are used today?
2. Imagine that you are a modern-day pioneer going to settle a new frontier. What items would you take?

Virginia's Continuing Growth

THINK ABOUT WHAT YOU KNOW
Has your neighborhood grown or decreased in size in the last few years? What changes took place as a result?

STUDY THE VOCABULARY
navigator

FOCUS YOUR READING
What was life like on plantations in Virginia in the 1700s?

A. Life on Plantations

The Agricultural Life In the 1700s, life in Virginia centered on plantations rather than on towns. This was due, in large part, to England's influence. English rulers wanted the people of Virginia to grow farm crops such as tobacco, wheat, and corn. They did not want Virginians to manufacture goods such as cloth or furniture. English factories wanted to sell such goods to the people who lived in America.

Like a Small Town As time went by, planters' small farms grew into larger and larger plantations. In many cases, the plantations were set up like miniature towns. The people on the plantations grew most of their own crops. Their own cattle and wild game also provided food. They made most of their own clothes. To build their houses, they cut down trees on the plantation. They used the clay that they found

Life in eighteenth century Virginia centered on plantations.
▶ How are these plantation houses alike?

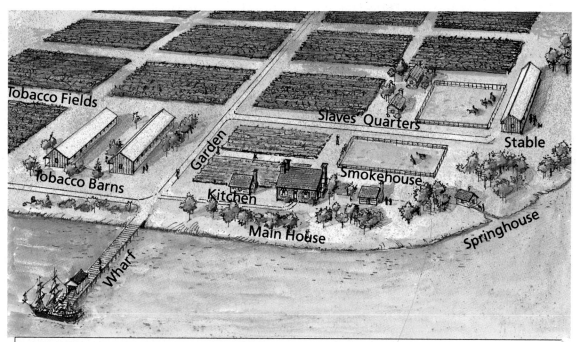

Some plantations were so large they were more like small villages. In addition to the tobacco fields, the main house, and the slave quarters, many plantations had workshops and stables.
▶ What is the advantage of being located near water?

along the river banks for making bricks. Many plantations even had their own workshops and their own carpenters and blacksmiths.

People who lived on the plantations rarely left home, except to go to church on Sundays and to town once a month. Even the children were taught at home.

B. Slavery

Many planters spent much of their time supervising workers. These workers chopped trees and tended the fields. They did many other chores on the plantation.

But who did the planters use to do this work? The answer is provided in a book by Julius Lester. The title of the book is *To Be a Slave.*

Gradually the English colonists turned to Africans as the ideal [best] solution. Because they were black, it would be difficult for them to run away and escape detection [being discovered]. Too, they could be bought . . . and held for as long as they lived. And finally, the supply was [endless].

Black slaves were trained for different trades. Some were trained

GROWTH OF SLAVE POPULATION IN VIRGINIA, 1630-1710

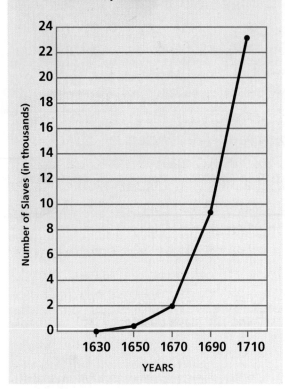

This graph shows how Virginia's population increased between 1630 and 1710.
▶ About how many slaves were in Virginia in 1690?

as carpenters or barrel makers. Some were spinners, weavers, or butchers. Others were blacksmiths or shoemakers. Some slaves built boats and sailed them to carry farm crops to the ports. A few slaves became ships' pilots. But most slaves were tobacco farmers.

Virginia grew and became rich during the 81 years that Williamsburg was its capital. But much of its wealth was based on the work of slaves. Slaves soon made up nearly one fourth of Virginia's people. Some big Virginia plantations had as many as 500 slaves. Many Virginians felt that it would not be possible to run the huge tobacco plantations without slaves.

C. Virginia's Trade

The King's Rule Although Virginia was growing rapidly, England still treated the colony as if it were just a large farm. The king was happy to receive shipments of wheat, corn, and tobacco. These crops grew well in the mild Virginia climate. In return, the king traded goods, such as tools, candlesticks, furniture, and cloth. The king refused to let the colony make its own goods or trade with any other country. By 1733, England had 13 colonies in America. The people in all of the colonies were forced to live by these same harsh and unfair rules.

Each fall, ships loaded with crops would set sail for England. Each spring, the same ships would return, filled with goods made in England. Many of the goods were bought with money from the sale of Virginia tobacco.

As time went on, **navigators** (NAV uh gayt urz) found better sea lanes across the Atlantic. Navigators were people who mapped out ocean routes. These new sea lanes made the ocean crossings shorter. At the same time, ships could steer clear of storms, and fewer passengers became ill.

Attacked by Pirates But new problems arose to replace the old ones. The worst of these problems was the threat of pirates. Pirates hid along the coast of North Carolina, in areas that were thick with trees.

Without warning, the pirates would dart out and raid the English ships.

One of the worst pirates was Edward Teach. His nickname was Blackbeard. Teach earned this nickname from his long black beard, which he used to twist into pigtails. He enjoyed the terror that he caused people to feel. When he attacked a ship, he put lighted matches under his hat so that smoke would come out around his ears and make him look terrifying.

Teach made his headquarters along the Pamlico River in North Carolina. There, he and his crew of 30 lived like savages. They raided

To frighten people, Blackbeard put lighted matches under his hat.
▶ Why do you think this story is or is not true?

PRODUCTS SENT FROM THE COLONIES TO ENGLAND

Wood

Fish

Rice

Furs

Tobacco

Goods made in colonial Virginia were sent to England each fall. In return, goods made in England were sent to the settlers each spring.
▶ Why do you think the English king would not let Virginia trade with any other country?

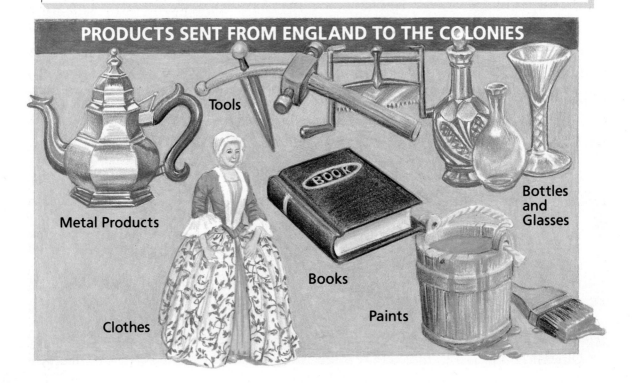

PRODUCTS SENT FROM ENGLAND TO THE COLONIES

Tools

Metal Products

Book

Bottles and Glasses

Books

Clothes

Paints

This picture, painted in 1773, shows Virginia ships off the coast of England. The ships carried corn, wheat, and tobacco to England and brought English-made goods back to the colony.
▶ Why do you think the ships sailed for England in the autumn?

ships as they pleased. They also forced nearby planters to give them food and drink.

After a time, the unhappy and desperate planters appealed to Virginia's Governor Spotswood for help. The governor decided to mount an attack against the pirate. In that bloody battle, Teach was killed. His head was cut off and paraded along Hampton Roads. Fifteen members of Blackbeard's captured crew were tried in Williamsburg, and thirteen of them were hanged. This event made Governor Spotswood so hated among pirates that he said he didn't dare sail for England in anything but a king's ship.

LESSON 2 REVIEW

THINK AND WRITE

A. Why did plantations become such a big part of life in the 1700s?
B. Why were slaves used to supply labor needed by Virginia planters?
C. What rules of trade did the king of England make?

SKILLS CHECK

MAP SKILL

Turn to the map of the United States on pages 354 and 355. Find North Carolina. Describe the location of North Carolina in relation to Virginia.

Moving Westward

THINK ABOUT WHAT YOU KNOW
What are some qualities that would make a trip an adventure?

STUDY THE VOCABULARY
treaty   militia
ferrier

FOCUS YOUR READING
What advantages and challenges faced the people who settled west of the Blue Ridge Mountains?

A. Knights of the Golden Horseshoe

Moving Westward By the early 1700s, the Piedmont Region was becoming home to more and more settlers. And the number of settlers continued to increase. Aware of a need for more space, Virginians looked westward for new frontiers.

To the west of the Piedmont Region lay the Blue Ridge Mountains. England had already claimed the land beyond those mountains as its own. But no Virginians had actually gone there to settle. Virginia's Governor Spotswood was eager to have Virginians settle that new frontier. Some French fur trappers were already there. Governor Spotswood was afraid that the French would settle beyond the Blue Ridge Moun-

tains before the English. He did not want France to claim that land. He therefore announced that he himself would lead a mission across the "Great Mountains."

This was not the first time an English settler had crossed the mountains. A settler named John Lederer had made the trip 47 years

Governor Spotswood led an expedition across the Blue Ridge Mountains in 1716.
▶ What are some of the things the people brought with them?

earlier. However, this journey across the Blue Ridge Mountains was going to be made "in style." Governor Spotswood's group of 63 men even took servants to carry their comforts.

The Start of the Journey   In August 1716 Governor Spotswood was saddled and ready. He wore a suit of rich green velvet and boots of the finest leather. At one o'clock in the afternoon, the group began its journey. By five o'clock they had already set up camp. They ate a delicious dinner by the banks of a stream.

After a good night's sleep, the group started out in the morning. Again, they rode only a short distance before stopping. But this slow, easy pace did not last forever. Soon the men found themselves struggling up the mountainside. Governor Spotswood's handsome green suit became torn and dirty. The group was forced to leave behind some of its heavier belongings.

Two Weeks Later   Finally, after about two weeks of traveling, the group reached the mountaintop. There, spread far below them, was a beautiful valley. The land was covered with a thick carpet of grass. A deep blue river wound along the valley floor. All around were bright yellow and red flowers.

Once they reached the valley, the men hunted and fished. They swam in the icy waters of the Shenandoah River. Their trip of 438 miles (705 km) had delivered them to yet another promised land.

The trip had been a great success. As a reminder of the adventure, Governor Spotswood gave each man a golden horseshoe. The gifts were symbolic because horseshoes had been important to that trip. It was one of the first times in America that horseshoes were used on a journey.

Alexander Spotswood gave all his men golden horseshoes.
▶ Why were the horseshoes important?

Spotswood called the men his Knights of the Golden Horseshoe. Now he felt that Virginia's claim on this western land was even stronger.

A Peace Treaty   Governor Spotswood was especially interested in making it safe for settlers to move west. So he and the governors of two other English colonies signed a peace **treaty** with the Indians in

1722. A treaty is an agreement between two groups. The Indians promised not to harm settlers who came to these western lands.

Despite the treaty, settlers in the west continued to be afraid. They remembered hearing that Indians had attacked Jamestown colonists when the Indians had been forced off their land. They feared that the same thing might happen to them. They were, after all, moving into Indian land.

B. Settling Western Virginia

New Wave of Settlers Virginia's earliest settlers had come from England. A handful of black people had come from Africa and the islands of the West Indies. But soon, people from other European countries began to join the Virginians who were moving west.

People from Germany began to settle in the lands west of the Blue Ridge Mountains. The Germans had fled their own country after they were denied freedom to worship God in their own way. First they had moved to Pennsylvania. Then some German families headed south into Virginia's Great Valley. The Great Valley is still home to many people of German background.

The governor and the House of Burgesses were glad to have the

Germans in western Virginia. They believed that the new people would help keep the French out of Virginia's land. They knew that the Germans were good farmers.

Hardworking People People from Scotland also went to western Virginia. They were called Scotch-Irish because they had lived for a while in Ireland. They went to Virginia to practice their own religion and to own their own land. The Scotch-Irish settled along the Blue Ridge Mountains from Pennsylvania all the way to Georgia.

William Gooch became governor of Virginia in 1727. He was happy that the Scotch-Irish had set-

Settlers built homes to protect themselves from wild animals and cold weather.
▶ Where did settlers get the logs they used to build their homes?

tled in Virginia. He knew that they were hardworking farmers and strong people. He hoped they would be able to live peacefully and successfully in Indian country.

The new settlers built houses, barns, churches, and schools. They planted fields and raised families. They worked long and hard to help Virginia grow.

C. Frontier Life

Pluses and Minuses Life on the frontier had a few pluses and many minuses. One plus was that western Virginia frontier land was cheap. Sometimes it was free for the asking. Among the many minuses was the constant fear of Indian attacks. Wild animals also posed a serious threat. Life was very difficult, and few things made life comfortable.

What to Do First Imagine that you are a settler new to the frontier. Your first task is to build a home. You notice that the first homes everyone is building are three-sided log huts. You see that the spaces between the logs are filled with clay. This, you learn, is to keep out the rain. In cold weather, the fourth, or open, side of the hut is covered with the skins of buffalo, bear, and deer. This helps to keep out the cold.

Inside the huts you find little furniture. There are beds of fur and leaves. The furs are for warmth during the bitter cold nights. The leaves are a cushion against the hard earth. Above all else, you find that your neighbors are friendly.

Working Together Frontier people stuck together. They helped each other build their homes. Sometimes they built their cabins close together for protection against enemy attacks. Some people built cellars in their houses so that they could hide. They feared that Indians might set fire to their homes. Others built their homes inside a log fort. Both forts and cabins had narrow holes in the walls that were used as peepholes to spot approaching enemies. Settlers could also fire guns at enemies through the holes.

Aside from their homes, the western settlers had few possessions. They did not have any shops to browse in. They did not have any money either. Their few possessions had been brought with them when they crossed the Blue Ridge Mountains. They had to rely on their brains and their hands for everything they needed. They learned how to make things, or they traded animal furs for them.

D. Growing Counties

Travel in Virginia The General Assembly, the group that made laws for the state of Virginia, divided Virginia into counties in 1634. There were eight counties at that time. As Virginia grew and people moved westward, the lawmakers formed more counties.

The people of the county took care of the county roads. Roads often grew out of paths that wagon wheels had made. But roads were still scarce. To avoid struggling over rough, narrow paths, travelers often used Virginia's waterways. The ferryboat was a popular form of transportation. By 1700 51 ferryboats were crossing Virginia's creeks and rivers. All were run by families that had been approved by the county.

Crossing by Ferryboat Suppose that you had been there in the early 1700s. You might have watched a scene like the following one.

"Hello, there!" I heard someone call out.

Ferry boats were a common sight on Virginia's waterways. They transported goods and people.
▶ How were the boats moved?

The voice came from the other side of the river. The water shimmered in the setting sun. My father explained that the people on the far bank were calling to the **ferrier.** The ferrier was the man who ran the boat for the county. Father said that the passengers were letting the ferrier know that they wanted to be taken across the river.

"Sometimes," my father said, "the passengers ring a bell to let the ferrier know they are there. Some-times they fire a gun." He looked toward the water. "Now you keep watching, Peter," he said to me. "Any minute you'll see the ferrier using a long pole to push his boat across the river."

As I watched, the ferryboat crossed the river and stopped so the people could get aboard. Then the boat returned, and I saw that there were animals on it.

"You mean you can take animals with you on the ferryboat?" I asked my father.

"You sure can," he said, "as long as you pay for their passage. Horses have one price. Cows have another. People have another. The county tells the ferrier how much to charge for the ferry rides."

He picked up our belongings. "Well," he said, "we'd better get down to the landing."

We would be crossing the river in the other direction. Father told me that there was an inn on the other side of the river where we would stay for the night.

Soon we were underway. Several other passengers were on the ferry. There were also some two-wheeled carts and a wagon.

"Are you planning to spend the night at the inn?" the ferrier asked my father. Father nodded his head in answer to the question.

"The rooms cost 20 cents for the night," the ferrier said. "Dinner costs another 6 cents."

Towns often grew up around ferry crossings and many of them were named for the families that ran them. Such towns are a reminder of one of Virginia's oldest means of transportation.

Besides trying to provide roads and ferryboats, the counties in early Virginia did other things. Each county trained a group of soldiers. These soldiers were there to protect the colony. They saw to it that laws were obeyed. The soldiers were called the **militia** (muh LIHSH uh). All young men except slaves were required to serve in the militia. George Washington and Patrick Henry first became soldiers by serving in the militia.

Each county also made laws for its people. Those laws were made at a county courthouse. The village or town where the courthouse stood was called the county seat, just as it is called today.

Each county had a group of citizens who were trained to fight and help in emergencies. Today the militia is called the National Guard.
▶ Who is training this group of militiamen?

County business was discussed during court days. But many people attended court days for other reasons.
► Why did many people attend court days?

A Festive Time Certain days each month were set aside as court days. On court days people came to the county seat to hear different kinds of county business. The business was discussed at the courthouse. Court days were festive times. People came to the county seat to buy and sell goods. They watched races. They took part in all kinds of games and contests. Court days were like a county fair.

LESSON 3 *REVIEW*

THINK AND WRITE

A. Why did Governor Spotswood want to explore the lands west of the Blue Ridge Mountains?

B. What reason did both the Germans and Scotch-Irish have for coming to Virginia?

C. Why was life hard for many of the western settlers?

D. What services did the county provide for the people who lived in it?

SKILLS CHECK

THINKING SKILL

In what ways were the lives of the first settlers and of the western settlers alike? In what ways were their lives different?

A War for a Continent

Suppose two people want the same thing. What is the best way for them to settle their differences? What is the worst way to settle them?

surveyor   **tax**
surrender

What conditions led to the fighting of the French and Indian War?

A. French Settlers

A Vast Land The first Englishmen who reached Virginia had been given many tasks to perform. One of those tasks was to find a shortcut to the Pacific Ocean. They thought the James River might provide that shortcut. They had no idea how large North America was. They had no idea that the continent could hold nearly 185 Englands!

In time, however, the English settlers began to understand the new land's vastness. They also understood that having land is having power. And they wanted all the land and power that they could get.

Their old European neighbors, the French, wanted land too. The French had come to North America around the same time as the English. They had begun to settle what is now Canada. By 1750 the French had pushed south from the Great Lakes into the Ohio River valley and beyond. The French were getting very rich from the fur trade there.

Trading for Furs The French wanted beaver skins to send back to France. The Indians liked the French because the French did not clear the land and make the Indians leave as the English did. The Indians

This French fur trader is trapping beavers.
▶ What will he do with the beavers after he catches them?

were very happy to trade their animal furs for things they wanted from the French. French soldiers built forts from Lake Erie to the Ohio River to protect their land. Find the French forts called Le Boeuf (luh BUF) and Duquesne (doo KAYN) on the map on page 189.

However, the English believed that these western lands were theirs. They felt strongly that the French had no right building forts on "English" soil.

Virginia's Governor Robert Dinwiddie decided to send a message to the French. He would warn them to leave English land at once! He realized that delivering the message to the French would be a dangerous mission. He knew that the job of messenger required a brave and dependable soldier.

B. A Message to the French

The scene that took place at the French fort might have started this way: Young Pierre Dupres began the evening watch. He had been in the French army only a year. And he had been shipped here, to Fort Le Boeuf, only six months ago.

Pierre had just turned to gaze out toward the east when something caught his eye. Pierre studied the trees until his eyes again picked up the moving dot.

"Look!" Pierre called out to the guard in the southeast tower. Pierre pointed toward the speck, which kept growing bigger. Soon the guards could see that it was a man on horseback.

Finally, the man on horseback reached the entrance to the fort. The guards saw that he wore the uniform of a soldier in the Virginia militia. His rank was that of major. He came, he said, with a message for their general. When the guards asked his name, the man told them he was George Washington.

Washington was born on a farm in Westmoreland County on February 22, 1732. When he was a boy, he liked to hunt and fish and swim. He also liked to ride horseback. People liked George because he was always polite, honest, and fair.

When he was 17, he became a **surveyor.** That is someone who measures land and makes maps. Washington learned a great deal about Virginia's land. He learned how to camp and live outdoors. He knew the forests and the trails.

As a major in the militia, Washington trained other soldiers to fight in Indian country. He was the right person for a dangerous job.

C. The French and Indian War

Washington delivered Governor Dinwiddie's message in 1753. But the French refused to leave the Ohio River valley. The next year the governor gave George Washington another job to do. He was sent to the Ohio River country with a small group of Virginia soldiers. His orders were to drive the French out of their forts.

Washington's plan was to attack Fort Duquesne. But first he built his own fort. He called it Fort Necessity. Find Washington's fort on the map on the facing page. Can

Washington led an attack against the French at Fort Duquesne.
▶ What kinds of weapons did the soldiers use?

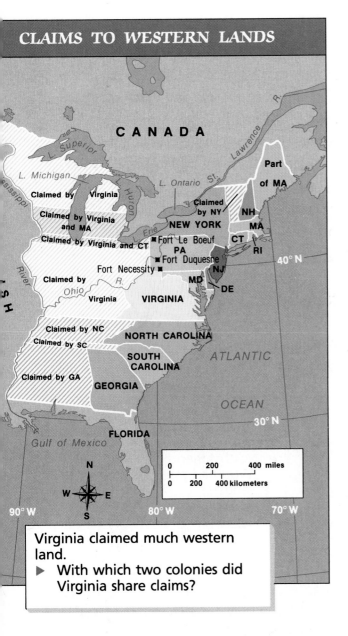

CLAIMS TO WESTERN LANDS

Virginia claimed much western land.
▶ With which two colonies did Virginia share claims?

they were outnumbered. In the end, Washington had to **surrender,** or give up the battle. The French had admired the courage of the Virginia soldiers. They allowed the soldiers to march back to Williamsburg with their guns and flags.

This battle marked the beginning of a ten-year war called the French and Indian War. On one side were England and its 13 American colonies. On the other side were the French and most of the Indian groups. The war was fought for a large part of the American continent.

D. General Braddock

Brave Leader England had lost the first round, but the English were not ready to give up. In 1755, England sent an army to help Virginia fight the French. The person in charge of the English forces was General Edward Braddock. General Braddock was a brave man. He had led the English to victory in a large number of battles at home.

General Braddock was not prepared for frontier fighting. Braddock was used to more "civilized" behavior during wartime. He had his men cut a road through the dense forest. He ordered his men to march along the road as if they were on parade. George Washington, now a colonel, warned Braddock to be cautious.

you guess why Washington decided to call it Fort Necessity?

A large group of French soldiers attacked Fort Necessity. For the next ten hours the air was thick with smoke and the smell of gunpowder. Washington and his brave Virginia soldiers fought hard, but

189

But the general refused to heed this advice. He and his troops marched out in the open in straight lines. Their bright red uniforms made them easy targets. French soldiers and Indians shot at the British troops from behind trees. It was easy for the French and the Indians to surprise the British with sudden gunfire. Washington and his 450 colonial soldiers hid behind trees and rocks to fire back at the enemy. But Braddock ordered them back into line. Washington knew it was a mistake, but as a soldier it was his duty to obey a command. Washington fought as well as he could.

Many Deaths When the smoke of battle cleared, many British soldiers lay dead. Among them was their leader, General Braddock. Washington had escaped injury, but two of his horses had been shot from under him. Once again, the English and their colonists had been beaten.

E. A Victory for England

The Continuing Battle Although they had lost twice, by 1758 the British soldiers were ready to do battle again. Their goal this time was to take Fort Duquesne from the French. Again, George Washington and his Virginia soldiers fought alongside the British army.

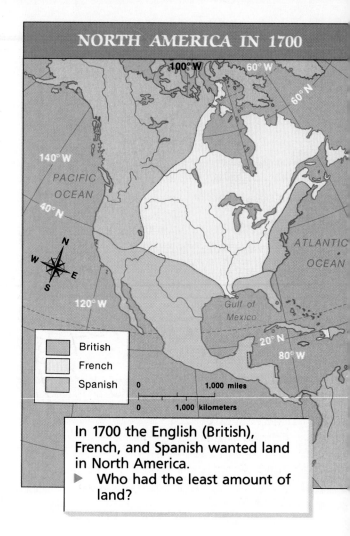

NORTH AMERICA IN 1700

British
French
Spanish

In 1700 the English (British), French, and Spanish wanted land in North America.
▶ Who had the least amount of land?

This time, however, the battle came out differently. This time the British won. And in all the battles that followed, the British army was victorious over the French. The French forces continued to grow weaker until they finally surrendered to England.

In 1763 France and England signed a peace treaty. The French agreed to give up Canada. They agreed to give up all the lands west

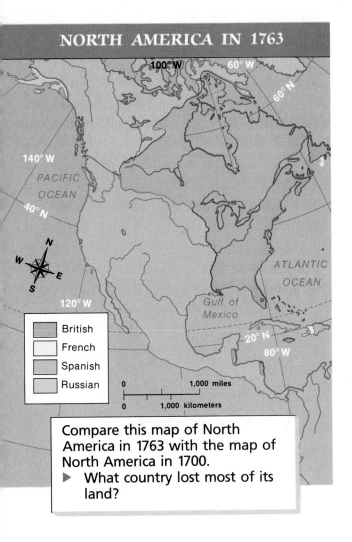

NORTH AMERICA IN 1763

British
French
Spanish
Russian

0   1,000 miles
0   1,000 kilometers

Compare this map of North America in 1763 with the map of North America in 1700.
▶ What country lost most of its land?

of the Appalachian Mountains as far as the Mississippi River.

Even though the war had officially ended, fighting between the Virginians and the Indians went on. Many more people were killed in the continued fighting.

New Problems At the time, other problems were also brewing. Virginia and the other colonies had fought on the same side as England during the war. But now the colonists were unhappy with England for several important reasons. England increasingly limited the production of certain products in the colonies. The English government also passed a series of tax laws. A tax is money that people pay their government. The Virginians began to talk of rebelling against King George III of England.

LESSON 4 REVIEW

THINK AND WRITE

A. What were relations like between England and France in the mid-1700s?

B. What characteristics did George Washington have that made him a good choice as Governor Dinwiddie's messenger?

C. Why did Washington and his soldiers lose the first battle against the French?

D. In what ways did the British make it easy for the French to win the second battle?

E. What problems did Virginians have after the war?

SKILLS CHECK

WRITING SKILL

Look at the maps on pages 190 and 191 and compare them. Write a paragraph describing their differences.

USING THE VOCABULARY

capitol	ferrier
stable	militia
restore	surveyor
navigator	surrender
treaty	tax

On a separate sheet of paper, write the best word to complete each sentence below. Choose your answers from the vocabulary words above.

1. The building where government leaders meet to conduct business is called the _____.
2. In early Virginia, all of the young men who were able to fight served in the _____.
3. George Washington and his men fought bravely at Fort Necessity, but they were forced to _____ to the French.
4. The Indians agreed not to harm the settlers and signed a peace _____ with them.
5. Money that people must pay their government is called a _____.

REMEMBERING WHAT YOU READ

Write your answers in complete sentences on a separate sheet of paper.

1. In what ways were the homes in Williamsburg different from those in Jamestown?

2. Why does Williamsburg today seem to be a lot like it was in colonial days?
3. Why did the English rulers keep the Virginia settlers from making cloth, furniture, and other goods?
4. What kinds of trades did black slaves learn?
5. Who was Edward Teach and why were people afraid of him?
6. Why were the frontier settlers afraid of Indians?
7. How did settlers try to protect themselves from Indian attack?
8. What were court days?
9. Why did the Indians like the French settlers better than the English settlers?
10. Who was Edward Braddock?

TYING LITERATURE TO SOCIAL STUDIES

Find a biography of George Washington in your school library. A biography is an account of the life of a well-known person. Write the name of the biography on a sheet of paper. Also write the name of the author. Look through the biography to find out things about George Washington that you have not learned before. Write three interesting things about George Washington on your paper. Share what you learned with the class.

THINKING CRITICALLY

Write your answers in complete sentences on a separate sheet of paper.

1. Why was Williamsburg a more impressive capital than Jamestown?
2. How did slaves help Virginia become rich?
3. How did Governor Spotswood make it easier for settlers to settle in western Virginia?
4. How did the Germans and Scotch-Irish help to build Virginia?
5. How was the battle for Fort Duquesne a turning point in the French and Indian War?

SUMMARIZING THE CHAPTER

On a separate sheet of paper, draw a graphic organizer that is like the one shown here. Copy the information from this graphic organizer to the one you have drawn. Under the main idea for each lesson, write three statements that support it. The first one has been done for you.

CHAPTER THEME
As the colony grew, there were many changes in the way the settlers lived.

LESSON 1

The new capital at Williamsburg was a grand place.

1. A college, the capitol, and the Governor's Palace
2. Shops and inns
3. Handsome homes of wood and brick

LESSON 2

People who lived on plantations in the 1700s lived differently from those in towns.

1.
2.
3.

LESSON 3

People who settled west of the Blue Ridge Mountains had advantages and faced challenges.

1.
2.
3.

LESSON 4

England and France fought against each other in the French and Indian War for several reasons.

1.
2.
3.

CHAPTER 6
VIRGINIA AND THE WAR FOR INDEPENDENCE

Many Virginians worked hard to protect the colonies from England. But war was the only answer. The patriots organized under George Washington's command. After years of fighting, the final battle was fought and won in Virginia.

Colonists in Rebellion

THINK ABOUT WHAT YOU KNOW

What might people do when they are treated unfairly?

STUDY THE VOCABULARY

treasury
Stamp Act
repeal
Townshend Acts

patriot
Committee of Correspondence
Continental Congress

FOCUS YOUR READING

What actions did Virginia and the other colonies take against England's unfair laws?

A. The Stamp Act and Patrick Henry

New Taxes England won the French and Indian War and gained some western lands. However, wars are very costly. And this one left the British **treasury** nearly empty. A treasury is the place where a country keeps its money.

The English lawmakers met with King George III. They explained that the French and Indian War had been fought to protect all the American colonies. They felt that the colonies should help pay for the war. They agreed that England would collect money from the colonists through new taxes.

One morning in 1765, Virginians awoke to the pounding of hammers. Small sheets of paper were being nailed to trees and fence posts. The papers told of a new law passed by the British government. The law said that Americans had to begin paying for tax stamps. These stamps were to be placed on all newspapers, calendars, and playing cards. The stamps were required on certain legal papers too. Americans could not get married or buy or sell land unless a tax stamp was placed on a certain paper.

Patrick Henry protested the Stamp Act. He spoke out at a meeting of the burgesses.
► Where did the women sit at the meeting of the burgesses?

195

Reaction in the Colonies Angry people from the 13 colonies began to protest. They said that the new law, called the Stamp Act, was unfair. Virginia led the other colonies in opposing the Stamp Act. They said that since the colonists had no say in making English laws, the English had no right to tax them.

One of the angriest Virginians was a man named Patrick Henry. Patrick Henry was a lawyer. He was also a member of the House of Burgesses. At a meeting of the burgesses on June 2, 1765, Henry's voice boomed. He said: "I know unfairness when I see it. It is unfair to ask us to send tax money to England. Our young colony needs money. Why should we send our money to the king? He will use our money for his fancy palace."

Speaker for the Colonists Patrick Henry was born in Hanover County, Virginia, in 1736. As a young boy, he liked to go fishing and hunting. He also liked music.

Until he was ten years old, Patrick Henry went to a one-room school. He was not a very good student. But he was very good at speaking. He loved talking to people, so he decided that he would become a lawyer. At the time, there was no law school to attend, so Patrick Henry taught himself the law. He studied hard and passed the law examination at Williamsburg.

Henry was elected to the House of Burgesses in 1765. That was the year England passed the Stamp Act. It was also the year Henry spoke out so strongly against the new law. People throughout the colonies followed Henry's lead. They refused to buy the tax stamps. Some people even burned the stamps. In 1766 England had to repeal, or take back, the Stamp Act. That meant the Stamp Act was no longer law.

B. The Townshend Acts

Repealing the Stamp Act England repealed the Stamp Act. But the king and his lawmakers were not finished yet. To them, the war over taxes was just beginning.

Still needing money, England passed the **Townshend Acts** in 1767. These laws said that Americans had to pay a tax when they bought certain goods from England. These goods were paint, lead, paper, glass, and tea. England issued a threat with the new law. The threat said that any American who did not pay these taxes would be punished by English courts.

Angry Again Now Americans were even more angry than they were before. They felt that their rights were being taken away from them. But Americans were afraid that England might use its power to make them obey the new laws.

In 1769 the House of Burgesses declared the Townshend Acts unfair. They said that only the Virginia Assembly had the right to tax Virginians. They said that the English courts had no right to punish colonists. Only American courts had the right to decide whether an American had broken a law. They told Virginians to stop buying taxed goods from England.

The King's Defeat Again Virginia led the other colonies in speaking out against unfair laws. That year England sold only about half the goods to Americans that it had sold in other years. In 1770 England repealed most of the Townshend Acts. The king and his lawmakers had been beaten again.

The Townshend Acts said that Americans must pay a tax on certain goods that came from England.
▶ How did Americans react to this?

C. Virginia's Patriots

Virginia had some strong leaders. Among them were George Washington and Patrick Henry. These men were called **patriots**. Patriots are people who have a special love for their country and work for its good. Some other Virginia patriots were Thomas Jefferson, Richard Henry Lee, and George Mason.

Virginia's leaders were aware that their problems with England were growing. The Virginia leaders feared for the safety of their people. They knew England must be aware that it was losing control of its colonies. They thought England might try regaining its control by taking away more American rights.

In 1773 Richard Henry Lee suggested a way to protect his fellow Virginians. He presented his plan to the House of Burgesses. The plan called for a colony-wide **Committee of Correspondence**. This group was set up to help Virginia protect itself against trouble from the English. Again, the other colonies followed Virginia's lead. They set up their own Committees of Correspondence.

The different groups could now keep in touch with one another by letter. They could warn one another if they thought that England was about to take away any American rights or liberties.

Richard Henry Lee (top) and Benjamin Harrison were Virginia representatives of the first Continental Congress.
► Where was this meeting held?

D. The First Continental Congress

The Virginia Committee of Correspondence and the House of Burgesses became more and more worried about England's acts against the colonies. They thought England might even take further

On September 5, 1774, representatives from all 13 colonies met in Philadelphia, Pennsylvania. This important meeting was known as the **Continental Congress.** Virginia sent seven men there. Among them were George Washington, Richard Henry Lee, Patrick Henry, Edmund Pendleton, Richard Bland, and Benjamin Harrison. The seventh Virginian, Peyton Randolph, had been Speaker of the House of Burgesses. Randolph was a wise and honorable man. He had spent much of his life becoming an expert on the law. The men at the meeting agreed that Randolph should be the president of the Continental Congress.

The Continental Congress asked King George to repeal all the remaining unfair laws. It asked him to give the colonists all the rights and freedoms they were supposed to have as English people. But King George refused to answer.

Edmund Pendleton (top) and Peyton Randolph also represented Virginia at the First Continental Congress.
▶ Who else represented Virginia?

E. Liberty or Death

It was harvest time. The days were growing colder. John Lydecker, a Richmond farmer, carried his tools to his shed. Then he headed to the farmhouse where his family was waiting for him.

Inside, his sons William and Andrew were arguing. "I tell you," said William, "we'll soon be at war."

steps against the colonies. It became clear that the colonies must now band together more tightly than ever. So Virginia asked all the other colonies to choose some men who would meet and talk about the problems they were facing.

Andrew shook his head. "I say you're wrong. We colonists are simple people. What match are we for the king's army?"

John Lydecker took his seat at the head of the table. "What's this talk of war?" he said to his teenage sons. His wife brought over a steaming pot of soup.

William spoke up. "I say that war is the answer, Father. The king won't hear our demands. He won't grant us our freedoms. We have no other choice."

John Lydecker was afraid that his son was right. Several days ear-lier, on October 26, the Continental Congress had come to a close. During the meeting, the members had agreed that colonists should gather rifles. The Congress wanted the colonists to be prepared for war.

"I hope you're wrong, William," John Lydecker said. "But we will have to wait and see."

In March 1775, Virginians held another meeting. This one was at St. John's Church in Richmond. War was still on the minds of most patriots. Many believed that war was the only answer. One of those patriots was Patrick Henry. At that

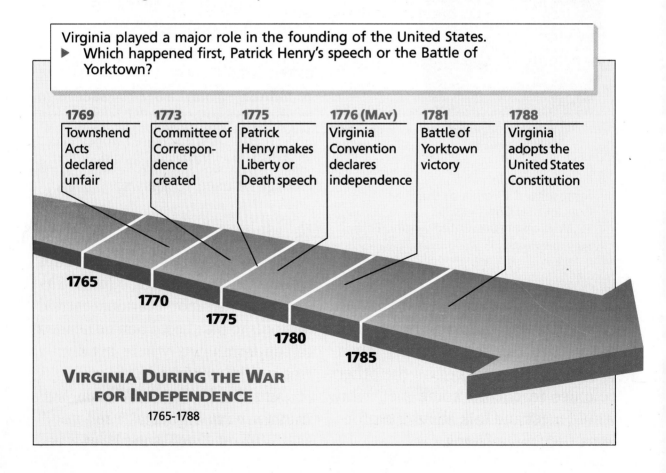

Virginia played a major role in the founding of the United States.
▶ Which happened first, Patrick Henry's speech or the Battle of Yorktown?

1769	1773	1775	1776 (May)	1781	1788
Townshend Acts declared unfair	Committee of Correspondence created	Patrick Henry makes Liberty or Death speech	Virginia Convention declares independence	Battle of Yorktown victory	Virginia adopts the United States Constitution

1765   1770   1775   1780   1785

VIRGINIA DURING THE WAR FOR INDEPENDENCE
1765-1788

Patrick Henry made a speech at a meeting held by the Virginians. He thought that war was the only answer to the unfair English laws. His speech became very famous.
▶ How can you tell that many of the men agree with Patrick Henry?

meeting he made a famous speech. In his speech he asked the patriots, "Is life so dear, or peace so sweet, as to be purchased at the price of chains and slavery? Forbid it, Almighty God!" Then he declared, "I know not what course others may take; but as for me . . . give me liberty or give me death." The patriots went wild with excitement.

LESSON **1** *REVIEW*

THINK AND WRITE

A. Why did Virginians feel that the Stamp Act was unfair?

B. Why did England repeal most of the Townshend Acts?

C. What was the purpose of Virginia's Committee of Correspondence?

D. Why did the colonies establish a Continental Congress?

E. Why did the colonists think that war was the answer to their problems with England?

SKILLS CHECK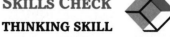

THINKING SKILL

What might have happened if Patrick Henry had not become a member of the House of Burgesses?

201

The Fighting Begins

THINK ABOUT WHAT YOU KNOW

Name some heroes you know of. What makes these people heroes?

STUDY THE VOCABULARY

Virginia Convention

Declaration of Independence

FOCUS YOUR READING

What happened during the early years of America's fight for independence?

A. America at War

It was an early spring morning in Concord, Massachusetts. The air was filled with the usual sounds. Birds were chirping. Horses were clip-clopping, and wagon wheels were creaking. You could hear the iron clang of the blacksmith's hammer and the laughter of children.

But there was another sound that morning. It was a sound the people of Concord were not used to hearing—the crackle of gunfire.

British soldiers had come to destroy or capture guns and gunpowder that patriots had hidden in Concord. American soldiers there tried to stop them. Some Americans were killed in the shooting.

Earlier that morning British soldiers had wounded and killed other Americans in the nearby village of Lexington. Ralph Waldo Emerson, a famous American poet, later called this gunfire "the shot heard 'round the world." April 19, 1775, was the day America and England first fired at each other.

B. America's Fighting Forces

Commanding the Forces In May 1775, men from the 13 colonies met in Philadelphia for the Second Continental Congress. A month had passed since that morning when the war started. But the gunshots were still fresh in the minds of the patriots. The Congress drew up plans for armed forces to fight England. It decided to form a Continental army and a Continental navy.

This cartoon shows the British as a mighty force against the much smaller Continental army.
▶ What is the artist saying?

The Second Continental Congress chose George Washington to lead the army. This painting shows Washington taking his command at Cambridge, Massachusetts, on July 3, 1775.
▶ How is Washington showing respect to his army?

Congress chose George Washington as commander in chief of the army. Washington was then 42 years old. He owned a plantation called Mount Vernon on the Potomac River in Fairfax County. He loved his plantation. But he also loved his country. When duty called, Washington knew he must serve.

Washington's army had few trained soldiers. But brave men from all over Virginia and the other colonies came to join the army. There were farmers and merchants. There were craftsmen and traders. Even

ministers went to join General Washington. One minister who went was a Virginian named John Peter Muhlenberg.

John Peter Muhlenberg was pastor of a church in Woodstock, in the Shenandoah Valley. One Sunday morning, the Reverend Muhlenberg gave a special sermon. In it, he said: "There is a time for everything. . . . There is a time to speak and a time to keep silent. There is a time to fight and a time for peace. This is the time to fight!" He threw off his long black preacher's robe. Under it was a

John Peter Muhlenberg asked the men in his congregation to join him in the fight for independence.
▶ How do you think the men reacted to his call?

soldier's uniform. John Peter Muhlenberg asked for men to go with him to join General Washington in the fight for independence. This pastor led his men well.

Leading the Navy The Continental navy was headed by another well-known patriot. That brave captain's name was John Paul Jones. He is known today as the Father of the American Navy.

Virginia formed its own navy of small armed vessels. These ships kept watch over Chesapeake Bay. At night small Virginia ships sometimes sneaked past the great English warships. Once in open water, they headed for French and Dutch islands in the Caribbean Sea. There, they traded Virginia farm crops for guns and other war supplies.

The navy took part in many battles. During one battle with a British ship, John Paul Jones was ordered to surrender. Instead he replied, "I have not yet begun to fight." He went on to win the battle, scoring a great victory for the American side.

C. The Virginia Convention and Independence

On May 6, 1776, a group of Virginia patriots met in Williamsburg. This meeting is known as the **Virginia Convention.** The patriots felt that the American colonies should no longer be a part of England. They sent a message to the Second Continental Congress, which was then meeting in Philadelphia. The message asked the Congress to declare that the colonies were "free and independent states." Richard Henry Lee of Westmoreland County gave the Congress this message.

The result was the **Declaration of Independence.** Most of this very important paper was written by Thomas Jefferson, a Virginian. It stated that all people are created equal and have rights to life, liberty, and the pursuit of happiness. All members of the Congress signed the paper. On July 4, 1776, the American colonies became the United States of America, a free new land.

D. The Early War Years

Shouts of joy rang out through the colonies when the Declaration of Independence was signed. At last Americans would be free!

But before they could be truly free, they would have to prove themselves on the battlefield. A long, hard fight lay ahead of them. Washington's army was much smaller than the British army. And the colonies' ships would be up against the strongest navy in the world — the British navy.

Still, Virginians and other Americans had great faith in George Washington. They fought hard for him. Some of these men were much feared by the English soldiers. One of them was Daniel Morgan of Winchester. Ninety-six men from the Shenandoah Valley served under him at first.

The soldiers who fought under Captain Morgan were given the nickname Morgan's Rifles. They did not have fancy uniforms. Most of them wore homemade hunting shirts. Many had the words *Liberty or Death* printed across their shirt fronts. Some reports say that the British soldiers feared Morgan's Rifles more than any other American soldiers.

Despite the help of such brave patriots as Daniel Morgan and many others, America won few battles at first. However, George Washington did not give up. He believed America would win the war for freedom. His soldiers believed this too. They refused to give up even when they were cold and sick and hungry.

Daniel Morgan commanded a group of men in the army. They were known as Morgan's Rifles.
▶ What kind of uniform is Daniel Morgan wearing?

E. The Northwest Campaign

Western Lands During the French and Indian War, the colonists had fought with England to keep their claims to western lands. Now the colonists had to fight for these lands again. This time, however, they had to fight against England.

A new English law said that Virginians were not allowed to settle west of the Allegheny Mountains. But many Virginians already lived there. To chase them out, the English began sending Indians to attack the settlers. The Indians were sent from three forts that the English held in the Ohio River valley.

Two Virginia patriots agreed on a plan to end the attacks. The plan called for the Americans to take over the three forts where the English were living. One of the patriots behind this plan was Patrick Henry, who was then the governor of Virginia. The other was George Rogers Clark. Clark was born in central Virginia, but he loved the frontier and had moved to western Virginia. Clark wanted to lead the attack.

Capturing British Forts In the spring of 1778, Clark set out with about 350 of his Virginia frontiersmen. That summer they captured the English forts at Kaskaskia (kas KAS kee uh), Cahokia (kuh HOH kee uh), and Vincennes (vihn SENZ). In December the English Colonel Henry Hamilton won back the fort at Vincennes. But in February 1779, Clark and 170 of his men made a surprise raid on Vincennes. The fort was in American hands again.

Because of the work of Clark and his troops, the Americans gained control of the land north of the Ohio River, from the Appalachian Mountains to the Mississippi River. This land was later called the Northwest Territory.

F. Helping to Win the War

Advancing British Soldiers Imagine that you are an American soldier in the War for Independence. You

Clark offers the Indians a choice between war and peace.
▶ Which color, do you think, means peace?

Women took an active part in the war. They served as nurses and cooks, and they made war supplies.
▶ What is this woman doing?

and other soldiers are hiding behind trees. Ahead of you is a hill. And over it pour waves of British soldiers in bright red uniforms.

Such sights were common during the war. But the bravery of the American soldiers was not easily shaken. The Americans were skilled fighters. They came from many different backgrounds, and all had something special to offer. Mountain fighters from the Appalachians, for example, used squirrel rifles. The rifles had been made by Germans from the area. With these crude weapons, the mountain fighters could outshoot the English soldiers.

General Washington greatly admired these patriots.

Help from All It was not only soldiers who made a difference in the war effort. Farmers from the Great Valley served as wagon drivers and mechanics for Washington's army. Women played an important part too. Women rode with the army supply trains. Some drove wagons. Others were nurses or cooks. Still others made gunpowder or uniforms for the soldiers. Most important, women ran many farms that grew food for the army.

Black people also played a key role in the War for Independence. About 1 soldier in every 60 was black. Black sailors also fought bravely on American ships. A great many of these black fighters were from the state of Virginia.

Only free blacks were allowed to serve in Virginia's armed forces. However, Virginia slaves also helped win the war.

James Armistead was a slave from New Kent County. During the war, he became famous by delivering letters to other spies. He kept his eyes and ears open. Because he worked for a French general named Lafayette, the spy took the name James Lafayette.

At the end of the war, James Lafayette was given his freedom. He was also given $40 a year as pay for the work he had done.

James Lafayette was a slave who worked as a spy during America's War for Independence.
► Why did the spy decide to use the name Lafayette?

2

THINK AND WRITE

A. What happened in Concord, Massachusetts, in April 1775?

B. What was the tough decision that George Washington had to make in May 1775?

C. What part did Virginia play in the events that ended with the signing of the Declaration of Independence?

D. Why was the signing of the Declaration of Independence only a beginning for the people of the American colonies?

E. How did George Rogers Clark help stop the Indian raids on the western frontier?

F. How did blacks help win the War for Independence?

SKILLS CHECK

WRITING SKILL

Look up the city of Philadelphia in the Gazetteer in the back of the book. In your own words write two important facts about the city of Philadelphia, Pennsylvania.

Victory on the Chesapeake

THINK ABOUT WHAT YOU KNOW

What reasons can you think of for moving something from one place to another?

STUDY THE VOCABULARY

Treaty of Paris

Virginia Statute for Religious Freedom

FOCUS YOUR READING

How did the Americans finally defeat the British in the War for Independence?

A. Another New Capital for Virginia

In 1779 the General Assembly voted to move the capital once again. Eighty years earlier, the capital had been moved from Jamestown to Williamsburg. This time the move was taking place because of safety. Norfolk, a city on the coast, had been burned to keep it from the British. The nearby cities of Portsmouth and Suffolk had also been attacked from the sea. Virginians feared that because Williamsburg was near the coast, it would be next.

The small town of Richmond was chosen for the new capital of Virginia. Richmond was chosen because it was located safely inland, and it looked grand, perched above the James River falls. In 1780 the government of Virginia now led by Governor Thomas Jefferson, moved to Richmond.

B. Jack Jouett

In Charlottesville The sun had just risen. And so had Mike Halsey. He was up at daybreak as he had been each morning of his 70 years. Mike went outside into the early morning air. It would be another hot June day for sure. He looked around. The town of Charlottesville was slowly beginning to wake up.

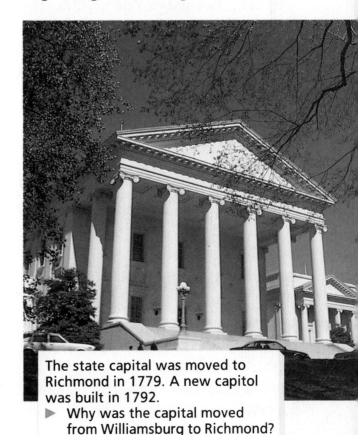

The state capital was moved to Richmond in 1779. A new capitol was built in 1792.
► Why was the capital moved from Williamsburg to Richmond?

Mike Halsey had lived in Charlottesville all his life. He had gone to school there. He had married there. He and his wife, Anne, had raised their three daughters there. He had watched each of his daughters grow up, get married, and then raise families of their own.

Mike's grandson Jerrod was walking to work when he saw his grandfather standing outside. "Hello, Grandfather, how are you?" he called out.

"Oh, hello, Jerrod," Mike muttered. "I'm fine."

"You don't sound like you're fine," Jerrod said.

"Oh, I'm just puzzled," Mike replied. "These days Charlottesville seems like a different town to me. For instance, a few weeks ago, Governor Jefferson and the General Assembly arrived. Why did they come here when they just moved to Richmond last year?"

"I can tell you," Jerrod said. Jerrod explained how an English general named Cornwallis and his army had invaded Virginia and done great damage. He said that they had burned James River plantations. They had destroyed warehouses and war supplies. And Cornwallis had captured Richmond.

"Well, that certainly explains why Jefferson left Richmond," Mike

Jouett raced to Charlottesville. He told Jefferson that British soldiers were headed there.
▶ Why were the British marching to Charlottesville?

said. But Mike still wondered why Governor Jefferson did not hide somewhere else. Why did he come to Charlottesville?

Mike started to go into the house when he heard a noise from down the road. Suddenly, something burst out of the mist. Mike jumped back. It was a man on horseback! As the man rode by, Mike saw that his clothes were torn and his face was scratched.

Captain Jack's Ride The man Mike Halsey saw ride by was Captain John (Jack) Jouett. The night before, Jack Jouett had been sitting in an inn in Louisa County. He noticed hundreds of British soldiers ride by. He wondered where the soldiers were headed.

Then he realized that Cornwallis had sent these men. They were on their way to Charlottesville to try to capture Thomas Jefferson and the other patriots.

Jack Jouett wasted no time. He leaped onto his horse and rode off toward Charlottesville. He had to warn the governor.

Jack knew every shortcut and back road. He rode all night across the hills. Tree branches ripped his clothes and scratched his face. But still Jack Jouett rode on.

Finally, at dawn, he reached Thomas Jefferson. He told Jefferson that the British were coming. Jack Jouett was just in time. Jefferson could see the English soldiers riding in the distance. But Jefferson and the men of the General Assembly were able to escape.

C. The Battle of Yorktown

Rough Time in Virginia   In early 1781, America's chances for victory did not look good. Like most colonies, Virginia was having a rough time. The colony was running out of supplies and money. The people's spirits were low.

Then an offer came from France. France promised to send extra troops if America wanted them. France's navy would also be ready to support the patriots' cause.

The French and General Washington worked out a plan. They knew that General Cornwallis and most of his army had moved to Yorktown after their raids in central Virginia. General Washington would fool Cornwallis into thinking that the Americans were going to attack New York.

Cornwallis would then send his troops north to stop the colonists. Washington would swoop down on Cornwallis from the north. At the same time, a small American force would swoop down on Cornwallis from the northwest. Those soldiers were led by a French major general, the Marquis de Lafayette.

Meanwhile, the French navy could seal off the Chesapeake Bay. That action would prevent British warships from rescuing General Cornwallis and his army.

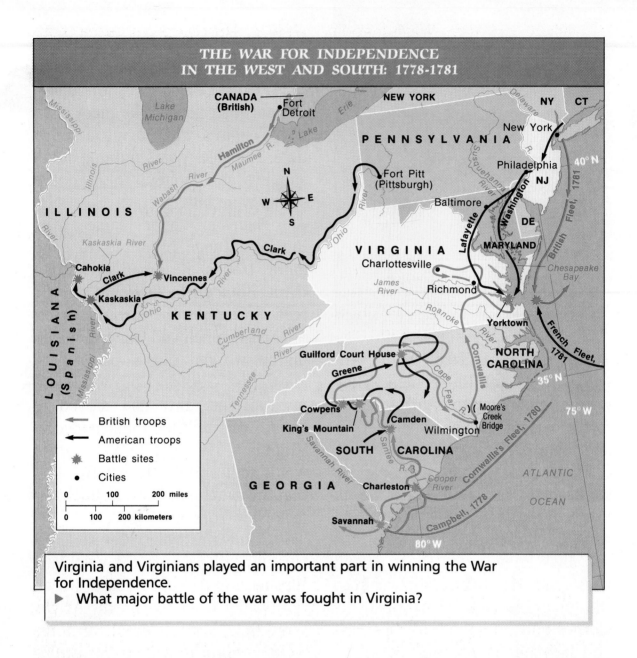

THE WAR FOR INDEPENDENCE IN THE WEST AND SOUTH: 1778-1781

Virginia and Virginians played an important part in winning the War for Independence.

▶ What major battle of the war was fought in Virginia?

Setting the Trap If the plan worked, the unprotected English general would be trapped. He might be forced to surrender. To help the plan along, Washington planted word of a New York attack so that enemy spies heard it. As he had hoped, the spies told Cornwallis.

By early September, there were 20 to 30 French warships in Chesapeake Bay. American and French soldiers had surrounded Yorktown. The Americans and the French had a total of 16,000 troops. That was more than double the number that Cornwallis had at Yorktown.

Night and day, Washington's soldiers fired on the English. Cornwallis's soldiers returned fire, but it was no use. The combined French and American forces were too strong. Soon the English used all their food and water. Finally, on October 19, 1781, Cornwallis surrendered. It was America's most important victory of the war!

D. The Treaty of Paris

Fighting went on for a while in other parts of the country and at sea. But the war was really over when Cornwallis's army was beaten.

In 1783 leaders from England and the United States met in Paris, France. They signed a peace treaty called the **Treaty of Paris.** In it, England said the United States was a free nation. The colonies became the independent United States of America. The treaty also gave the United States the land between the Atlantic Ocean and the Mississippi River from Canada to Florida.

E. Freedom of Religion

Virginia had played an important part in encouraging the colonies' wish for freedom. Virginia had

In this painting, Washington watches Cornwallis's army surrender at Yorktown.
▶ Which army is on the left and which is on the right?

played a part in winning an American victory. Now Virginia took the lead in making religious freedom part of American life.

Thomas Jefferson drew up a paper called the **Virginia Statute for Religious Freedom.** This paper said that all people must be free to worship in any way they pleased. It said that no one could be punished for religious beliefs. It also said that a person's rights could not be taken away because of religious beliefs.

The Virginia Statute for Religious Freedom was made a law by the General Assembly in 1786. Now all Virginians were truly free to worship as they chose. In 1789 Virginia's first Jewish congregation was formed. Catholics were also free to worship as they pleased. The same was true for Presbyterians, Quakers, Baptists, and members of all other religions.

Virginia led the nation in making religious freedom part of American life.
► What kind of religious building is this?

LESSON 3 REVIEW

THINK AND WRITE

A. Why was Virginia's capital moved from Williamsburg to Richmond?

B. Why might Jack Jouett be described as a great patriot?

C. In what way was the battle of Yorktown an important victory for America?

D. What did England agree to in the Treaty of Paris?

E. What did the Virginia Statute for Religious Freedom say?

SKILLS CHECK

MAP SKILL

Find the map of Virginia in the Atlas on page 356. Use the mileage scale in the key to figure out how far west Richmond is from Williamsburg.

214

Forming a Nation

THINK ABOUT WHAT YOU KNOW

What qualities does a team need to succeed?

STUDY THE VOCABULARY

federal
architect
Constitutional
   Convention
constitution

Virginia
   Declaration
   of Rights
Bill of Rights
statesman

FOCUS YOUR READING

How were the problems facing the new nation solved?

A. Winning the Peace

The colonies had been able to stand together in war. But now they had to work together to build a new nation. The idea of a strong government frightened some people. Some states wanted to protect their own rights and powers. They feared that a strong government might take away their rights, just as England had tried to do.

But other Americans had different ideas. Some states such as Virginia wanted a strong **federal,** or national, government. They argued that the United States needed a strong government. Without a strong government, the United States would be destroyed.

All agreed that the United States needed a new form of government. They knew that this government should be strong enough to lead a young and growing nation. At the same time, the government should respect the individual rights of each state. But how would the country form such a government?

B. The Constitutional Convention

Planning the Nation Like a house, a government should be built using **architects** (AHR kuh tekts). Architects are people who draw up plans. They make sure that the building will be strong and that it will stand the test of time.

The architects of the government of the United States met in Philadelphia in 1787. Each state had sent its finest leaders. Virginia sent

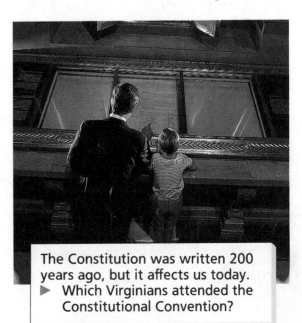

The Constitution was written 200 years ago, but it affects us today.
▶ Which Virginians attended the Constitutional Convention?

George Washington, who was chosen to head the meeting. This important meeting became known as the **Constitutional Convention.**

The Laws The important business of this meeting was to write a new plan for the United States government. It was called the United States Constitution. A **constitution** is a set of laws by which a country is governed. The Constitution called for a Congress of two houses and a President. The President would carry out the laws made by Congress.

Leading Lawmakers James Madison was a member of the Constitutional Convention. Madison was a famous, and humorous, storyteller. But he was even more famous as a brilliant political scholar.

Like Thomas Jefferson, James Madison had fought for religious freedom in Virginia. And like Jefferson, Madison loved his country. He wanted the United States to have the best government possible. The Constitution is based in large part on Madison's hard work and great ideas. His contributions earned him the title Father of the Constitution.

In addition, Madison kept a record of what was said and done at the Constitutional Convention. Thanks to him, we know much about that important meeting.

The Virginia Plan Other important Virginians, such as George Wythe of Williamsburg and Edmund Randolph of Richmond, added their ideas to the United States Constitution. Edmund Randolph was the governor of Virginia at that time. Many of Edmund Randolph's ideas went into a plan that was called the Virginia Plan. Part of the Constitution of the United States was based on the Virginia Plan.

George Mason was a great patriot. He wrote the Virginia Declaration of Rights.
▶ What were two of the rights listed in this paper?

C. The Virginia Declaration of Rights and the Constitution

Virginia already had a constitution that had been created by Virginia patriots in 1776. One important part of the Virginia constitution was a paper known as the Virginia Declaration of Rights. It was written by George Mason. Mason was famous for being a great patriot. His paper stated that no one could take away the rights of any Virginian. Two of the rights listed on this paper were freedom of speech and freedom of religion.

Members of the Constitutional Convention read the Virginia Declaration of Rights. They agreed that all Americans should have those rights. They voted to add George Mason's ideas to the Constitution of the United States. Those ideas are known as the Bill of Rights. The Bill of Rights lists the basic rights granted to all Americans by the United States Constitution.

D. Adopting the Constitution

The men of the Constitutional Convention worked hard at writing the Constitution. They worked all through the hot summer of 1787. On September 17, 1787, it was finished. Then it had to be sent out to all the states to be voted on.

Members of the Constitutional Convention had many discussions.
▶ What is the Bill of Rights?

Virginia agreed to the Constitution after a very close vote. Many Virginians, such as Patrick Henry, were against it. They felt that it gave too much power to the national government and that it took too much power away from the states. However, many other Virginians, such as Edmund Randolph and John Marshall, were in favor of the new Constitution. The Constitution became the law of the land in 1788. Today, the Constitution is still the law of the United States.

E. Virginia, Home of Great Leaders

Virginia was the home of many great leaders during the American War for Independence. Patrick Henry, George Washington, Thomas Jefferson, and Richard Henry Lee were all great patriots who led the American colonies into, and safely through, the War for Independence. And who could ever forget the brav- ery of Captain Daniel Morgan or George Rogers Clark? And, of course, there was the great loyalty of Virginians like James Lafayette and Jack Jouett.

After the War for Independence, Virginia continued to give great leaders to the new nation. Four of the first five United States Presidents came from Virginia. As the country grew, Virginia provided still more leaders. In time, Virginia came to be known as the mother of states and **statesmen**. A statesman is a wise government leader.

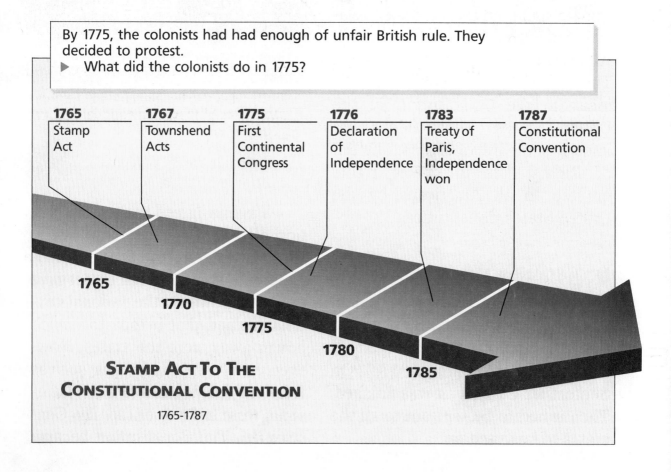

By 1775, the colonists had had enough of unfair British rule. They decided to protest.
▶ What did the colonists do in 1775?

| 1765 | 1767 | 1775 | 1776 | 1783 | 1787 |
| Stamp Act | Townshend Acts | First Continental Congress | Declaration of Independence | Treaty of Paris, Independence won | Constitutional Convention |

1765
1770
1775
1780
1785

STAMP ACT TO THE CONSTITUTIONAL CONVENTION
1765-1787

When the Constitution was signed in 1788, it became the law of the United States. Today, more than 200 years later it is still the law of the land.

▶ Why was Patrick Henry at first against the Constitution?

To honor these great Virginians, Americans have named counties after them. Thirty-one counties in the United States are named after George Washington. Thomas Jefferson has twenty-six counties named after him. Patrick County and Henry County in Virginia were named for Patrick Henry.

LESSON 4 REVIEW

THINK AND WRITE

A. How did Americans feel about the kind of government the new nation needed?

B. Why is James Madison known as the Father of the Constitution?

C. How did the Virginia Declaration of Rights affect the Constitution?

D. Why were some people against the Constitution?

E. Why is Virginia known as the mother of states and statesmen?

SKILLS CHECK

WRITING SKILL

Virginians played an important role at the Constitutional Convention. Write a paragraph describing the ways in which Virginians helped to write the Constitution.

USING THE VOCABULARY

treasury	Treaty of Paris
Stamp Act	Constitutional
Townshend	Convention
Acts	constitution
Continental	Virginia
Congress	Declaration
Declaration of	of Rights
Independence	Bill of Rights

You have learned that the colonists performed many brave actions to win their freedom from England. They also had to set up a new government for the young and growing nation. On a separate sheet of paper, write the names of *three documents* that guarantee important freedoms to Virginians. Next, write the names of *two meetings* where colonists talked about freedoms that people thought were important. Choose your answers from the vocabulary words above.

REMEMBERING WHAT YOU READ

Write your answers in complete sentences on a separate sheet of paper.

1. Which items required tax stamps under the Stamp Act?
2. What goods were taxed by the Townshend Acts?
3. Who were five Virginia patriots?
4. Which Virginia patriot stated "give me liberty or give me death" in his famous speech before the War for Independence?
5. Who was commander in chief of the Continental army?
6. What document made the United States a new country?
7. Who was the leader of the Northwest Campaign?
8. What city became the new capital of Virginia in 1779?
9. Where was the final battle of the War for Independence fought?
10. Which two Virginians added ideas to the Constitution?

TYING MATH TO SOCIAL STUDIES

The First Continental Congress was held in Philadelphia, Pennsylvania. The representatives came from many different places to attend this important meeting. Look at a map of the United States. Locate the following places from which the representatives came: Jamestown, Virginia; Trenton, New Jersey; Boston, Massachusetts; New York City, New York. Use a ruler and the map scale to figure out the distance between each of these cities and Philadelphia. Which representatives traveled the longest distance? Which traveled the shortest distance?

THINKING CRITICALLY

Write your answers in complete sentences on a separate sheet of paper.
1. How were the Stamp Act and the Townshend Acts alike?
2. How would you explain what Patrick Henry meant by the words quoted on page 201?
3. Why were the shots fired in Lexington on April 19, 1775, so important?
4. How did General Washington trick General Cornwallis?
5. Why was building a new nation after the war a difficult task?

SUMMARIZING THE CHAPTER

On a separate sheet of paper, draw a graphic organizer that is like the one shown here. Copy the information from this graphic organizer to the one you have drawn. Under the main idea for each lesson, write three statements that support it. The first one has been done for you.

CHAPTER THEME

Virginians worked with people from other colonies to declare their independence from England.

LESSON 1

Virginia and the other colonies took actions against England's unfair laws.

1. Rebellion against the Stamp Act
2. Organization of a

   Committee of Correspondence
3. Request by colonists at

   Continental Congress that

   England repeal unfair laws

LESSON 2

In the early years of the War for Independence, many things happened.

1.
2.
3.

LESSON 3

The Americans defeated the British in the War for Independence.

1.
2.
3.

LESSON 4

The new nation of the United States solved the problems it faced.

1.
2.
3.

SETTLERS AND RELIGIOUS FREEDOM

In some countries, most people belong to one religion and worship in the same way. Sometimes these people think that their religious beliefs are the only correct beliefs. They feel that other religions and other ways of worshiping are wrong. In many of these countries, the religion of the majority of the people is officially recognized as the religion of the state.

In the past, people who did not share the religious beliefs of the majority were mistreated. Often, they had to move from place to place to avoid abuse. Some left their homelands in order to find places where they could practice their religion freely.

In the 1600s, most European countries had a state religion. In England most people belonged to the Church of England. Anyone living in England who did not belong to the Church of England was mistreated, or persecuted. Eventually, some of these people left England. They came to America where they hoped to practice their religion freely. Many of the first settlers in Virginia were such people.

In the late 1700s, our nation's leaders thought that freedom of religion was very important. In fact, they decided to make it part of our Constitution. The first amendment of the United States Constitution states that "Congress shall make no law respecting an establishment of religion, or prohibiting the free exercise thereof . . ." This means that the United States will have no official state religion. The people of the United States may practice any religion they choose or no religion at all. As a result, the United States is a nation where people from all religious backgrounds can worship openly and freely.

Thinking for Yourself

On a separate sheet of paper, answer the questions in complete sentences.

1. How does respect for the religious beliefs of others benefit everyone?
2. Imagine that you are a member of the Constitutional Convention. Develop an argument for making freedom of religion part of our country's Constitution.
3. In what ways might our country be different if we did not have freedom of religion?

7 VIRGINIANS LEAD THE NATION

Thomas Jefferson was the third President of the United States and the second Virginian to hold that office. With wisdom and leadership, Virginians continued to guide the young nation as it grew and expanded westward.

A New Kind of Nation

THINK ABOUT WHAT YOU KNOW
Think of a team captain or other leader you have helped choose. Why did you choose that person?

STUDY THE VOCABULARY
elect   Cabinet
oath of office   term

FOCUS YOUR READING
What happened as the new nation developed?

A. Bill of Rights

A New Government The Constitution set up a new government for the United States of America. In this nation's government, the power would be in the hands of the people. From now on, the people would be free to make their own laws. And they would be free in other ways. Many of their new freedoms were spelled out in the United States Constitution. These freedoms are in the section of the Constitution known as the Bill of Rights.

The First Amendment In Chapter 6 you learned that the Bill of Rights helps keep us all free. The first part of the Bill of Rights is called the First Amendment. It lists five things that the government cannot do.

1. The government cannot keep people from having their own religion. That is called freedom of *religion.*

2. The government cannot stop people from speaking freely about their own ideas. That is called freedom of *speech.*

3. The government cannot stop people or newspapers from printing what they believe is the truth. That is called freedom of the *press.*

4. The government cannot stop people from meeting together peaceably to talk about their problems. That is called freedom of *assembly.*

5. The government cannot stop people from requesting the government to do something to help them. That is called freedom of *petition.*

Do you remember the name of an important Virginia paper that gave some of these ideas of freedom to the Bill of Rights?

B. Washington as President

No Kings Here The United States would not have a king. The Constitution gave the people the right to govern themselves. They could elect the people they wanted to lead them. Electing means choosing leaders by voting for them.

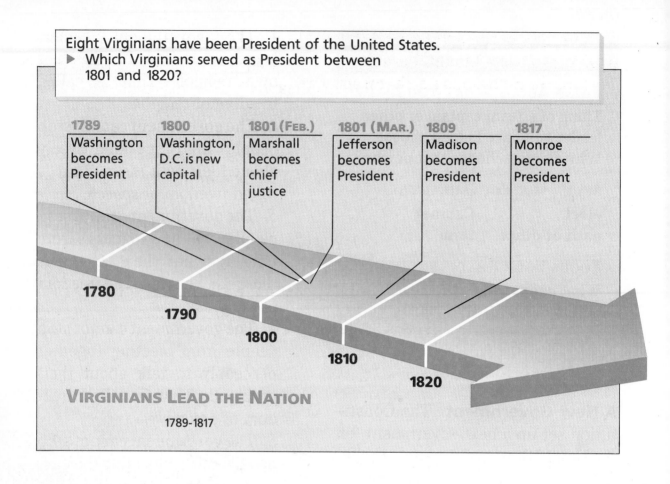

Eight Virginians have been President of the United States.
▶ Which Virginians served as President between 1801 and 1820?

1789
Washington becomes President

1800
Washington, D.C. is new capital

1801 (FEB.)
Marshall becomes chief justice

1801 (MAR.)
Jefferson becomes President

1809
Madison becomes President

1817
Monroe becomes President

1780
1790
1800
1810
1820

VIRGINIANS LEAD THE NATION
1789-1817

The first job facing the people of the new nation was to elect a top leader. Most people agreed that the new leader should be a person of great strength. He also should possess courage and wisdom. Above all else, he should be a great patriot.

An Easy Choice For most people the choice was easy. In their minds, words like *courage* and *patriot* described one person better than anyone else—George Washington. Another Virginian, "Light-Horse Harry" Lee, said Washington was "first in war, first in peace, and first in the hearts of his countrymen." So, in 1788, George Washington was chosen to be the first President.

Away from Home Washington had mixed feelings about his election. He was pleased that his fellow Americans honored him so much. But his heart was with his family and home in Virginia. Once again this great patriot put his love for his country before his own wishes. He agreed to accept the job he had been chosen to do. He did so, however, on one condition. He would not take any pay as President.

In the early spring of 1789, Washington left Mount Vernon on horseback. He headed north toward New York City, the nation's first capital city. Along the way, crowds of Americans, eager for a glimpse of the new President, lined the roads. People cheered wildly as Washington rode into view. Children threw flowers in his path.

On April 30, after completing his journey, George Washington took the **oath of office** in New York City. With these words, the President promises to do the job well. After taking the oath, George Washington of Virginia was President of the United States.

C. Washington's Cabinet

Washington was a very wise man. He knew he needed a great deal of help running the new government. He chose four men to help him. They were Alexander Hamilton of New York, Henry Knox of Massachusetts, and Thomas Jefferson and Edmund Randolph of Virginia.

These men helped Washington make important decisions. They became known as his **Cabinet.** Ever since then, each President of the United States has had a Cabinet to help him run the government. Over the years, the number of Cabinet members has increased.

D. Washington's Return Home

George Washington made a fine President. But his thoughts were never far from the plantation he loved. He made trips back to Mount Vernon as often as he could. He looked forward to the day when he could return there and be a farmer.

But that was not to happen as soon as he had hoped. Washington had been elected for a **term** of four years. A term is the length of time a President stays in office. At the end of his term, the people of America

When George Washington was elected President, he traveled on horseback to New York City.
▶ Why did Washington go to New York City after his election?

The United States Capitol stands high above the city of Washington, D.C. This place is now called Capitol Hill. This is where United States senators and representatives meet to make laws for the nation.
▶ What is the name of the architect who designed this building?

asked him to serve another term. Again, Washington was loyal to his country. He agreed to stay on.

George Washington completed his second term and left office in 1797. He had been a strong leader. But at the age of 65, he was tired and ready to go home.

E. A New Capital

George Washington suggested the idea for a new capital city in 1791. At that time the nation's capital was Philadelphia, Pennsylvania.

Washington suggested using a piece of land 10 miles (16 km) square on the banks of the Potomac River. The land lay between Virginia and Maryland and was called the District of Columbia. A French architect named Pierre L'Enfant (pyair lahn FAHN) was asked to design plans for the city. He had also planned part of Paris, France.

L'Enfant's plan showed the capitol building at the highest point in the new city. In 1792 the government asked different architects to draw plans for the capitol building. The architect who drew the best plan would win a prize of $500, and his design would be used. The winner was a man named William Thornton. The capitol building that

This is the United States Capitol as it looks today.
► In what ways has it changed since the early 1800s?

we know today is the one William Thornton designed.

The planning and building of the new capital took nearly ten years to complete. Finally, in 1800, the United States government moved to the District of Columbia. A year earlier, George Washington had died. He never saw the new capital finished. To honor our first President, the capital city of the United States was named Washington, D.C.

LESSON *1* REVIEW

THINK AND WRITE

A. What five freedoms are spelled out in the First Amendment to the Constitution?

B. Why did George Washington have very mixed feelings about his election?

C. What does George Washington's need for a Cabinet tell you about him?

D. Why did the American people want George Washington to serve a second term?

E. How was the design for the capitol building chosen?

SKILLS CHECK

MAP SKILL

Turn to the map of the United States in the Atlas on pages 354–355. Find the cities of Philadelphia, Pennsylvania, and Washington, D.C. on the map. Use the mileage scale in the key to estimate how many miles apart they are.

Jefferson and the Exploration of the West

THINK ABOUT WHAT YOU KNOW

Name some famous people who are good at many different things. How do you feel about these people?

STUDY THE VOCABULARY

**Louisiana   explorer
   Purchase**

FOCUS YOUR READING

How did the United States of America grow under the presidency of Thomas Jefferson?

A. Our Third President

President and Chef A waiter came into the kitchen carrying a tray of dishes. As the kitchen door swung shut, the noise from the dining room faded. Tonight the President of the United States was hosting a big state dinner. Many important people had been invited.

The waiter set down the tray of dishes on the counter. He nearly knocked over a large can that rested at the edge of the counter. "Be careful!" scolded the chef.

"What's in there anyway?" asked the waiter.

The chef removed the lid from the can. The waiter looked in and saw what looked like firmly packed snow. "What is it?" he asked.

"It's called ice cream," the chef explained. "It's a type of dessert. President Jefferson learned about it when he was in France. He told me how to make it."

Thomas Jefferson was now President. He had become President in 1801. John Adams of Massachusetts had followed Washington as President. And now Jefferson had followed Adams.

"President Jefferson has so many interests," the waiter said. "He's a remarkable man."

Thomas Jefferson, our nation's third President, was interested in many things.
► What were three of Jefferson's interests?

Thomas Jefferson was an architect. He designed his home at Monticello. He was also an inventor.
► For what other things is he known?

"Yes, he is," agreed the chef. "He knows more about food than I do. He speaks several languages. And he's an inventor."

An Architect "I hear he designs buildings as well," the waiter added. It was true. In his day, Jefferson was one of the country's leading architects. He designed some of Virginia's buildings.

Jefferson also gave America its system of money. Before Jefferson's system, the colonies had paid for goods with money like the British used, called pounds.

A Great Leader Above all else, Jefferson was a great leader of people. He had been a lawyer, a member of the House of Burgesses, and the governor of Virginia. You learned earlier that Jefferson wrote most of the Declaration of Independence. You also read about his Virginia Statute for Religious Freedom.

Yet, with all that he knew and did, Thomas Jefferson always was eager to learn and do even more. Jefferson especially loved the outdoors and was very interested in farming. He knew a great deal about seeds, plants, and trees. Jefferson was always interested in learning more about new and different places, people, plants, and animals.

B. The Louisiana Purchase

Under the leadership of America's first two Presidents, America grew. But under America's third President, Thomas Jefferson, the country doubled in size!

In 1803 Jefferson made a bargain with the leader of France. Up to that time, much of the land west of the Mississippi River belonged to France. The French called the area they owned Louisiana (loo ee zee AN uh). Jefferson persuaded the Congress to buy this land from the French. He agreed to pay the French government $12 million in cash. That may sound like a lot of money,

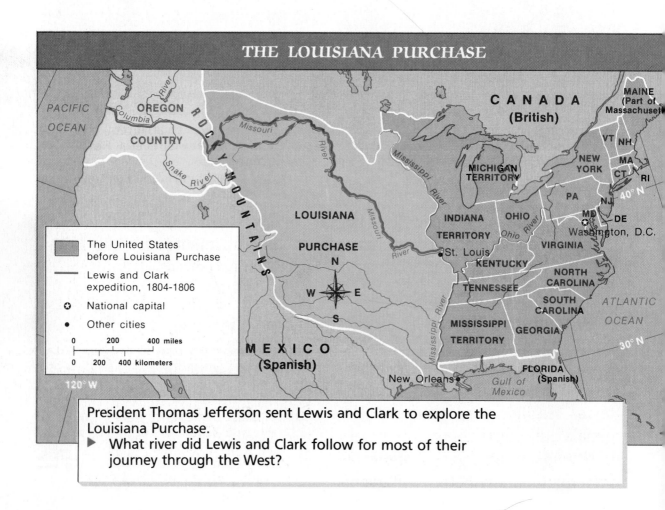

THE LOUISIANA PURCHASE

President Thomas Jefferson sent Lewis and Clark to explore the Louisiana Purchase.
▶ What river did Lewis and Clark follow for most of their journey through the West?

but the land was worth many times that amount. The deal was known as the **Louisiana Purchase.** It has been called the greatest bargain in American history.

With the Louisiana Purchase, America's western frontier now stretched as far as the Rocky Mountains. Find the Louisiana Purchase on the map on page 232.

C. Lewis and Clark

Unexplored Land Jeremy Perkins gazed up the wide Missouri River. He thought about the adventure that lay ahead. He had heard about mountains so tall they scraped the sky. And somewhere beyond was the shiny blue Pacific Ocean!

"Look lively, Perkins!" Sergeant Mell barked. "Captain Lewis wants the men to start raising the sail on the big boat."

"Yes sir," replied Perkins. He saluted smartly.

Private Jeremy Perkins had signed up for a special journey. Its purpose was to learn more about the lands beyond the Mississippi River. No one knew much about these lands. President Jefferson was curious to see what he had bought with the $12 million he had persuaded the people of America to pay to France. He wanted maps of the region. He also wanted to know about the Native Americans who lived there. And he wanted to find out about the area's plants and animals.

Leading Explorer The journey was to be headed by Captain Meriwether Lewis. Captain Lewis was from Albemarle County, Virginia. He had been a captain during the War for Independence. At one time, Lewis lived with the Indians in the western part of Virginia.

Lewis was a childhood friend of Thomas Jefferson. But the President had not chosen Lewis because of friendship. The President had felt

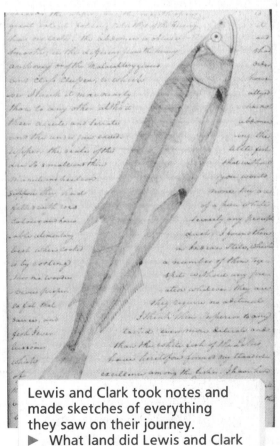

Lewis and Clark took notes and made sketches of everything they saw on their journey.
▶ What land did Lewis and Clark explore?

that the journey called for a keen **explorer.** It needed someone who could find his way through the thickest woods. It needed someone who could live off the land. Above all, it needed someone who was fearless. Lewis was such a man.

Younger Brother As Perkins and the other men worked, a strong-looking man with bright red hair strolled up. He took one of the ropes. At Captain Mell's next signal, the man pulled with all his strength.

This man was William Clark. Lewis had chosen him as a partner in the exploration. Clark was also a Virginian, from Caroline County. He was the younger brother of George Rogers Clark. Do you remember what you read about George Rogers Clark in Chapter 6?

D. An Unknown Land

Finding a Guide In 1804 the big boat with the canvas sail left the dock in St. Louis. The people on the riverbanks cheered wildly as the boat passed them. The inside of the boat was filled with food, guns, and medicine. It also contained glittering rings, brass kettles, and strings of beads. These gifts were for any Native Americans that the explorers might meet on their journey.

By fall, the voyagers had traveled nearly 2,000 miles (3,218 km) along the Missouri River. They had reached what is now the state of North Dakota. They decided to camp there for the winter. All along the way, friendly Indians had served as guides. Now they met a very wise Indian woman with long dark hair and a gentle smile. Her name was Sacagawea (sak uh juh WEE uh).

Sacagawea belonged to the Shoshone (shoh SHOH nee) people. She spoke the language of many of the western Indians. She told the explorers that the high mountains were in the West. Lewis and Clark asked if she would come with them to show them the way.

Sacagawea, a Shoshone Indian, helped guide Lewis and Clark as they traveled west.
► What kind of weapons did the explorers carry with them?

Reaching the Sky When the group started the trip again in the spring, it had three new members. Sacagawea was one of them. The other two were her French-Canadian husband and her son. With their new guide, Lewis and Clark journeyed through bear country. Sacagawea helped them speak with the Indians they met on the way. They gave the Indians gifts from President Jefferson.

The group had to leave their boat and continue on horseback when the river became shallow. Then one day they saw the Rocky Mountains in the distance. The trip through the mountains was very difficult. The Rocky Mountains were too steep for the explorers to climb straight up. Instead, they had to make broad circles to reach the tops of the peaks.

The explorers made it over the Rocky Mountains and continued on their way. Next, they came to the wide Columbia River. The explorers had to build canoes.

Finally, on November 7, 1805, Lewis and Clark reached their destination. The Pacific Ocean stretched as far as they could see. Two Virginians had led the first Americans across the continent.

Lewis and Clark brought back maps they had made of the western lands for President Jefferson. They told him about the people they had met. And they brought him samples of the plants they had found and two little bear cubs!

The people of the United States felt they now had a claim to the lands west of the Rocky Mountains.

E. The End of the Jefferson Presidency

While Jefferson was President, England and France were at war again. English and French ships had even attacked American ships. In 1807 a British ship attacked the American navy ship *Chesapeake* near Chesapeake Bay. Jefferson

Thomas Jefferson drew the plans for the buildings of the University of Virginia, including this rotunda.
▶ What shape is the rotunda?

knew his country was not strong enough to fight both England and France. He kept the United States out of the European war.

Jefferson's final term as President ended in 1809. He went home to Monticello. There, he drew the plans for the buildings of the University of Virginia. He had worked on the idea of a university for many years. Thomas Jefferson, a great Virginian, died on July 4, 1826.

LESSON 2 REVIEW

THINK AND WRITE

A. Why might a person say that Thomas Jefferson was a remarkable man?

B. Why was the Louisiana Purchase called the greatest bargain in American history?

C. Why did President Thomas Jefferson choose Meriwether Lewis to head the exploration of the western lands?

D. In what ways did Sacagawea help Lewis and Clark?

E. Why did President Thomas Jefferson choose to keep America out of England's war with France in 1807?

SKILLS CHECK

WRITING SKILL

Find the Missouri River in the Gazetteer and on the United States map on pages 354–355. Then, in your own words, list some facts about this river that Lewis and Clark traveled on.

Guiding a Young America

THINK ABOUT WHAT YOU KNOW

If a disaster such as a hurricane were about to hit your school, what one item would you take with you to safety?

STUDY THE VOCABULARY

Era of Good   Supreme Court
   Feeling   chief justice
Monroe
   Doctrine

FOCUS YOUR READING

What important leadership roles did Virginians have in the nation in the early 1800s?

A. Madison and the War of 1812

A New Leader In 1809 America had a new leader. He lived in Orange County, Virginia, and was a man who had devoted his whole life to making America a free country. He was James Madison, the Father of the Constitution.

Madison greatly admired the Presidents who had served before him. His job, he felt, was to continue their good work.

Taking Our Sailors Like Jefferson, Madison wanted to keep America out of the war between France and England. However, this was becoming harder and harder to do. The nation's wounds from the British attack on the *Chesapeake* had not healed. The American people remembered with bitterness that three of their sailors had died. They had not forgotten that 18 others had been injured. British navy ships continued

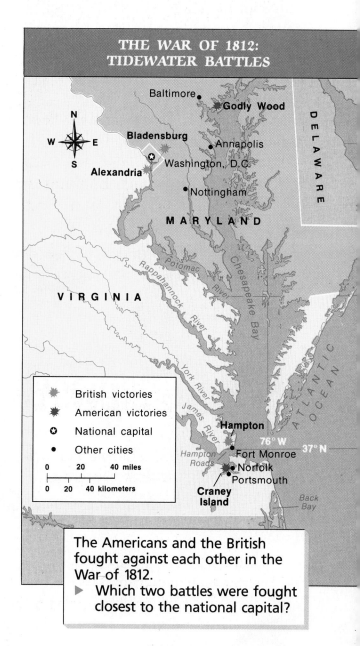

THE WAR OF 1812: TIDEWATER BATTLES

Baltimore
Godly Wood
Bladensburg
Annapolis
Washington, D.C.
Alexandria
Nottingham
MARYLAND
DELAWARE
Rappahannock River
Potomac River
VIRGINIA
Chesapeake Bay
York River
James River
ATLANTIC OCEAN
Hampton
76° W   37° N
Hampton Roads
Fort Monroe
Norfolk
Portsmouth
Craney Island
Back Bay

* British victories
* American victories
○ National capital
• Other cities
0   20   40 miles
0   20   40 kilometers

The Americans and the British fought against each other in the War of 1812.
▶ Which two battles were fought closest to the national capital?

to attack American ships off Virginia's coast. And now the British were kidnapping American sailors and forcing them to work on British ships. The American people were getting very angry with the British.

In 1812 America once again went to war with England. British ships and soldiers attacked Virginia several times during the War of 1812. America's handful of ships had a difficult fight against the large, strong British navy.

In 1813 a large British fleet sailed into Hampton Roads to attack Norfolk. Virginia soldiers pushed back the English at the battle of Craney (KRAY nee) Island on the way to Norfolk. But the angry British then attacked the nearby port of Hampton and burned it.

B. The Burning of Washington

Marching to Washington On a hot day late in August 1814, the people living near Chesapeake Bay saw a frightening sight. Four thousand English soldiers, with orders to burn the new capital, were marching toward Washington.

Dolley Madison was afraid the British would destroy the White House. She wanted to protect possessions that were important to Americans.
▶ What were some of the things she took when she fled?

American troops under General Winder rushed to Maryland, near Washington, D.C. Their plan was to form a wall of soldiers to hold off the British. But reports on the size of the British forces reached the general. The wall would not be strong enough! The general ordered his men back to Washington, D.C. Meanwhile, the British set up camp in Maryland.

Waiting for News Back in the capital, President Madison's wife, Dolley, anxiously awaited news from her husband. A day earlier, the President had gone out to inspect his army. Dolley Madison now feared that the White House would be destroyed by the British soldiers. The White House meant a great deal to her. She had made it a center of hospitality by giving many dinners.

A Heroic Act With 100 guards standing outside the White House, Dolley Madison began packing. She did not pack her own precious possessions. Instead, she gathered together things that were precious to the nation. Among the things she packed were important government papers and a full-length portrait of George Washington.

Later that day, the British soldiers invaded the capital. President and Mrs. Madison and members of the government escaped into

The British burned the White House and most of the city of Washington, D.C., in 1814.
▶ During which war was this?

Virginia. By nightfall, most of the new government buildings stood in flames. The White House was among these buildings.

C. The Peace Treaty

After the burning of Washington, there were a few more battles. But both sides were growing tired of the long and bitter war. They were ready for peace.

That peace came on December 24, 1814. On that day, America and England signed a peace treaty called the Treaty of Ghent (gent).

Neither side could really claim to have won the War of 1812. However, America had come away with some important knowledge. The country now knew the strength of its own fighting forces. It had fought the mighty British navy. And it had not been beaten.

D. President Monroe

Former Governor Virginia had given America three of its first four Presidents. In 1817, following James Madison's term, Virginia produced another President.

James Monroe, the nation's fifth President, was from Westmoreland County. He had been an officer in the War for Independence. He had studied law under Thomas Jefferson. And, like Jefferson, Monroe had served as governor of Virginia.

Monroe was eager to serve his country. After a stormy four years under James Madison, America was ready for a change. Monroe believed he could bring about that change. He said that if elected, he would improve life in America. He promised to build canals, roads, and forts.

Improving the Nation Monroe honored his promise. During his two terms as President, things went smoothly in the United States. In fact, they went so smoothly that those eight years became known as the Era of Good Feeling.

President Monroe encouraged roads and canals to be built so that the United States would be truly united. The canals were especially important to Virginia.

This painting, hanging in the United States Naval Academy Museum, shows a battle during the War of 1812.
► How did the War of 1812 end?

This is Fort Monroe at Old Point Comfort.
▶ Why were many forts built near water?

President Monroe also strengthened America against enemy attack by building strong new forts. The largest of the new forts was Fort Monroe at Old Point Comfort in Virginia. Fort Monroe was built so that the United States Army could easily fire on enemy ships in Hampton Roads. Fort Monroe is still an army base today.

President Monroe also added another large piece of land to the United States. He did this in 1819 when he bought Florida from Spain.

E. The Monroe Doctrine

The sale of Florida to the United States had both good results and bad results for Spain. It was

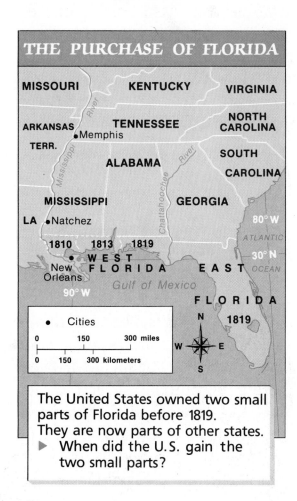

THE PURCHASE OF FLORIDA

The United States owned two small parts of Florida before 1819. They are now parts of other states.
▶ When did the U.S. gain the two small parts?

President Monroe is explaining the Monroe Doctrine to his cabinet.
► What country is shown on the wall map behind Monroe?

thought to be good because Spain needed money badly. Spain's treasury was nearly empty because of a war in Europe.

The sale was bad because Spain was slowly losing all its colonies in America. While Spain had been fighting in Europe, several of its American colonies had demanded their independence.

Now Spain turned to its European neighbors. It asked for help in stopping its American colonies from breaking free. Offers of support came from France and Russia.

President Monroe was upset. He felt that Europe should no longer take part in the affairs of the Americas. In 1823 he sent the countries of Europe a warning. He warned them against ever trying to take over any country in North America or South America. This warning is called the **Monroe Doctrine.**

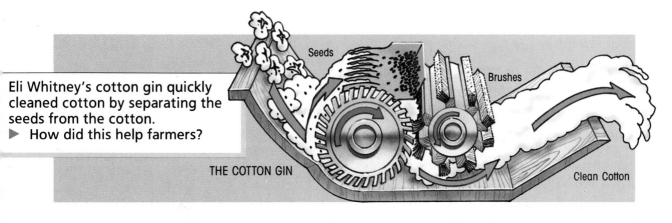

Eli Whitney's cotton gin quickly cleaned cotton by separating the seeds from the cotton.
▶ How did this help farmers?

Seeds

Brushes

THE COTTON GIN

Clean Cotton

machine did the work of many humans in readying cotton for market.

Cotton was the boost that some Tidewater farmers needed. But cotton also led to Virginia's loss of many of its planters. They moved farther south. Or they moved southwest. They wanted to go where there was plenty of land for raising cotton.

C. New Farming Ideas

Making Better Soil One of Thomas Jefferson's interests was making the most of Virginia soil. Like Washington, Jefferson was a farmer at heart. Unlike Washington, Jefferson was also a scientist. If there was a way to make the soil produce better crops, he would find it.

Working alongside Jefferson were several men who understood much about growing things. All of these men were Virginians. One was John Taylor of Caroline County.

Imagine that you were a Virginia planter in the early 1800s. You might first hear of John Taylor from a neighbor who had read one of Taylor's papers on growing crops. Soon you would begin reading these papers. You would find out that fertilizers can make the soil grow stronger. You might also learn that plowing more deeply helps the soil.

Newspaper for Farmers Another man who worked with Jefferson on new farming ideas was Edmund Ruffin of Prince George County. Ruffin, like John Taylor, had attended the College of William and Mary.

Edmund Ruffin published a journal called *Farmer's Register*. This journal greatly influenced farmers in the South. One of Ruffin's important findings was that most of the worn-out soil needed a powder called lime. Lime would help the soil to grow better crops.

Men such as John Taylor and Edmund Ruffin gave much to Virginia. Thanks to them, Virginia farmers learned new ways to make the soil better. Crops began to grow larger and stronger.

D. Voting

Farms were not the only things that had changed in Virginia. Americans now had the right to vote to elect their own leaders. This was one of the main things that made the United States different from many other countries.

Election days were exciting for Americans. Most men took a holiday from work. They drove to the county seat in horse-drawn wagons. At the county seat they would put their **ballot** in the box where the votes were collected. A ballot is the paper on which a vote is marked down.

These men are electing government leaders by written ballot.
▶ What are some ways that voting is different today?

Women were not allowed to vote in these elections. Neither were slaves. Not even all free men could do so. Only free men who owned land were allowed to vote.

Some unfair laws still remained even after the War for Independence. However, Virginians in the 1800s were learning to trust their national government.

E. Black People in Virginia

By 1800 more than 300,000 slaves lived in Virginia. And many more were in other southern states.

Not all Virginians liked the idea of slavery. Many, in fact, spoke out strongly against it. In 1779 Thomas Jefferson asked the General Assembly to free Virginia's slaves. However, Virginians were not willing to go that far. Thomas Jefferson's request was turned down.

Of course, not all blacks in Virginia were slaves. Many blacks were free. Most free blacks lived in towns. They kept shops. They worked at different trades. Blacks made and sold furniture. They made silverware and ironwork. They made bricks and sewed clothes. They were noted for the fine work they did.

But even these "free" blacks were not as free as whites. Some slave owners feared that free blacks might lead slaves to revolt. So laws were passed to try to stop that from happening. Though free blacks were good citizens, they were not free to own guns. Though they ran businesses, they were not free to go out at night. Though they worked very hard, they were not free to learn to read and write.

Then, in 1816, John Marshall, James Monroe, and other Virginians came up with a plan. They raised money to send free blacks to live in a country of their own on the western coast of Africa. The country was called Liberia. The first boat sailed for Liberia in 1821. Several thousand people went there to live.

In 1829 Joseph Jenkins Roberts left for Liberia. He had been born a slave in Virginia. In 1841 he was made governor of Liberia. Seven years later, he was chosen as Liberia's first president.

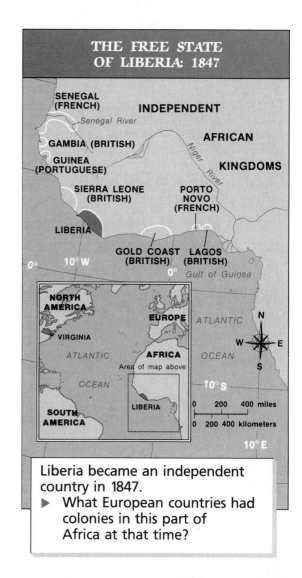

Liberia became an independent country in 1847.
▶ What European countries had colonies in this part of Africa at that time?

LESSON 4 REVIEW

THINK AND WRITE

A. Why were many Tidewater farmers eager to move to other parts of Virginia?

B. Was there more or less land for growing cotton in Virginia than farther south?

C. What important discoveries did Virginians John Taylor and Edmund Ruffin make?

D. Who was allowed to vote in Virginia, and who was not?

E. Where is Liberia?

SKILLS CHECK

THINKING SKILL

Why did some blacks leave America and go to Liberia? Why did many blacks stay in America?

USING THE VOCABULARY

oath of office	Era of Good
Cabinet	Feeling
term	Monroe
Louisiana	Doctrine
Purchase	Supreme Court
explorer	chief justice
	ballot

On a separate sheet of paper, write the best word to complete each sentence below. Choose your answers from the vocabulary words above.

1. The time when James Monroe was President is called the _____.
2. The President of the United States is elected to serve a four-year _____.
3. President Jefferson made a deal called the _____, in which he bought land from the French.
4. Jefferson chose Captain Lewis to be a fearless _____ of the land that made up the Louisiana Purchase.
5. The four men President Washington chose to help him make decisions became known as his _____.

REMEMBERING WHAT YOU READ

Write your answers in complete sentences on a separate sheet of paper.

1. What kind of person were the people of the new nation looking for to be the first President?
2. Who were the members of Washington's first Cabinet?
3. Where was the new capital of the nation located?
4. What offices had Thomas Jefferson held before being elected President of the United States?
5. How was President Thomas Jefferson able to double the size of the United States?
6. What did Lewis and Clark bring back with them from their journey into the Western lands?
7. What war was fought against the British during the time James Madison was President?
8. What was the purpose of issuing the Monroe Doctrine?
9. What new farming practices helped Virginia planters?
10. Who was Joseph Jenkins Roberts?

TYING LANGUAGE ARTS TO SOCIAL STUDIES: WRITING TO LEARN

From the chapter choose one of the following people whom you would like to be: George Washington, Thomas Jefferson, Meriwether Lewis, Sacagawea, or Dolley Madison. Write a paragraph explaining why you chose that person. Give reasons why you admire the person you selected.

THINKING CRITICALLY

Write your answers in complete sentences on a separate sheet of paper.

1. What is one idea of George Washington's that continues today?
2. Why was the Louisiana Purchase so important for the nation?
3. Why did Lewis and Clark set out on their expedition?
4. How were James Madison's years as President difficult ones?
5. How did farming change in Virginia after the War for Independence?

SUMMARIZING THE CHAPTER

On a separate sheet of paper, draw a graphic organizer that is like the one shown here. Copy the information from this graphic organizer to the one you have drawn. Under the main idea for each lesson, write three statements that support it. The first one has been done for you.

CHAPTER THEME
The new United States government gave important powers to the people.

LESSON 1

As the new nation developed, many things happened.

1. George Washington elected first President
2. Washington chose a Cabinet
3. New capital built in the District of Columbia

LESSON 2

The United States grew and improved while Thomas Jefferson was President.

1. _____
2. _____
3. _____

LESSON 3

Many changes took place in America as it began its second 100 years.

1. _____
2. _____
3. _____

LESSON 4

Many changes took place in Virginia after the War for Independence.

1. _____
2. _____
3. _____

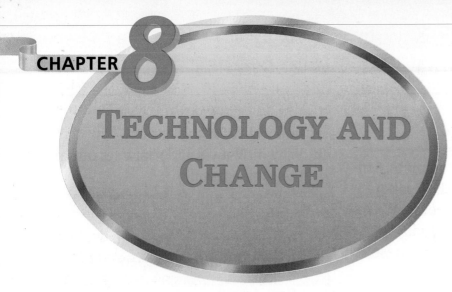

CHAPTER 8

TECHNOLOGY AND CHANGE

During the 1800s machines were invented that made life easier. Railroads and steamboats changed the ways people and goods traveled. Serious disagreements arose that would soon separate Virginians.

Machines to Make Work Easier

Name two inventions you know of. How has each made life easier for the people who use it?

technology	shingle
harpoon	barrel stave
steamboat	

What new forms of transportation became popular in America during the 1800s?

A. Inventions and a Changing Virginia

Scientific Advances Technology (tek NAHL uh jee) is a very useful word. It is used to describe all the ways people have of making and using the things they need and want. High technology is technology that makes use of many machines. It uses advanced scientific knowledge to produce special equipment. This equipment includes computers, digital watches, and calculators.

In the United States today we have high technology. But we did not become a nation of high technology overnight. Little by little people began to find better ways to get work done. They invented machines to help them do work more easily and faster. Many of these machines were invented in the 1800s. Many were invented by Virginians.

A New Machine One machine invented in the 1800s made the life of the farmer easier. That machine was the McCormick reaper. Its inventor, Cyrus McCormick, was a Virginian.

As a child, Cyrus McCormick liked to watch the wheat blow gently in the fields. He also liked to watch his father harvest the wheat. In those days, harvesting was done by hand. Cyrus's father always believed that someday there would be a machine to do the job. He did not know, back then, that his son Cyrus would invent that machine.

Cyrus McCormick first tried out his new harvesting machine in 1831. He used it on a neighbor's grain field, and it worked. From then on, harvesting could be done much more quickly. The machine could cut wheat more easily and faster than ever before.

The Grain Barrel The Valley of Virginia came to be called the grain barrel of the nation. Because of the invention of the McCormick reaper, the amount of wheat grown was increased. More mills were then needed to grind the wheat into flour.

Cyrus McCormick first tried his new machine on a neighbor's wheat field in 1831. McCormick's reaper completely changed the way grain was harvested.
► What effect did the reaper have on wheat production in Virginia?

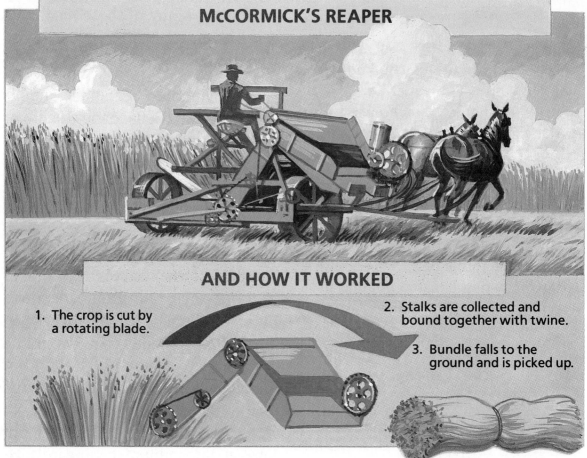

McCORMICK'S REAPER

AND HOW IT WORKED

1. The crop is cut by a rotating blade.

2. Stalks are collected and bound together with twine.

3. Bundle falls to the ground and is picked up.

Many flour mills were built between 1830 and 1850. They ground both wheat and corn. The mills used the fast-moving waters of the James River to turn the mill wheels. The flour from the mills was then used to make bread and other foods.

Many other mills and factories were built during these years. In 1836 Virginia's first cotton mill was built. Furniture shops were also built. They made their products from Virginia's many forests.

This statue honors Lewis Temple. He invented a special harpoon.
► How did Temple earn his living?

254

A Safe Tool for Whalers Virginians were also finding ways to improve other businesses. Lewis Temple was a black man born in Richmond in 1808. In 1829 he moved to Massachusetts, the whaling center of the country. He ran his own blacksmith shop and made iron tools for the whaling industry. Whaling was an important industry. Whale oil was used to make candles. There were no electric lights then.

In 1848 Temple invented a special **harpoon.** A harpoon is a kind of spear that is used for catching whales. Temple's harpoon is thought to be the most important invention in the history of whaling. Whaling became less dangerous, and the industry grew.

B. Steam Instead of Sails

Without Sails I could feel my heart pound as the **steamboat** drifted toward us. In all my years as a newspaper reporter, I had never seen anything like it. This boat had no sails or oars. It moved by steam power.

"Steady as she goes!" a boat worker on the dock shouted. Soon the big boat was up against the dock.

My boss at the newspaper had sent me to Hampton Roads to cover the story. I had already thought of the headline: *Steam, The Future of Virginia's Waterways.*

Suddenly I felt a big shove from behind. Everyone was pushing forward. Everyone wanted to be one of the first to ride.

Steamboats and Engines After I got on the boat I checked the notes on my note pad. The steamboat had been introduced three years earlier, in 1807. Its inventor was a New York man named Robert Fulton. He had

Steamboats became an important means of transportation.
► Who was the inventor of the steamboat?

used another important invention, the steam engine, to drive his boat. The steam engine had been invented in England. It burned wood or coal to heat water. The heated water made steam. The power from the steam could run many machines.

Steamboats began to carry people and goods up and down Virginia's rivers. They also ran between Hampton Roads and other ports on the Atlantic Coast. Ships big enough to steam across the ocean began to run from Norfolk and Alexandria to Europe. At first, steamboats were not as fast as the big sailing ships. But soon they could make a voyage in much less time than sailboats. They brought Virginia closer to the rest of the world.

C. Dismal Swamp Canal

In the 1800s most of the farm products raised in North Carolina were sent to Virginia on canal boats. The boats traveled along the canals built in the Dismal Swamp. North Carolina's goods were shipped from Norfolk to the rest of the country and to other parts of the world. This was necessary because North Carolina had no deep harbors that big ships could use. In 1826 Norfolk became even more important to North

Travelers on the Dismal Swamp Canal often stopped at Lake Drummond Hotel. Small boats still use the canal.
▶ What types of boats are in this picture?

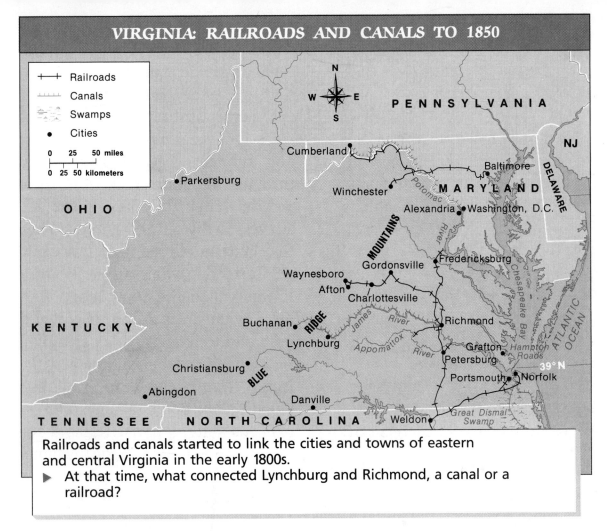

Railroads
Canals
Swamps
• Cities

0 25 50 miles
0 25 50 kilometers

PENNSYLVANIA

NJ

Cumberland

Parkersburg

Winchester

Baltimore

MARYLAND

DELAWARE

OHIO

Alexandria • Washington, D.C.

Potomac

River

MOUNTAINS

Fredericksburg

Gordonsville

Waynesboro

Afton

Charlottesville

Richmond

Chesapeake Bay

ATLANTIC OCEAN

James River

KENTUCKY

Buchanan

RIDGE

Lynchburg

Appomattox River

Grafton

Hampton Roads

Petersburg

39° N

Christiansburg

BLUE

Portsmouth • Norfolk

Abingdon

Danville

TENNESSEE   NORTH CAROLINA

Weldon

Great Dismal Swamp

Railroads and canals started to link the cities and towns of eastern and central Virginia in the early 1800s.
▶ At that time, what connected Lynchburg and Richmond, a canal or a railroad?

Carolina. In that year the Dismal Swamp Canal from North Carolina to Norfolk was cut wider and deeper.

Then steamboats, as well as the older, smaller canal boats, could use the canal. They carried loads of lumber, tar, wood **shingles,** and **barrel staves** from North Carolina's forests. Shingles are thin pieces of wood used to cover the roofs and sides of buildings. Barrel staves are strips of wood used to make barrels. The steamboat greatly helped Virginia businesses. But another invention changed Virginia even more.

D. Railroads

Travel by Land By 1833 Virginia had joined the growing number of states to welcome the railroad, which was a better form of travel. Track was laid connecting Richmond to North Carolina. During the 1830s, Portsmouth, Norfolk, Petersburg, and Fredericksburg also had short railroads. Railroads could move people and goods faster than wagons or canal boats could.

Like steamboats, the early locomotives were powered by steam. The tracks were very close together,

257

Railroads soon replaced travel by wagon and canal boat.
▶ What did the early passenger cars look like?

and the trains were small. Most of the cars were wagons that had been made to be pulled by horses. The cars were tied together behind puffing steam engines that gave off sparks and smoke. Passengers usually arrived from their journeys covered with soot.

Building a Tunnel Another problem of early rail travel was that trains could not go far. This was partly because they could not cross mountains. In the 1840s a man named Claudius Crozet (kroh ZAY) solved that problem. Colonel Crozet was a railroad builder who had served in the French army. He was given the challenge of laying a rail line across the Blue Ridge Mountains. The line would connect Gordonsville and Waynesboro.

Some of the peaks were too steep for Crozet's work crew, so they dug tunnels. They blasted holes through the hard rock with gunpowder. Then they used picks and shovels to dig out the tunnels. Then they laid the railroad tracks. One tunnel Crozet dug was nearly a mile long. It was called the Blue Ridge Tunnel. It went from Afton to Waynesboro and took eight years to build.

Once Crozet's rail line was finished, trains came to Virginia's Great Valley. Soon, rail lines were all over the state. And the trains themselves were better made. Engines were stronger and built to haul heavier loads. The railroad cars were big-

The Blue Ridge Tunnel allowed trains to cross steep mountains.
▶ Why did the builders have to go through the mountain?

ger. Railroads seemed to bring Virginia's coast and mountain regions closer together. Farmers could ship their goods to towns and cities. People could travel with ease.

E. The Age of Coal and Iron

The years after 1830 were called the age of coal and iron. Railroads and steamships needed coal to run their engines. Coal was the fuel used to heat the water that produced the steam. Virginia had rich coal fields beneath its surface. Some ships and railroad trains still run on Virginia coal today.

Iron ore was also plentiful in Virginia. And a great deal of iron was needed. The ore was put into hot furnaces. It came out as steel and iron. These strong metals were then

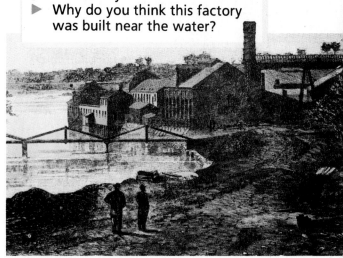

Tredegar Iron Works in Richmond was one of the largest iron works in the country.
▶ Why do you think this factory was built near the water?

hammered into new railroad cars or tracks or into steamboats.

Richmond was home to one of the biggest iron works in the country. It was called the Tredegar (TRED e gur) Iron Works. Railroad tracks, engines, and many other iron products were made there.

LESSON **1** *REVIEW*

THINK AND WRITE

A. How did the inventions of the 1800s make life in America better?
B. Why was the invention of the steamboat so important?
C. How did deepening the Dismal Swamp Canal improve trade between Virginia and North Carolina?
D. What were some good points and bad points of the early railroads?

E. Why have the years after 1830 become known as the age of coal and iron?

SKILLS CHECK

MAP SKILL

Turn to the map on page 257. What linked Cumberland and Washington, D.C.? What linked the city of Fredericksburg and the city of Richmond?

TRAINS THROUGH THE TIMES

First locomotive built in the United States, 1830

American railway scene, 1876

Turboliner, gas turbine 1978

Metroliner, electric 1990

The trains on this track are from different times. Follow the track from the top of the page to the bottom. You will see that trains have changed in many ways. One way they have changed is in the type of fuel they use. Think of some other ways in which trains have changed.

▶ How do you think trains will look in the future?

Changing Ways of Learning

THINK ABOUT WHAT YOU KNOW

What are your two favorite subjects in school?

STUDY THE VOCABULARY

seminary	current
mechanic	chart
fund	

FOCUS YOUR READING

What changes took place in education in America after 1800?

A. Jefferson and Education

Free Public Schools   Thomas Jefferson placed great value on education. He felt that all children should have a chance to learn. He believed that education was the main building block of a nation. At the time, though, there was no statewide system of free schools.

So Jefferson drew up a plan calling for free public schools in Virginia. He read his plan before the Virginia Assembly. But the Assembly refused to go along with it. Jefferson continued to fight for public education in Virginia.

A New University   Jefferson was successful in another of his goals for public education. He started a state university in Virginia. For this project, Jefferson used his skills as an architect. He drew the plans for the buildings himself. He also searched for the best possible teachers. The place chosen for the new university was Charlottesville.

This is a class at the University of Virginia today.
► How does it differ from Jefferson's public education plan?

Girls attended schools such as Miss Betty Carter's Seminary.
▶ How do these young women differ from young women today?

In March 1825, the University of Virginia opened its doors and began teaching pupils. Jefferson had planned for the university to teach science and other useful subjects. He wanted the university to train Virginians to become doctors, teachers, ministers, lawyers, engineers, and scientists.

For Men Only Besides Jefferson's University of Virginia, the state opened four new colleges in the 1830s and 1840s. One of these was the Virginia Military Institute. It was founded at Lexington in 1839. It taught scientists, engineers, and soldiers. A medical school was also opened in Richmond in 1837.

Colleges still taught only men. Some women went to schools called

seminaries. These were schools especially for young women. The women were not trained to work as scientists or engineers. Instead, the women were taught such subjects as French, English, math, music, and handwriting. Very few women worked at jobs outside their homes at this time.

B. A Thirst for Knowledge

Learning More   Thomas Jefferson played a key role in interesting Virginians in public education. But other factors were involved.

At the beginning of this chapter, you learned that the early 1800s were an age of invention. During that time, steamboats and trains became common sights throughout America. The cotton gin and McCormick's reaper made life easier. People were suddenly eager to know more. They wondered what other machines could make work easier and faster. As a result, many people started to become interested in science and technology.

New Subjects   The curiosity about these subjects was one reason the new schools and colleges were started in the 1830s and 1840s. Students at these schools studied to become builders, scientists, or **mechanics.** A mechanic is trained to work with tools and to make, repair, and use machines.

The importance of schools continued to grow. In the 1840s a few Virginia counties and towns started free schools. Then more children were able to go to school. In 1850 the Virginia Assembly approved a **fund** to be used for the education of poor children. A fund is money set aside for a special purpose. Jefferson's dream of free public schools throughout the state finally became a reality in 1869.

Teaching Reading   The most important subject Virginia children learned in the 1800s was reading. Once they could read, they could learn many new subjects.

A primer, or first reader, was used to teach reading and spelling.
▶ Who is helping Mary with her lessons?

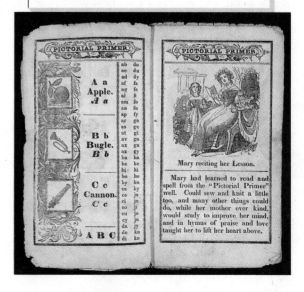

A great pioneer in the field of reading lived at that time. His name was William H. McGuffey (muh GUF ee). He was a teacher at the University of Virginia.

William McGuffey believed that reading was so important that the subject deserved its own special books. No such books were available. So McGuffey answered the need himself. In 1836 he started to write a series of seven reading books for young children. The books were called McGuffey's Readers. They became an overnight success among teachers. Teachers liked the books because children not only learned how to read. They also learned about their country and the world they lived in.

Throughout the 1800s, the popularity of McGuffey's Readers grew. By 1920, over 120 million copies of the books had been sold.

C. A Fine Writer

Moving to Virginia   Until the 1800s, Americans had been busy building a nation. They did not have the time to write many poems or books. Then more and more newspapers and books began to be printed. And in Virginia, a great writer was growing up. This writer's name was Edgar Allan Poe.

Edgar Poe was born in Boston in 1809. But he grew up in Virginia and always thought of himself as a Virginian. When he was two, his mother died. Edgar went to live in the home of John Allan, a wealthy Richmond merchant. Edgar later took the Allan family name as his middle name.

Edgar was a quiet little boy. He lived in a make-believe world of his own. Edgar spent much time making up stories and poems. He made up people and had them do exciting things. He liked ghost stories. When

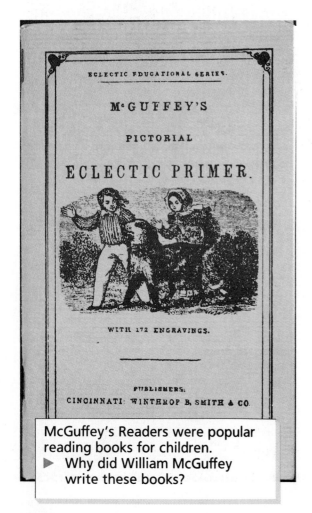

McGuffey's Readers were popular reading books for children.
▶ Why did William McGuffey write these books?

Edgar Allan Poe wrote many ghost stories. This painting shows a scene from one of his stories, *The Fall of the House of Usher.*
▶ Why was Poe so poor during his lifetime?

the night wind rattled his bedroom windows, he imagined that spirits were trying to get in.

When Edgar was 17 years old, he went to the University of Virginia. He also served in the army at Fort Monroe. However, he soon realized that all he really wanted to do was write. Poe sold some of his poems and stories, but he got very little money for his work. He was quite often hungry and sick.

Magazine Writer Then, in 1835, he was hired to work for a new magazine in Richmond. The name of the magazine was the *Southern Literary Messenger.* Poe became better known as a writer, although he still did not earn much money.

Poe died in 1849, when he was only 40. After he died, many people in America and Europe read his works. They admired his unusual and beautiful poems, his ghost stories, and his mysteries. Today Poe is thought of as one of America's greatest writers.

In the following passage from one of Poe's ghost stories called "The Pit and the Pendulum," the character was feeling his way around a dark dungeon.

I have observed [seen] that, although the outlines of the figures upon the walls were . . . distinct, yet the colors seemed blurred and indefinite. These colors had now assumed [had taken on] . . . a startling and most intense brilliancy, that gave to the spectral [ghostly] . . . [pictures] an aspect that might have thrilled even firmer nerves than my own. Demon eyes . . . glared upon me in a thousand directions, where none had been visible before.

D. Maury's Exploration of the Seas

Exploring the Sea Another important person from Virginia was Matthew Fontaine Maury (MAWR-ee). Maury was born on a farm in Spotsylvania County in 1806. He became an important scientist.

Maury loved the sea. As a young man, he served in the United States Navy. He spent many years at sea. His great interest in the sea caused him to study it carefully. He

Maury's charts taught sailors about the ocean bottom and the currents. His charts made sea travel safer.
▶ In what way did Maury's charts help sailors avoid shipwrecks?

became an expert on the shapes of oceans, bays, and rivers. He took measurements to learn how deep the waters were. He dreamed at night about the winds that blow over the water.

Maury came to understand that the earth's seas and oceans had **currents** that flow through them.

Currents are movements of the water within an ocean that follow steady, unchanging streams.

Sea Maps   Maury was eager to share what he had learned with the world. He drew scientific charts, or sailors' maps of the sea or other bodies of water. With these charts, sailors could guide their ships safely. Maury's charts helped them steer clear of dangerous waters and dangerous weather. The charts showed shallow or rocky spots in the ocean to be avoided. Many sailors lives were saved with the help of Maury's charts.

With Maury's maps, ocean travel also became faster. Using his charts, sailors could choose paths where the winds and currents would work in their favor. Because of his important work, Maury is called the Pathfinder of the Seas.

LESSON **2** REVIEW

THINK AND WRITE

A. What were Thomas Jefferson's two important goals for improving public education?

B. What factors were part of the movement toward public education in Virginia?

C. Why, do you think, was Edgar Allan Poe so good at making up stories and poems?

D. Why is Matthew Fontaine Maury called the Pathfinder of the Seas?

SKILLS CHECK

WRITING SKILL

Look at the photograph of the schoolroom on page 261. Write a paragraph about the differences and similarities between that classroom and your classroom.

Statesmen from Virginia

THINK ABOUT WHAT YOU KNOW

Have you ever known anyone who moved away from Virginia? What reasons might a person have for doing so?

STUDY THE VOCABULARY

Great Wagon Road   **Oregon Trail**

FOCUS YOUR READING

How did Virginia leaders help America expand its western frontiers?

A. New States and Statesmen

Statesman from Virginia   On its east, Virginia is bordered by water. To its west, the land spreads outward through Ohio and Kentucky and beyond. In the 1700s and 1800s, this land to the west was still frontier. Green forests and deep, misty valleys stretched as far as the eye could see. Several Virginians played key roles in helping to develop states out of the vast wilderness.

Because of its western explorers and leaders, Virginia is often called the mother of states and statesmen. One important statesman of this time was Henry Clay of Hanover County. Henry Clay was born in 1777. He studied in Richmond to become a lawyer. In 1797 he went to live in Kentucky. Just five years earlier, Kentucky had become the first new state west of the Appalachian Mountains. Find Kentucky on the map on pages 354–355.

In 1803 Henry Clay became a leader in the Kentucky state government. He worked hard for his new state and for his country the rest of his life. Henry Clay was Kentucky's leading statesman.

Guiding Soldiers   Another Virginian who became important in a new state was John Sevier (suh VIHR). He was born in 1745 in New Market,

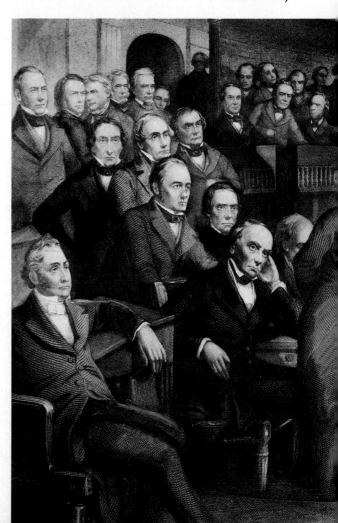

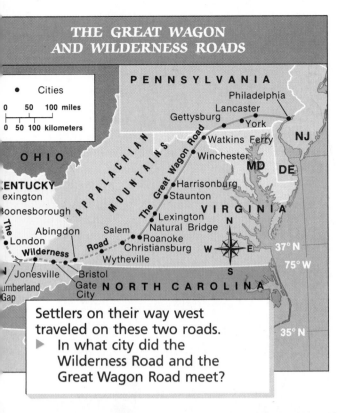

THE GREAT WAGON AND WILDERNESS ROADS

- Cities

0 50 100 miles
0 50 100 kilometers

PENNSYLVANIA

Philadelphia
Lancaster
Gettysburg
York
Watkins Ferry
Winchester

OHIO

MD   DE

NJ

KENTUCKY
Lexington
Boonesborough

APPALACHIAN MOUNTAINS

The Great Wagon Road

Harrisonburg
Staunton

VIRGINIA

Abingdon
London
Wilderness

Salem
Road

Lexington
Natural Bridge
Roanoke
Christiansburg
Wytheville

N
W   E
S

37° N

75° W

Jonesville
Cumberland
Gap

Bristol
Gate
City

NORTH CAROLINA

35° N

Settlers on their way west traveled on these two roads.
▶ In what city did the Wilderness Road and the Great Wagon Road meet?

Virginia. His family ran an inn on the **Great Wagon Road** in the Valley of Virginia. The Great Wagon Road ran from Philadelphia, Pennsylvania, as far south as Georgia. It connected with the Wilderness Road where present-day Roanoke is located. From Roanoke, the Wilderness Road ran westward into Kentucky. Over these roads hundreds of pioneers moved into Virginia and later into the western frontier lands.

In 1773 Sevier also moved west, into what is now part of Tennessee. Find Tennessee on the map on pages

Henry Clay studied law in Virginia. He went on to become an important leader.
▶ How can you tell that he was a powerful speaker?

John Sevier traveled west on the Wilderness Road to Tennessee. He became a hero during the War for Independence.
▶ What did Sevier have in common with Clay?

John Sevier

354–355. Sevier became an important leader in that area. He led soldiers from the Tennessee territory in the War for Independence. He and his men helped win the battle of King's Mountain in 1780. After Tennessee became a state in 1796, John Sevier became its first governor.

B. Two Statesmen and Texas

Pioneer in Texas   Another new state that was established in the western wilderness was Texas. Find Texas on the map on pages 354–355. Like Kentucky and Tennessee, this state was helped through its early struggles by pioneers from Virginia. One of those pioneers was Stephen Austin. He is known as the founder of Texas.

Stephen F. Austin was born in Wythe County, in southwestern Virginia, in 1793. He was a hard worker, and as a young man, he worked in his father's lead mine.

Austin had the restless spirit of an explorer. In 1822 he led a group of Virginia families west. They settled in the land that is now the state of Texas. These brave pioneers were the first Virginia settlers in Texas. The Texas city of Austin was named in honor of the pioneers' courageous Virginia-born leader.

Texas Governor   Sam Houston, another Virginian who helped Texas grow, was born the same year as Stephen Austin. Sam Houston's first home was in Rockbridge County, Virginia. When he was 13, he moved with his Scotch-Irish family to the Tennessee frontier.

In 1835 Sam Houston moved even farther west, to Texas. There he became a famous leader and soldier. He also worked hard to make Texas a part of the United States, and in 1845, Texas became a state. Later, Sam Houston was elected governor of Texas. The Texas city of Houston was named for this soldier and leader from Virginia.

C. "Tippecanoe and Tyler, Too"

A Political Meeting   Chester Carver's chair was on the stage of the meeting hall. As he looked out on the crowd, he saw many farmers. They were all talking. A man at the front of the stage was trying to get their attention.

"Ladies and gentlemen," the man shouted. "Could we get started please." He tapped a wooden hammer on the speaker's stand before him. The noise of the crowd began to die down. The man went on.

"Tonight," he said, "we are here to listen to Mr. Chester Carver. Mr. Carver, as you know, works for one of the two men running for President of the United States. He would like to tell us something about that man. Let's give Mr. Carver a warm Virginia welcome!"

The crowd cheered, and many hands clapped. Carver stood and walked toward the speaker's stand. He smiled at the crowd.

"In 1825," Carver began, "James Monroe's second term as President ended. In the 16 years since, there has been no Virginian in the White House. Now, at last, we have a chance to put a Virginian there once again!" Another loud cheer filled the room.

A Political Slogan   The man Carver spoke about was William Henry Harrison. William Henry Harrison

Sam Houston, born in Virginia, became a leader in Texas. He is shown here leading soldiers.
▶ In what ways did Houston help Texas?

271

A TIPPECANOE PROCESSION.

The presidential campaign of 1840 focused more on big displays than on important issues. This paper ball was rolled from city to city to gain support for Henry Harrison.

▶ How do you think the paper ball helped Harrison's campaign?

had been born in Charles City County, Virginia. His father, Benjamin Harrison, had been one of the seven Virginia signers of the Declaration of Independence.

As a young man, William Henry Harrison had gone west to seek his fortune. He had joined the army and become an officer. He had fought in the western wars against the Indians. In 1800 he had been elected governor of the Indiana Territory.

Carver looked out at the crowd as he finished making his speech. "And so, my fellow Americans," he said, "when you vote next week, I want you to remember four words. Those four words are *Tippecanoe and Tyler, too!*"

After these words were spoken, the crowd cheered more loudly than ever. They were remembering that on November 7, 1811, William Henry Harrison had defeated the Indians in the Battle of Tippecanoe. This important victory had made Harrison famous. People began to call Harrison Old Tippecanoe. *Tyler* referred to John Tyler, the man running for Vice President alongside

Harrison. Tyler, another leading statesman, had also been born in Charles City County.

Harrison and Tyler won the election. In 1841 William Henry Harrison became the ninth President of the United States.

A month after he became President, Harrison died of pneumonia. Vice President Tyler then became President. He was the first Vice President to take over for a President who died in office.

If you drive over the John Tyler Highway along the lower James River, you can see Tyler's home, Sherwood Forest. You can also see Greenway, the house where he was born. Nearby is Berkeley, where William Henry Harrison was born and lived before he moved west.

D. Heroes of the Mexican War

Part of Mexico When Sam Houston and Stephen Austin arrived in Texas, Texas belonged to Mexico. Find Mexico on the map on pages 354–355. As more and more settlers arrived, the Mexicans began to worry. The settlers talked of making Texas free from Mexico.

Even after Texas became a state, Mexicans thought Texas should remain part of Mexico. In 1846, the year after Texas was awarded statehood, Mexico went to war with the United States to try to get Texas back.

John Tyler lived in this house. It is known as Sherwood Forest.
▶ How can you tell that this house was located in a rural area?

Old Rough and Ready The United States sent armies to Mexico to fight for the new state. One of those armies was led by a fierce soldier from Orange County, Virginia. His name was Zachary Taylor. His troops called him Old Rough-and-Ready because of his toughness.

Zachary Taylor led his army to victory over Mexico and became a national hero. In 1849 he became President of the United States. Taylor was the seventh person born in Virginia to hold that office. After only 16 months in office, however, President Zachary Taylor died. His Vice President, Millard Fillmore, took over as President.

Strutting Proudly Another well-known Virginian who fought in the Mexican War was General Winfield Scott from Dinwiddie County. Like Zachary Taylor, Scott had a nickname. His troops called him Old Fuss and Feathers because he strutted so proudly in his uniform.

Serving as young officers under Winfield Scott were two other Virginians who were to become famous. They were Robert E. Lee and Stonewall Jackson.

The United States won the war for Texas, and a treaty was signed in 1848. By this agreement, the United States also gained the territories of California and New Mexico.

E. James Bridger

Virginia Trapper Some Virginians helped push the boundaries of our country farther west. One man who did was James Bridger. He was born in Richmond in 1804.

By trade, James Bridger was a hunter and fur trapper. In the early 1800s, the beaver hat was very popular. A search for skins is what brought Bridger and other frontiersmen as far as the Rocky Mountains. While they were there, they found passes through the towering mountain ranges. Later, these passes became the trails over which pioneers journeyed westward.

James Bridger, once a fur trapper, later became a guide for settlers traveling to the west.
► Which famous trail did Bridger map?

Mapping a Trail James Bridger made a map of one of the more famous trails, the **Oregon Trail.** The Oregon Trail was used by thousands of Americans who traveled west to the Pacific Ocean.

By 1840 the beaver hat was no longer in style. Then Bridger gave up trapping to become a full-time guide. He led wagon trains of hopeful settlers into the new promised lands of California and Oregon. In 1843 he built Fort Bridger on the Oregon Trail in what is now Wyoming.

It is said that James Bridger was the first white person ever to see the Great Salt Lake. Bridger helped make maps of the places he saw. On the map on pages 354–355, find Wyoming and the Great Salt Lake. In what state is the lake?

LESSON 3 REVIEW

THINK AND WRITE

A. In what two states did Henry Clay and John Sevier become important leaders?

B. In what way were Stephen Austin and Sam Houston honored for their leadership?

C. Whom did the words *Tippecanoe and Tyler, too* remind people of?

D. What was the main cause of the Mexican War?

E. Why did James Bridger go to the Rocky Mountains?

SKILLS CHECK

MAP SKILL

Turn to the map of the United States in the Atlas on pages 354–355. Give the direction of the following states in relation to Virginia: Kentucky, Tennessee, and Texas.

LESSON 4

A Divided State

THINK ABOUT WHAT YOU KNOW
When people disagree on a subject, what can happen?

STUDY THE VOCABULARY
abolitionist

FOCUS YOUR READING
What differences arose between eastern and western Virginia toward the middle of the 1800s?

A. Troubles Within

Disagreement During Virginia's first 200 years, its people had gone through much together. They had fought the British and the French. Later, they had fought alongside the French. They had worked hard to form a bond of friendship with the Native Americans.

But Virginians could not agree on everything. Over time, the needs and wants of people change. By the 1830s, people in the eastern and western parts of Virginia were sharply divided on several points. One of these points of disagreement was transportation.

Hearing Complaints Western Virginians complained that there were too few canals, roads, bridges, and ferries. They said that they needed canals to connect the Ohio valley with the eastern ports. The western

> Poor road conditions caused many disagreements between eastern and western Virginians.
> ▶ How are these travelers trying to solve their problem?

276

Virginia farmers needed better transportation because they were having a lot of trouble getting their crops to market.

But eastern Virginians were against these improvements. They argued that Virginia's treasury did not have enough money in it for improving western Virginia's roads.

B. Disagreement About Voting

Landowners Voting Virginians also disagreed on voting rights. Western Virginians believed that all white men should be able to vote even if they did not own any land. Eastern Virginians, many of whom owned huge plantations, disagreed with western Virginians.

Unfair Representation Western Virginians were also upset over the number of representatives they had in the General Assembly. Through the 1700s the number of people who settled in western Virginia had steadily increased. By the early 1800s, more free Virginians lived west of the Blue Ridge Mountains than lived east of the mountains. However, the number of representatives western Virginia had in the General Assembly had not grown. Western Virginians felt that they did not have the voice in Virginia's government that they deserved.

C. Disagreement Over Slavery

The Slavery Issue The point that divided Virginians the most was slavery. Eastern Virginia had large farms and plantations. Easterners felt that using slaves was the best and cheapest way to get plantation work done. Westerners felt differently. Their farms were smaller, and they did not need slaves.

Some eastern Virginians also felt that slavery was cruel and horrible. But to most, slavery was necessary to run the big plantations.

A few slaves were beginning to grow impatient. Some of them decided to revolt.

On a steamy August night in 1831, 60 to 70 slaves were led to revolt by a slave named Nat Turner.

Impatient for his freedom, Nat Turner led a violent revolt.
▶ What were the results of his actions?

People throughout the country began to speak out against slavery. Wendell Phillips speaks out at an anti-slavery rally in Massachusetts.
► What groups of people would have gone to an anti-slavery rally?

Two Terrible Nights For two nights Nat Turner and his followers roamed the countryside. They were armed with swords, razors, and pitchforks. They killed white men, women, and children as they slept.

Nat Turner and his followers were finally caught. Sixteen of them, including Nat Turner, were put to death for what they had done. But the matter was not over.

Supporting Freedom The Nat Turner uprising made the people argue even more about slavery. By 1850 the arguments had spread all over the United States. People in Virginia as well as in other parts of the country were very much against slavery. These people were called **abolitionists.** Abolitionists fought hard to end slavery. Even the slaves were ready to join the fight.

One important war had already been fought over freedom. But clearly not everyone in America was free. America was about to be turned upside down over the issue of slavery. And the state of Virginia was about to be torn apart.

D. Unhappy Western Virginia

Western Virginians threatened to separate from eastern Virginia if their needs were not met. They de-manded a meeting at the state capitol in Richmond. Western Virginians felt that the time had come to make some important changes in the Virginia constitution.

In 1850 a Virginia constitutional convention was held in the city of Richmond. The westerners got some of the things they had asked for. All white men were allowed to vote, regardless of whether they owned land. And western

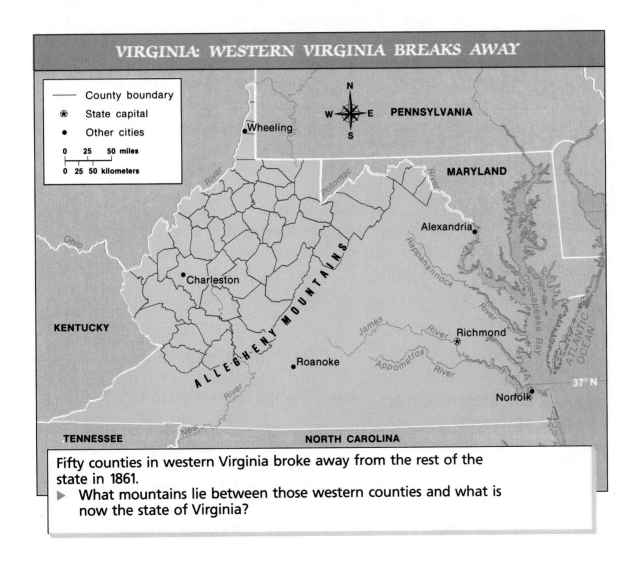

VIRGINIA: WESTERN VIRGINIA BREAKS AWAY

Fifty counties in western Virginia broke away from the rest of the state in 1861.
▶ What mountains lie between those western counties and what is now the state of Virginia?

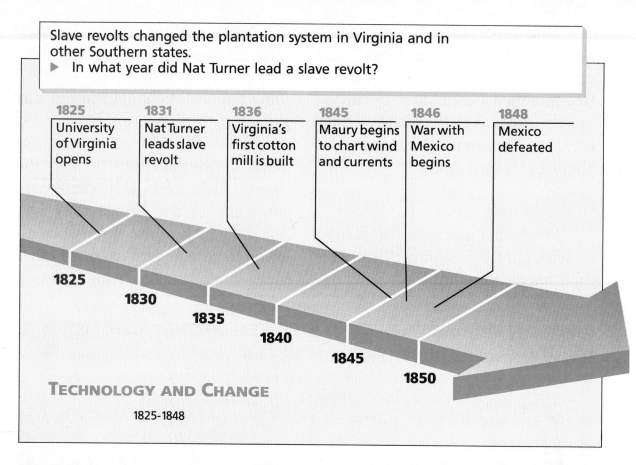

Slave revolts changed the plantation system in Virginia and in other Southern states.
▶ In what year did Nat Turner lead a slave revolt?

1825 University of Virginia opens

1831 Nat Turner leads slave revolt

1836 Virginia's first cotton mill is built

1845 Maury begins to chart wind and currents

1846 War with Mexico begins

1848 Mexico defeated

1825   1830   1835   1840   1845   1850

TECHNOLOGY AND CHANGE
1825-1848

Virginia got an equal say in Virginia's government. However, the most important demand on the western Virginians' list was ending slavery. And that demand was not met.

In a little over ten years, the people of western Virginia would break away from the rest of the state. They would form a new state called West Virginia.

LESSON **4** REVIEW

THINK AND WRITE

A. Why was better transportation important to the people of western Virginia?

B. What voting changes did western Virginians want?

C. How did eastern and western Virginians differ in their feelings about slavery?

D. What demand of western Virginians was not met at the convention in 1850?

SKILLS CHECK

THINKING SKILL

Imagine that you were a slave in Virginia. How would you have felt about Nat Turner's revolt?

280

USING THE VOCABULARY

technology	current
harpoon	chart
shingle	Great Wagon Road
seminary	Oregon Trail
mechanic	abolitionist

On a separate sheet of paper, write the word that best matches each definition below. Choose your answers from the vocabulary words above.

1. a person who was against slavery and fought hard to end it
2. a road that went from Philadelphia to Georgia
3. a map of the sea
4. a path used by Americans who traveled west
5. a special kind of spear
6. a steady stream that flows through the ocean
7. a thin piece of wood used to cover roofs and sides of buildings
8. a person trained to work with tools
9. knowledge used to make things
10. a school for young women

REMEMBERING WHAT YOU READ

Write your answers in complete sentences on a separate sheet of paper.

1. What items did Cyrus McCormick and Lewis Temple invent?
2. What were some of the goods that were transported by boat on the Dismal Swamp Canal?
3. How did Claudius Crozet's work help Virginia's transportation?
4. What subjects did Thomas Jefferson plan to be taught at the University of Virginia?
5. What subjects were taught at colleges for young women?
6. What was the important contribution that William McGuffey made to education?
7. How did Matthew Fontaine Maury change travel by water?
8. How was Texas helped by Stephen Austin and Sam Houston?
9. Why were eastern Virginians against transportation improvements for western Virginia?
10. What is Nat Turner known for?

TYING ART TO SOCIAL STUDIES

During the 1800s, many important new things were invented. Look back through this chapter to find out about these inventions. Draw a time line that shows the names of the inventions, the years in which they were invented, and the names of the inventors. You might also do library research to find information about some other inventions from the 1800s. Compare your time line with those of your classmates.

THINKING CRITICALLY

Write your answers in complete sentences on a separate sheet of paper.

1. How did the McCormick reaper lead to an increase in flour mills?
2. How did the invention of the steam engine affect the way Virginians got around in the 1800s?
3. In what ways were educational opportunities in the 1800s different for the men than for the women in the state of Virginia?
4. How did statesmen from Virginia help people in other states?
5. Why were there differences between the people in eastern and western Virginia?

SUMMARIZING THE CHAPTER

On a separate sheet of paper, draw a graphic organizer that is like the one shown here. Copy the information from this graphic organizer to the one you have drawn. Under the main idea for each lesson, write three statements that support it. The first one has been done for you.

CHAPTER THEME

The lives of Virginians were affected by technology and change.

LESSON 1

New forms of transportation became popular in America during the 1800s.

1. Steamboats
2. Canal boats
3. Railroads

LESSON 2

Many changes took place in education after 1800.

1.
2.
3.

LESSON 3

Virginia leaders helped America expand its western frontiers.

1.
2.
3.

LESSON 4

Several differences arose between eastern and western Virginia toward the middle of the 1800s.

1.
2.
3.

 REVIEW

COOPERATIVE LEARNING

You have just learned about the first English people who came to Jamestown in 1607. Now you are going to imagine that you are one of those early settlers. You have been in Jamestown for two years. Many of your friends have died. You must try to get other English people to come and join your settlement. You decide to make a poster to get people to come. A ship is sailing to England next week. The captain will take the poster to London and put it in a shop window.

REMEMBER TO:
- Give your ideas.
- Listen to others' ideas.
- Plan your work with the group.
- Present your project.
- Discuss how your group worked.

PROJECT

- Working with a group of two or three classmates, talk about what you will write on the poster. Remember, you are trying to get people to come to your colony.

- Choose a group member to look for more good things in the library about the Jamestown area.

- Pick three or four of the best reasons why people in England should move to Jamestown. Have another member of the group write down the reasons.

- Now ask one group member to write the final reasons on 12″ × 18″ poster board. Another group member might add a drawing or paste a picture to the poster.

PRESENTATION AND REVIEW

- Put the poster on the bulletin board.

- Ask your classmates what things they like best about the poster.

- Ask your classmates what things they would add to the poster.

A. WHY DO I NEED THIS SKILL?

This book has many special parts to help you learn about Virginia. To get the most from your textbook, you need to know how to use its special parts. You also need to know what kind of information is contained in each different part of your book.

B. LEARNING THE SKILL

The first special part of the book is the Table of Contents, or Contents. Look at the Contents at the front of this book. Notice that the book is divided into units and chapters. The Contents also lists the page number on which these units and chapters begin.

Other special parts are found at the end of the book. The Atlas is a special collection of maps. In the Contents you will find a list of the maps included in the Atlas. These maps show the location of physical features, boundaries, cities, and roads.

The Gazetteer gives information about the places and geographical features discussed in the book. The entries are listed in alphabetical order. For many of these places, the Gazetteer also gives latitude and longitude.

The Glossary is another important part of the book. It defines the vocabulary terms and special social studies words. These are the words that are listed at the beginning of each lesson. Like words in a dictionary, glossary words are listed in alphabetical order.

The Index is an alphabetical listing of the important topics in the book. The Index lists the page numbers on which these topics are discussed. Turn to the Index, starting on page 387. On what pages can you find information about the Monroe Doctrine?

C. PRACTICING THE SKILL

Use the special parts of this book to answer the following questions. After each answer, write the part of the book that helped you find the answer.

1. What states border Virginia?
2. What is the total number of chapters in this book?
3. On what page or pages is Jamestown discussed?
4. What is the meaning of *hornbook*?
5. On which pages does the Map Skills Handbook appear?
6. What is the longitude and latitude of Hampton?
7. What are the Grand Caverns?
8. What is the title of Unit 2?
9. What is it that makes the town of Smithfield famous?
10. Who was John Smith?

D. APPLYING THE SKILL

Select another textbook that you use in class. Examine the book carefully and make a list of its special parts. As you prepare your list, look for answers to the following questions:
- Does the book include a table of contents, a glossary, and an index?
- Does the book have any special parts that are not found in your social studies textbook?
- If it does, what are they?
- What information is contained in these other special parts?

Write your answers on a separate sheet of paper.

A. WHY DO I NEED THIS SKILL?

One thing sometimes causes something else to happen. For example, an earthquake in California in 1989 caused a bridge to collapse. We call this cause and effect. The cause of what happened was the earthquake. The effect was the collapse of the bridge. Identifying cause and effect relationships is part of thinking critically. It is especially important in social studies to learn how one event causes another to happen.

B. LEARNING THE SKILL

Read the following sentences.

> *Rats and insects had eaten what little grain the settlers could store away. By the end of the winter, many people had died of illness and starvation.*

To determine if a cause and effect relationship exists, ask yourself these two questions: What happened? Why did it happen? In this example, settlers died of illness and starvation. This is the effect. They died because rats and insects ate their grain. This is the cause.

Identify the cause and effect in the following example:

The colonists refused to buy England's tax stamps. In 1766 England repealed the Stamp Act. What happened? England repealed the Stamp Act. This is the effect. Why did it happen? The colonists refused to buy the stamps. This is the cause.

C. PRACTICING THE SKILL

In social studies you will read about many events that have cause and effect relationships. The American War for Independence occurred because the British taxed the colonists unfairly.

Fold a sheet of paper in half lengthwise. Label one column *Cause,* and label the other column *Effect.* Write the numbers from 1 to 5 at the left. Then read the following pairs of sentences. Identify the cause and the effect in each pair and write them in the correct column.

1. The settlers needed something in which to store food. They made wooden barrels.

2. John Smith brought gifts to the Indians. In return, the Indians brought food to the starving settlers during the winter of 1608.

3. After the Indian attack, the settlers punished the Indians. They forced them to move to the forests beyond the Fall Line.

4. The French settlers would not leave the Ohio Valley. The governor sent George Washington to drive them out of the region.

5. The British continued to attack American ships off the coast of Virginia. In 1812 America once again went to war against England.

D. APPLYING THE SKILL

Think about something that happened to you recently that has a cause and effect relationship. Write two paragraphs about the event. In the first paragraph describe the event and explain what caused it. In the second paragraph state what effects it had.

287

There is much to love in Virginia. From the Tidewater beaches to the Blue Ridge Mountains, Virginia has it all. ▶

Although the South fought bravely in the Civil War, their way of life was changed forever.

Virginia was important to the nation's war effort during World War II. Many new military bases were built here. ▶

UNIT 3 VIRGINIA: 1850 TO THE PRESENT

The Civil War lasted four years and tore the state apart. Many battles were fought in Virginia. After the war, Virginians sadly rebuilt the state.

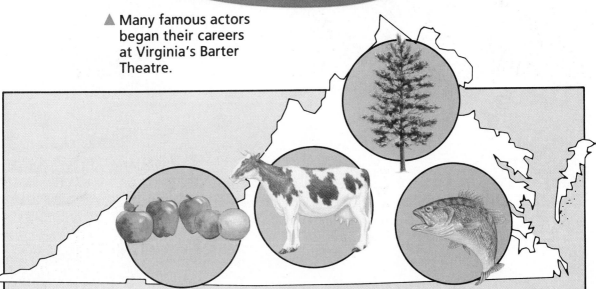

▲ Many famous actors began their careers at Virginia's Barter Theatre.

CHAPTER 9

FROM DIVISION TO REFORM

When the Civil War broke out between the North and the South, Virginia joined the Confederacy. After four long years of fighting, the North defeated the South. It took Virginians many years to rebuild their state.

Division in the United States

THINK ABOUT WHAT YOU KNOW

If you belonged to a club and were unhappy with how it was being run, what would you do?

STUDY THE VOCABULARY

secede	free state
Union	emancipate
slave state	

FOCUS YOUR READING

What were some causes of the Civil War?

A. North-South Differences

Dividing the Union The issue of slavery bitterly divided the Northern and Southern states. Most Southerners could not imagine life without slavery. Many Northerners could not accept life with it. Between 1800 and 1850, that division grew. Abolitionists called slave owners criminals. They felt that slave owners should be forced by law to free their slaves at once.

This angered many Southerners. They said that no one had the right to order them to free their slaves. They believed that even the federal government could not give them such an order. One Southerner, John Calhoun of South Carolina, felt the Southern states had to take strong action. He said that any state that felt bullied by the federal government had a right to **secede** (sih SEED). This meant that the state would leave the United States.

An Equal Number Another name for the United States was the **Union**. The Southern states in the Union were called **slave states** because they allowed slavery. The Northern states of the Union were called **free states** because slavery was not practiced in those states.

By 1850, there was an equal number of slave states and free states. Southerners were afraid that if more free states joined the Union, the North would have a stronger

Some slaves would do almost anything to escape slavery. This slave is traveling north in a box.
► Why did the men help him?

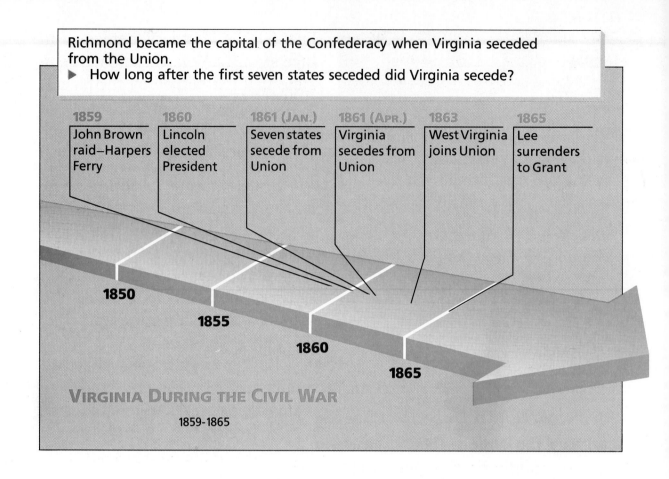

Richmond became the capital of the Confederacy when Virginia seceded from the Union.
► How long after the first seven states seceded did Virginia secede?

1859	1860	1861 (Jan.)	1861 (Apr.)	1863	1865
John Brown raid–Harpers Ferry	Lincoln elected President	Seven states secede from Union	Virginia secedes from Union	West Virginia joins Union	Lee surrenders to Grant

1850   1855   1860   1865

VIRGINIA DURING THE CIVIL WAR
1859-1865

voice in the federal government. Southerners worried that slavery and the Southern way of life would be abolished forever if the Northern states gained more power in the United States Congress.

B. A Growing Conflict

A New Free State In the 1850s, the issue of slavery caused even more troubles for the North and the South. The South was disturbed when California became the Union's newest free state. The North was very upset over a new law that or-

dered the return of runaway slaves to their masters.

In 1857 hatred between the two sides reached a new high. That year the United States Supreme Court declared that slaves were property. The Court said that slave owners could keep their slaves even when they moved to a free territory. Southerners were very happy about the new law. Northerners and abolitionists were against it.

John Brown's Raid On a cold and rainy October morning in 1859, the people of Harpers Ferry, Virginia, could relax at last. The "crazy abolitionist" named John Brown had been captured. John Brown hated slavery. He had often said he was willing to die to fight slavery.

Brown's Revolt Three days before, on October 16, Brown led 16 whites and 5 blacks into Harpers Ferry. He wanted to take over the federal gun supply. Brown was planning a slave revolt! The Virginia militia did what it could to hold off Brown. Finally, United States troops, under Colonel Robert E. Lee, arrived to stop Brown. Several weeks later, Brown was tried and put to death.

An Election John Brown's death increased the anger between the North and the South. Northerners and abolitionists thought of John Brown as a hero. Southerners felt that they needed to protect their right to have slaves more than ever before. Many Southerners saw hope in the presidential election of 1860. They believed that a President who favored slavery might be all the protection they needed.

But the winner of the election was not the leader the South had hoped for. Abraham Lincoln was a Northerner, and the South feared that its right to own slaves might be taken away.

John Brown wanted to get guns for a slave revolt. During the raid on Harpers Ferry, he was wounded and his two sons were killed.
▶ To whom is Brown speaking?

C. The Confederacy

Secession Within two months after Lincoln's election, seven Southern states made their feelings clear. South Carolina was the first state to secede from the Union. Within two months, Mississippi, Florida, Alabama, Georgia, Louisiana, and Texas followed. The seven states joined together under a government called the Confederate States of America.

The people of Virginia had trouble deciding whether to join the

293

Jefferson Davis hoped to lead the Confederate army. Instead he led the whole Confederacy.
▶ Why did Davis come to Virginia?

sometimes called the War Between the States. President Lincoln asked Virginia volunteers to fight against South Carolina. Virginians decided that they could never fight another Southern state. On April 17, 1861, Virginia seceded from the Union. Shortly after, Arkansas, Tennessee, and North Carolina seceded too.

Many people in the western part of Virginia were unhappy with Virginia's decision to secede from the Union. Fifty western Virginia counties broke away from Virginia in 1861. Two years later, they became part of the Union as the state of West Virginia. Harpers Ferry became part of West Virginia.

The Confederacy chose Jefferson Davis as its first president. Davis was born in Kentucky in 1808. He grew up in Mississippi. At 16, he attended the U.S. Military Academy at West Point, New York. He showed great bravery in battles against the Indians on the Wisconsin frontier. In 1845 Davis won a seat in the United States Congress.

Still, in his heart, Davis was a soldier first. After Mississippi seceded from the Union, Davis hoped to lead the Confederate army. But, instead, he was elected to lead the whole Confederacy. Robert E. Lee was chosen to lead the Confederate army of the South.

Confederacy, as the Confederate States of America was called. Virginians loved the Union they had helped to build. At the same time, however, they felt that their fellow Southerners were their family. They also believed that states had the right to secede from the Union if they felt that their constitutional rights were violated.

Virginia's Decision When the Civil War began, Virginia had to decide which path to take. The Civil War is

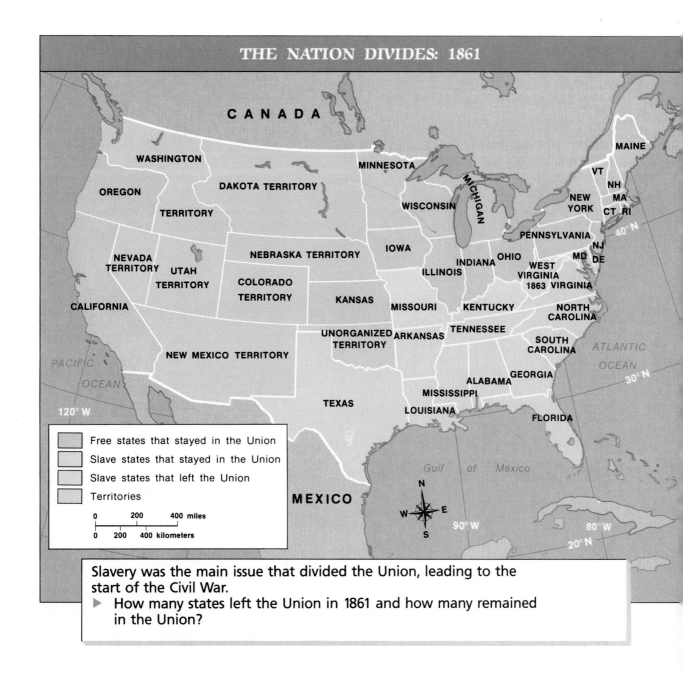

THE NATION DIVIDES: 1861

CANADA

WASHINGTON

OREGON
TERRITORY

MINNESOTA

DAKOTA TERRITORY

WISCONSIN

MICHIGAN

MAINE

VT
NH
NEW   MA
YORK   CT RI

PENNSYLVANIA

NEVADA
TERRITORY   UTAH
TERRITORY

NEBRASKA TERRITORY

IOWA

NJ

CALIFORNIA

COLORADO
TERRITORY

KANSAS

ILLINOIS

INDIANA OHIO
WEST   MD DE
VIRGINIA
1863 VIRGINIA

MISSOURI   KENTUCKY

NORTH
CAROLINA

NEW MEXICO TERRITORY

UNORGANIZED ARKANSAS
TERRITORY

TENNESSEE

SOUTH
CAROLINA

ATLANTIC
OCEAN

PACIFIC
OCEAN

TEXAS

ALABAMA

GEORGIA

MISSISSIPPI

120° W

LOUISIANA

FLORIDA

Free states that stayed in the Union
Slave states that stayed in the Union
Slave states that left the Union
Territories

0   200   400 miles
0   200   400 kilometers

MEXICO

Gulf   of   Mexico

40° N

30° N

90° W

80° W

20° N

Slavery was the main issue that divided the Union, leading to the start of the Civil War.

▶ How many states left the Union in 1861 and how many remained in the Union?

D. The Two Sides

The Armies The Confederate army and the Union army had different strengths and weaknesses. There were twice as many Union soldiers. But the Confederacy had better-trained officers. And the fighting took place in the South, so the Confederate soldiers knew the land better than the Union soldiers did. The Confederate soldiers were more used to outdoor living too.

Much of the fighting took place in Virginia. General Lee fought in

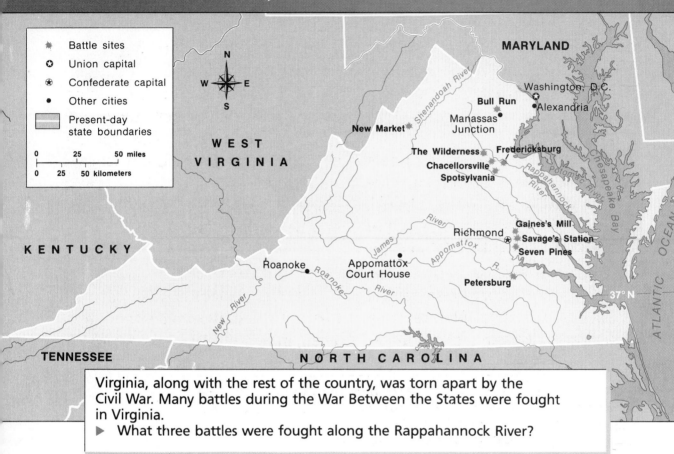

VIRGINIA: CIVIL WAR BATTLES

Legend:
- ✳ Battle sites
- ✪ Union capital
- ✺ Confederate capital
- • Other cities
- Present-day state boundaries

0   25   50 miles
0   25   50 kilometers

MARYLAND

Washington, D.C.
Alexandria

Bull Run
Manassas Junction

New Market

The Wilderness
Chancellorsville
Spotsylvania

Fredericksburg

WEST VIRGINIA

Shenandoah River

Rappahannock River

Potomac River

Chesapeake Bay

KENTUCKY

Roanoke

Appomattox Court House

Richmond

Gaines's Mill
Savage's Station
Seven Pines

Petersburg

James River

Appomattox R.

Roanoke River

New River

37° N

ATLANTIC OCEAN

TENNESSEE

NORTH CAROLINA

Virginia, along with the rest of the country, was torn apart by the Civil War. Many battles during the War Between the States were fought in Virginia.
▶ What three battles were fought along the Rappahannock River?

many of the important battles. Another Virginian who fought alongside him was General Thomas J. Jackson. In one famous battle, General Jackson earned the nickname *Stonewall* because he stood "like a stone wall" in the face of enemy fire.

Gains and Losses Lee had many victories. His greatest

Generals Lee and Jackson won many battles for the South.
▶ What important advantages did the Confederate army have?

was at Chancellorsville in 1863. Lee and his troops surprised and drove off a huge Union force. During the battle, however, Confederate soldiers shot Stonewall Jackson by mistake. He died later of pneumonia. Virginians were saddened by the general's death.

Even though the Confederate army fought well throughout the war, it was greatly outnumbered. The army was also running out of food and other supplies. Union ships blocked Confederate ports and made it hard for supplies to get through. As the Confederate army weakened, the Union army under General Ulysses S. Grant moved closer to its goal. That goal was to capture Richmond, which was the capital of the Confederacy.

Finally, on April 3, 1865, Richmond was captured by Union troops. Six days later, they surrounded Lee's army. Lee surrendered at Appomattox Court House. As a sign of respect for a great fighter, General Grant allowed General Lee to keep his sword.

E. Emancipation

At first, blacks had not been allowed to volunteer on either side. Then, in September 1862, President

General Robert E. Lee's army was surrounded by Union troops. He surrendered to General Ulysses S. Grant on April 9, 1865. The two generals met at the Appomattox Court House.
▶ How can you tell which man is General Lee?

Many freed slaves became soldiers and fought for the Union army during the Civil War.
▶ About how many former slaves joined the Union army?

Lincoln gave the South a warning. If they did not end the war by January 1, 1863, Lincoln would issue an order to free all Confederate slaves. The South did not end the war. On January 1 President Lincoln kept his word. He issued the formal order to emancipate (ee MAN suh payt), or free, all black slaves in areas captured by the Union army.

Some slaves remained loyal to their plantation owners. But since the beginning of the Civil War, over 31,000 Virginia slaves had escaped to freedom. Nearly 6,000 of these former slaves joined the Union army.

Blacks were still not permitted to serve in the Confederate army, however. That ruling changed in 1865 when the Confederate Congress agreed to make 300,000 slaves soldiers. But only a month after the law was passed, the war ended. The black Confederate soldiers never took part in the war.

F. Confederate Women

The Civil War was hard on the Confederate fighting men. But it was just as hard on the Confederate women at home. Everyday needs such as coffee, sugar, and firewood were in short supply. Many women were not able to feed their families.

Other women worked hard for the Confederate cause. Some risked their lives making bullets. Some, including free blacks and slaves, nursed the wounded. One woman,

Sally Tompkins, opened her own hospital in Richmond in 1861. In order for Sally Tompkins to treat Confederate soldiers, President Davis later made her a captain in the Confederate army.

A few women aided the Confederate war effort in a different way — by becoming spies. One of these women was Belle Boyd, a Virginian. As a spy, Belle Boyd learned important military secrets from Union soldiers. She then passed these secrets on to Confederate leaders. Though she was arrested four times, Belle Boyd was always clever enough to figure out a way to escape. Toward the end of the Civil War, Belle Boyd became the wife of a Union soldier.

Belle Boyd learned of the Union's plan to trap General Jackson and his soldiers.
▶ Which side did she spy for?

LESSON *1* REVIEW

THINK AND WRITE

A. Why were Southerners afraid of more free states joining the Union?

B. How did John Brown's actions and death increase the angry feelings between the North and the South?

C. Why did the people of Virginia have trouble deciding whether or not to join the Confederacy?

D. What were some of the strengths and the weaknesses of the Confederate army?

E. What did Lincoln's order do?

F. How did women help the Confederate war effort?

SKILLS CHECK

WRITING SKILL

Look at the map on page 295. Write a paragraph explaining what information the map provides. Be sure to include in your paragraph the number of slave states that stayed in the Union and the number that left the Union.

From: *Up From Slavery*

By: Booker T. Washington

Setting: Tuskegee, Alabama, 1881

Booker T. Washington was born in 1856 on a slave plantation in Franklin County, Virginia. His 1901 book, *Up From Slavery*, tells the story of his life. In the following passage, he describes his early days at Tuskegee Institute.

Before going to Tuskegee I had expected to find there a building and all the necessary apparatus [materials] ready for me to begin teaching. To my disappointment, I found nothing of the kind. I did find, though . . . hundreds of hungry . . . souls [people] who wanted to secure [get] knowledge. . . . My first task was to find a place in which to open the school. After looking the town over with some care, the most suitable [best] place . . . seemed to be a [rundown shack] near the [black] Methodist church. . . . Whenever it rained, one of the older students would very kindly leave his lessons and hold an umbrella over me while I [taught]. . . .

Booker T. Washington helped build Tuskegee Institute into an important training school.

Reconstruction

THINK ABOUT WHAT YOU KNOW

What problems do people have to deal with after a natural disaster, such as a fire or a hurricane, is over?

STUDY THE VOCABULARY

sharecropper   Reconstruction
freedman   carpetbagger
Vagrancy
  Law

FOCUS YOUR READING

How did Virginians start to rebuild their homes and their state after the Civil War?

A. Rebuilding Virginia

A New Life Cyrus Knox reached the Keenan farm by dusk. As he got down from his horse, he told himself he was home. His own farm in the Shenandoah Valley had been destroyed during the war. His farmhouse and barn had been burned. There were big holes in his fields from the battles. But he was lucky compared to some Virginians. There were 15,000 people who would not be coming home. Those brave soldiers had died on battlefields.

Cyrus Knox was starting over. He had made plans to become a **sharecropper** for the Keenans. As a sharecropper, he would farm a small part of the Keenans' land. In return, he would get to keep a share of the crops he raised. He would receive no money for his work. The Keenans had none to give him.

A Tragic Death For Virginia, like other Southern states, rebuilding the state went slowly. It went even more slowly following the tragic murder of President Lincoln shortly after the war. Lincoln had planned to help the states rebuild quickly. After his death, representatives in the United States Congress slowed down those plans.

Freed slaves in the Southern states began to earn their own livings by sharecropping.
► What crop is being harvested in this picture?

The Hampton Institute, founded in 1868, was established as a training center for blacks.
▶ Why was education important to the newly freed slaves?

B. Changes for Blacks

Slaves now had their freedom. They dreamed about a better life. But for freed blacks, or **freedmen,** the good life was not easy to get. They had not been educated. Many of them did not have any skills. Those who had skills were often denied jobs by whites.

Blacks had other problems too. A law called the **Vagrancy** (VAY grun see) **Law** was passed. Now people could arrest any stranger who arrived in their town without a job. Blacks who sought work in towns where they were not known could end up in jail! Because of angry reactions from Northerners, the Union military commander in Virginia erased the Vagrancy Law from the books.

In 1865 Congress set up a special board to help freedmen. The board saw to it that freedmen received food and a place to live. Northern teachers came to states like Virginia to educate freedmen. Schools like the Hampton Institute were founded. By 1870 over 200 schoolhouses had been built. Blacks were now able to become educated. Education was the first step toward achieving their dream of freedom with dignity.

C. Virginia's New Constitution

Statehood Again Both the North *and* South had to struggle to put America back together again. This time of struggle was known as **Reconstruction** (ree kun STRUK shun). Both sides wanted to end their differences. The North was ready to welcome Virginia and other Southern states back into the Union.

Before Virginia could become a state again, however, it had to agree to two things. One was to give the right to vote to all men. Before then, black men had been denied this right. Women were still unable to vote. This right did not come to them until 1920.

Virginia also had to agree to draw up a new constitution. In 1867, 105 elected representatives met in Richmond for this purpose. The meeting was headed by Judge John Underwood, a federal judge from the North who had gone to the South to live. Those people from the North were called **carpetbaggers.** They

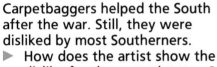

Carpetbaggers helped the South after the war. Still, they were disliked by most Southerners.
▶ How does the artist show the dislike for the carpetbaggers?

earned this nickname because they carried their belongings in suitcases made of carpeting material.

Carpetbagger Rule Most carpetbaggers favored fair treatment for blacks. Underwood was one of them. He felt that Virginia's new constitution should give all men the right to hold office. Underwood also felt that the constitution should deny the vote to all men who had fought for the Confederacy during the war.

Many Virginians were upset over this plan. They said that it opened the door to a Virginia government controlled by blacks. It would also hurt the Confederate veterans, whom most Virginians greatly admired.

It seemed that the only way to solve their differences was for each side to give a little. On July 6, 1869, the constitution was passed by Virginians. The constitution gave vot-

A new Virginian Constitution was passed in 1869. It gave black men the right to vote.
▶ When did women first vote?

ing rights to all male United States citizens regardless of race, color, or previous conditions of slavery.

LESSON *2* REVIEW

THINK AND WRITE

A. Why was sharecropping necessary in Virginia?
B. What did Congress do to help newly freed slaves?
C. What problems did Virginians face in writing a new constitution for their state?

SKILLS CHECK

WRITING SKILL
Life for Southern blacks changed after the Civil War. Do you think it became easier or more difficult? Write a paragraph giving reasons for your answer.

Changes in Virginia

THINK ABOUT WHAT YOU KNOW
What would life be like if there were no cars?

STUDY THE VOCABULARY
cash crop   toll road

FOCUS YOUR READING
In what ways did Virginia grow after the Civil War?

A. Growth and Change

New Fortunes Virginia's coal supply gave the state hope and wealth at a time when both were badly needed. Land that had been pasture for sheep became worth thousands of dollars when coal was mined there. Hundreds of new mining jobs sprang up. Virginia grew as people moved there to get those jobs. Towns such as Norton and Wise doubled in size very quickly.

Coal had helped the first trains run. Now the trains helped take the coal to market. In the 1880s, more railroads were built. By 1910 eight rail lines were carrying coal from Virginia's mines to the port cities.

Law and Order The coal boom also had its disadvantages. Towns grew so fast that there were sometimes more people than the sheriff or police could handle. Townspeople began to take the law into their own hands. Some of Virginia's best-known outlaws lived in these early mining towns.

One of these was Dr. M. B. "Doc" Taylor. Doc Taylor had been a Confederate army scout in the Civil War. As a doctor, he had some strange ways. He used wild plants as medicine. People claimed he could talk a person out of being sick.

Taylor also helped the government catch lawbreakers. This job got him in trouble when he arrested a man who threatened his life. Before the man could act, Taylor killed him and seven others. Taylor was hanged for the murders.

Doc Taylor thought that he was outside the law. He decided to live by his own rules.
▶ Why is taking the law into your own hands a bad idea?

305

COAL PRODUCTION IN VIRGINIA 1900-1920

1900

1905

1910

1915

1920

= ONE MILLION SHORT TONS
(907,000 metric tons)

By 1910 eight rail lines were bringing coal to Virginia's ports.
▶ How did coal production change between 1900 and 1920?

B. Rural Area Problems

Hard Times   In its early days, Virginia had been a land of farms and farmers. In 1890 it was still a farming state. Reports from 1890 show that about nine of every ten Virginians lived in rural areas.

But life was not easy for Virginia's farmers. They had a hard time earning a living. That was because of old-fashioned ways of farming, low crop prices, and high railroad charges. The growth of new farms in the new western and southern states created new competition for Virginia's farmers.

Making Changes   The farmers had to make some changes, both in Virginia and in other states as well. They formed a group so they could make their needs known. As a group, farmers made sure that the railroads charged them fairly for carrying the crops to market.

Another change was the founding of colleges such as the Virginia Agricultural and Mechanical College, which became Virginia Polytechnic Institute. These schools taught modern ways of farming so farmers could raise better crops.

The invention of the refrigerated railway car was a positive change. Crops could be taken to the market and arrive as fresh as the day they were picked. Farmers began to pay attention to cash crops. These were crops that they could sell in large amounts. Tobacco was a major cash crop. Other cash crops were potatoes, lettuce, and apples. By 1920 Virginia farmers were selling $3 million worth of apples alone. The hard times seemed to be over for farmers in Virginia.

C. A Special Place

Town Meeting   The town hall of Big Lick, a village in Roanoke County, was filled with people. It looked like just about all 669 of the townspeople were there.

The mayor began, "I've called this town meeting for a special reason. The head of the Norfolk and Western Railroad made an announcement today. He said that his rail line and the Shenandoah Valley line are planning to cross. They are searching for a place for the crossing. I would like that place to be our town—Big Lick."

The people began talking so loudly that the mayor had to ask them to be quiet.

"If Big Lick is chosen," he went on, "it will mean more jobs in town. It will mean more money in the town treasury. We must do whatever we can to get the railroad to notice us."

The townspeople raised $7,875, which they gave to the railroad as a gift. When Big Lick was chosen as the place where the two railroads would cross, the townspeople decided to change the town's name to Roanoke. Roanoke soon became the major railroad city in southwestern

Most of Virginia's apples are grown in the Shenandoah Valley.
▶ What are some things that can be made from apples?

Virginia. Within 20 years, the population in the town had grown from only 669 to 24,495.

Urban Growth   The railroads caused similar growth in the cities of Norfolk and Newport News. Norfolk became one of the most important ports in the country. Newport News, once a quiet farming village, became a major shipbuilding center.

Virginia's railroads and rich coal supply made the state a strong industrial force. In the 1880s the tobacco industry grew at an amazing rate. Virginia also became an important leader in the textile, or cloth-making, industry.

D. Automobiles and Transportation

In 1899 the first horseless carriage reached Virginia. The car, a shiny black Locomobile, had rubber tires. It broke down often, and its engine made an awful smell. But it was truly something to see!

At first, cars could be driven only in town. But problems remained even after cars were allowed in the countryside. Roads were dusty in dry weather and muddy in wet weather. Many roads were **toll roads.** Drivers had to pay private owners to use the roads. Sometimes payment was made in produce.

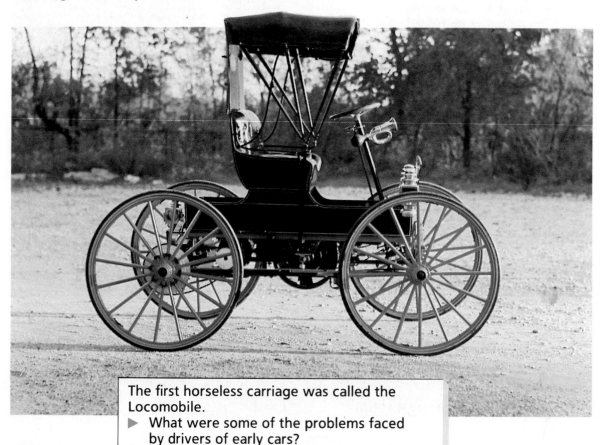

The first horseless carriage was called the Locomobile.
▶ What were some of the problems faced by drivers of early cars?

Cars became popular in the early 1900s. This car was built in 1906.
► What was the speed limit for cars in 1906?

was set at 15 miles (24 km) an hour. Drivers also had to stop for horse-drawn wagons.

That was only the beginning. As more and more Virginians bought cars, new and hard-surfaced roads were needed. The state provided over 2,000 miles (3,218 km) of new gravel and dirt roads. Within a year, Virginia had begun plans for a state highway system. The car was here to stay.

The number of car owners was small at first. But before long, everyone wanted one.
► When did the greatest increase in registrations occur?

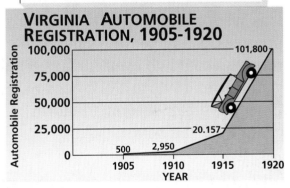

VIRGINIA AUTOMOBILE REGISTRATION, 1905–1920

Despite these problems, the car became popular. Many Virginians became proud owners of Fords and Oldsmobiles. By 1906 there were 500 car owners in Virginia. That year, the state set up its first rules of the road. The speed limit for cars

LESSON **3** REVIEW

THINK AND WRITE

A. How did coal help Virginia through rough times after the Civil War?

B. How did refrigerated railroad cars improve farmers' lives?

C. Why did towns want to have new rail lines built through them?

D. What were the problems of early car travel?

SKILLS CHECK

THINKING SKILL

In what ways did the development of railroads affect many of the industries in Virginia?

Working Toward Reform

THINK ABOUT WHAT YOU KNOW

What things about your school or your town would you improve if you could?

STUDY THE VOCABULARY

reform   civil rights
Jim Crow laws

FOCUS YOUR READING

How did reformers improve life for Virginians?

A. Changes Through Reform

Education Changes Most Virginians were pleased with their state's progress. Many people believed the progress could go even further. The years from 1890 to 1917 became a time of great **reform.** Reform is change for the better.

Education was improved by reform. In 1900 Virginia's schools were poor and inadequate. Many schools were open only four months a year. Less than half the children in the state attended.

Lila Meade Valentine and Mary Cooke Munford brought about some needed changes. In 1900 these women succeeded in stretching the school year to 118 days. They won higher pay for teachers and opened Virginia's colleges to women.

Another pioneer in education was Virginia E. Randolph, a black teacher from Henrico County. She taught her pupils to read and write. She also taught them to cook and clean. Her bold new ideas won her a gift of money. With this money, she traveled throughout Virginia, sharing her ideas with other teachers.

Public Health Virginia reformers also took the lead in the battle to improve public health. Many diseases were caused by unclean living habits. Again, Lila Valentine helped bring about change. Together with Sadie Heath Cabaniss (kuh BA-nihs), of Dinwiddie County, she formed a group of teacher-nurses. These nurses went into homes to

Before child labor reforms, many children had to work long hours in mines or factories.
▶ What are these boys carrying?

teach Virginians how to avoid these health problems.

Protecting Young Workers Child labor was another problem taken up by reformers. Through the early 1900s, small children were forced to work long hours in dirty factories. With the help of the reformers, that was no longer allowed. In 1908 Virginia passed strict laws that stopped business owners from taking advantage of children.

B. Women's Struggle for Equality

Women reformers in Virginia had achieved much but not their goal of equal rights for all women. Women were still not allowed to vote. In 1909 a group headed by Lila Valentine worked to reform voting laws. But another 11 years passed before the laws changed.

Women were also denied the chance to hold the same jobs as men. Only a few women were doctors. By law, none could be lawyers. One or two women did rise to the top of the business world. Maggie Lena Walker, a black woman from Richmond, became the first woman bank president in the United States. But most women who worked held low-paying factory jobs.

C. The Struggle for Civil Rights

Black Leader In the late 1800s, many hard-working blacks became well known. With the help of the black vote, many were elected to office. One important black, Booker T. Washington, became a leader in education. Washington had been born into slavery near Roanoke in 1856. After winning his freedom, he attended Hampton Institute and studied to become a teacher.

In 1881 Washington was asked to run Tuskegee (tus KEE gee) Institute, a school for freed slaves in Alabama. Booker T. Washington spent

Booker T. Washington was a black educator and reformer.
▶ How did he help Tuskegee Institute?

his life making Tuskegee Institute a fine school. He also worked hard to help blacks get ahead in America.

Bad Times In the 1890s, the negative feelings that whites had toward blacks suddenly resurfaced. Many whites began to feel that blacks should not vote after all. A meeting was held in Virginia in 1901 to figure out new ways to keep blacks from being allowed to vote.

New laws, called Jim Crow laws, were passed. Blacks could not fully enjoy their civil rights because of these laws. Civil rights are the basic rights to which all Americans are entitled. The Jim Crow laws were meant to make blacks feel unwanted. Blacks were no longer allowed to ride in the same railway cars as whites. They could not use the same public restrooms or drinking fountains. And mobs of bitter whites often killed blacks suspected of offenses. All these changes took away civil rights from blacks.

D. World War I

Overseas War In 1914 American newspapers carried headlines announcing the start of a war in Europe. But to most Americans, it was business as usual. In fact, in Virginia, business was *better* than usual. The countries that were at war needed coal for their factories

Although denied their rights, many blacks made great sacrifices for their country during the war.
▶ How were blacks denied their rights?

and ships. They needed food for their armies. Virginia's coal fields and farms helped meet the demand. Virginia sent goods to countries the United States was friendly with.

Germany, a powerful country fighting against America's friends, tried to stop America from sending supplies. German warships sailed in the waters of Chesapeake Bay. They attacked supply ships leaving Virginia ports. These attacks angered Americans, who wanted to stay out of the war. On April 6, 1917, Congress declared war on Germany. Scenes like the one described on the next page were very common.

At Home Uncle Fred played the piano as Frank Delahoe wiped a tear from his eye. He loved his family. He also loved his country. That was why he had signed up to fight in the war in Europe.

Frank was one of the thousands of brave Virginians to fight in the war. Some became medics. Others joined to fight on the ground, on the sea, or in the air. Many people trained at Virginia bases such as Camp Lee and Langley Field.

Virginians at home did their share for the American war effort. Women and men and blacks and whites all worked together making weapons and clothing. Some people packed food for war victims. Other people drove trucks and worked in Virginia's shipyards.

During World War I, Virginia's railroads improved. New loading docks and factories were built. Vir-

This memorial in Richmond was built to mark World War I.
▶ How did World War I help the industries in Virginia?

ginians learned new skills in factories. When the war ended in November 1918, Virginia had strong industries and qualified workers. The state was well prepared for the twentieth century.

LESSON **4** REVIEW

THINK AND WRITE

A. How did the Virginia reformers help people?
B. What rights were women denied in the early 1900s?
C. How did Jim Crow laws hurt blacks in the South?
D. Why did Virginia grow stronger during the war?

SKILLS CHECK

MAP SKILL

Turn to the map of the world in your Atlas on pages 352–353. Find the country of Germany, located in Europe. Which ocean did the Germans have to cross to get their ships to Virginia?

USING THE VOCABULARY

secede	carpetbagger
Union	cash crop
emancipate	toll road
sharecropper	reform
freedman	civil rights

On a separate sheet of paper, write the best word to complete each sentence below. Choose your answers from the vocabulary words above.

1. A change for the better is a _____.
2. A nickname for someone from the North who came to live in the South was a _____.
3. A law that set slaves free would _____ them.
4. A person who raised crops on another's land was called a _____.
5. A black who had been freed from slavery was called a _____.

REMEMBERING WHAT YOU READ

Write your answers in complete sentences on a separate sheet of paper.

1. How did John Calhoun feel about the federal government giving orders to the states?
2. What was the difference between slave states and free states?
3. How did General Thomas J. Jackson get the nickname *Stonewall*?

4. What problems did slaves face after they were freed?
5. What was the Vagrancy Law?
6. Why was it very difficult for most Virginia farmers to earn a living in the 1890s?
7. How were the townspeople of Big Lick able to get the owners of the railroad to build a new railroad through their town?
8. How did Lila Meade Valentine and Sadie Heath Cabaniss improve public health in Virginia?
9. How did Booker T. Washington become known as a leader in the field of education?
10. How did Virginians at home help in the American war effort?

TYING MUSIC TO SOCIAL STUDIES

Two songs that are well known to Virginians are about railroading. One is a work song called "I've Been Working on the Railroad." The other tells a story about a famous train wreck. It is called "The Wreck of the Old '97." Ask your school librarian or your music teacher to help you find a copy of these songs or a record. Your class will enjoy singing these songs when you have learned all of the verses.

Can you find other songs that are about work? Can you find other songs that are about tragic events?

THINKING CRITICALLY

Write your answers in complete sentences on a separate sheet of paper.

1. How did disagreements on the issue of slavery lead to the Civil War?
2. What were some factors that led to the defeat of the Confederacy?
3. How did Virginians rebuild their state after the Civil War?
4. How was the coal mining industry both good and bad for Virginia?
5. In what areas were women reformers active between the years 1890 and 1917?

SUMMARIZING THE CHAPTER

On a separate sheet of paper, draw a graphic organizer that is like the one shown here. Copy the information from this graphic organizer to the one you have drawn. Under the main idea for each lesson, write three statements that support it. The first one has been done for you.

CHAPTER THEME

Differences between the North and South led to division, reunion, and reform in the United States.

LESSON 1

There were several causes of the Civil War.

1. Slavery divided the
   Northern and Southern states
2. Laws about slavery
   angered Northerners
3. Southern states
   seceded from the Union

LESSON 2

Reconstruction was a period of rebuilding after the war.

1. _____
2. _____
3. _____

LESSON 3

Virginia grew after the war.

1. _____
2. _____
3. _____

LESSON 4

Reformers improved life in Virginia.

1. _____
2. _____
3. _____

315

CITIZENSHIP AND AMERICAN VALUES

YOU DECIDE:

If you are like most students, you probably visit your local public library from time to time. You probably use the reference books there for homework assignments. You may also check books out and bring them home to read. And it costs you nothing!

Have you ever wondered who paid for all the books at the library? Who pays the librarians' wages? Who pays for the library's heating and lighting?

The answer is that everyone in your community pays. The money for public libraries comes from the local taxes that homeowners and wage earners pay. Local taxes are also used for such services as road maintenance and repair, street lighting, and other services that benefit everyone. However, not everyone benefits directly from the public library.

Some people whose money is used for funding the library never even set foot inside the building. Some simply do not read books. Other people prefer to buy their own books.

Do you think it is right that everyone should contribute to a service that is not used by everyone? What if libraries were made into private institutions instead of public ones? Then they would be funded only by the people who choose to give them money. Private libraries could only be used by those who gave money for them. They would probably have less money—and fewer books and services to offer. But people who did not want to use them would not be paying for them.

You decide — should libraries be public or private? The questions below should guide you in reaching your decision.

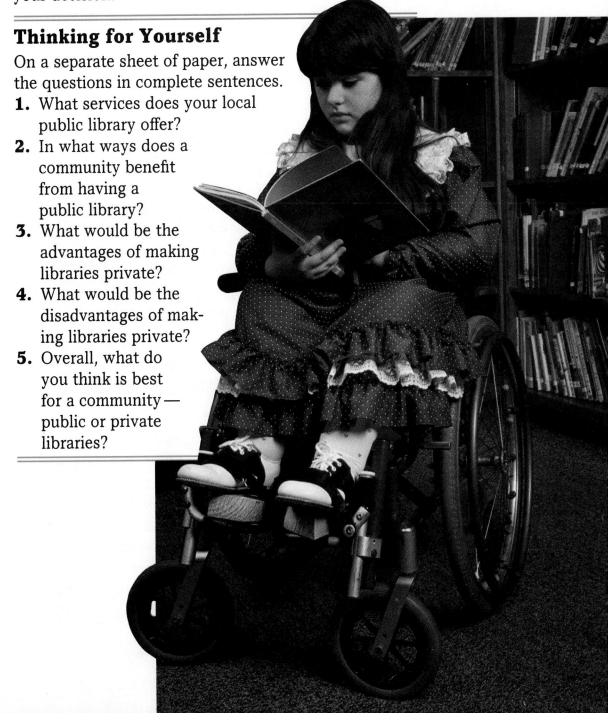

Thinking for Yourself

On a separate sheet of paper, answer the questions in complete sentences.

1. What services does your local public library offer?
2. In what ways does a community benefit from having a public library?
3. What would be the advantages of making libraries private?
4. What would be the disadvantages of making libraries private?
5. Overall, what do you think is best for a community — public or private libraries?

10

VIRGINIA IN THE 1900s

The twentieth century has been a time of great change for Virginia. Through good times and hard times, Virginians have led the way. The people of the state look forward to the future — a time to live, work, and play together in peace.

The Byrd Family

THINK ABOUT WHAT YOU KNOW

What could you or your family do to make your state a better place to live?

STUDY THE VOCABULARY

pay-as-you-go

FOCUS YOUR READING

What contributions did the Byrd family make to the governments of Virginia and America?

A. The Byrds of Virginia

One of the most important family names in Virginia history is Byrd. William Byrd was one of the first European people to reach Virginia. After his arrival in the early 1600s, William Byrd was elected to the House of Burgesses. Later, he was a part of the governor's council.

His son, William Byrd II, also became a member of the House of Burgesses. At the time, William II was only in his early twenties. But his age did not keep him from becoming a strong leader.

Through the 1700s and 1800s the Byrd family was involved in Virginia's government. The Byrd family continued to be important in Virginia politics even in the 1900s. It was during that time that Harry Flood Byrd helped bring about change in Virginia's government.

B. Harry Byrd's Role in Government

Early Career Harry Flood Byrd grew up in Winchester in the late 1800s. From the time he was small, Harry Byrd was energetic. At 15, he left school to save his father's failing newspaper. Within a few years, the paper was doing well.

In 1908 Harry Byrd was elected to the Winchester City Council. Seven years later, Byrd became one of the youngest members of the

William Byrd came to Virginia to work for his uncle.
▶ What political office did he hold?

319

Virginia State Senate. Scenes like the following probably took place.

The people of Hampton Roads had come to hear Senator Harry Byrd speak. Many of them held signs that read "pay-as-you-go." This was the senator's motto. It meant that the senator did not like Virginia's plan to borrow money for road repairs. He believed that borrowing money would cause problems for Virginia. He said that the money should come instead from a gasoline tax.

The people of Virginia liked Byrd's plan. They voted for it over the plan to borrow money.

Governor and Senator   Several years later, in 1925, the people of Virginia elected Harry Byrd governor of the state. As governor, Byrd improved Virginia's roads and its state government. Harry Byrd was the first governor to work for the protection of Virginia's many natural resources. Harry Byrd also favored the development of Shenandoah National Park.

In 1930 Byrd's term as governor ended. Three years later, he became a United States Senator, a job he held for 32 years. During those years he became a very powerful and respected leader.

Governor Byrd began the development of Shenandoah National Park.
► In what ways does Shenandoah National Park help Virginia?

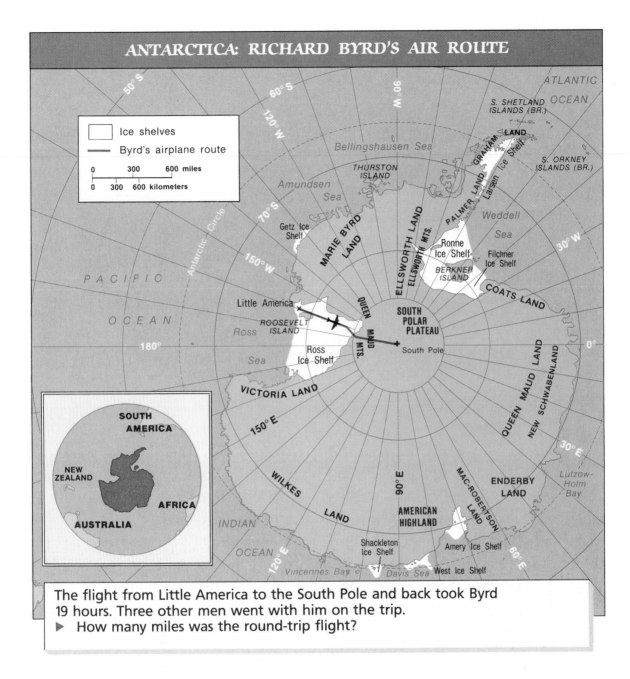

ANTARCTICA: RICHARD BYRD'S AIR ROUTE

Ice shelves

Byrd's airplane route

0   300   600 miles

0   300   600 kilometers

The flight from Little America to the South Pole and back took Byrd 19 hours. Three other men went with him on the trip.

▶ How many miles was the round-trip flight?

C. Rear Admiral Richard E. Byrd

Richard Byrd loved adventure as much as his older brother Harry loved government work. By the age of 12, Richard had already traveled halfway around the world.

Richard studied at several Virginia colleges. He also attended the U.S. Naval Academy at Annapolis, Maryland. After he became a navy pilot, he flew over the North Pole with a friend. They were the first people to try this daring deed.

Richard Byrd was a polar explorer. He was the first man to fly over both the North and South poles.
► What are the men in this picture doing?

1262.46

Richard's next frontier was the South Pole. On January 1, 1929, his plane landed on the frozen wasteland called Antarctica (ant AHRK tih kuh). He and his crew set up camp there and named it Little America.

By November, they were finally ready to fly over the South Pole. On November 29, the plane passed over the South Pole. The crew members took photographs and dropped an American flag there.

Richard Byrd returned to the United States, as a hero. President Herbert Hoover presented him with an important award.

LESSON 1 REVIEW

THINK AND WRITE

A. When did the Byrd family come to Virginia?
B. What improvements did Harry Byrd make as governor?
C. Why did Richard E. Byrd receive an award?

SKILLS CHECK

WRITING SKILL

Which policy do you prefer, borrowing or pay-as-you-go? Write your answer to this question in one or more complete sentences.

The Great Depression and World War II

THINK ABOUT WHAT YOU KNOW

Imagine that you get an allowance, and it is the only money you receive. How would you feel if you stopped getting your allowance?

STUDY THE VOCABULARY

depression   salary
drought   barter
New Deal   riveter

FOCUS YOUR READING

How did the Great Depression and World War II affect Virginia?

A. A National Disaster

A Sad Time One night in 1930, Jamie Keller awoke because he was thirsty. On his way to get a drink of water, he heard his parents talking.

"Robert, what are we going to do?" Robert's wife Anne asked, crying softly. "We have so little money left, and until this is over there is no hope of either of us getting a job. We have three children to feed."

"Don't cry, Anne. Everything will be all right. It just has to be," Robert said.

"Oh, Robert. I wish I could believe that. But this is such a disaster," Anne said. "Many of our friends are hungry. I don't want that for our family. I don't want to have to leave our home."

"Soon we will be back on our feet. These hard times will pass. We will make it through," Robert said. "I won't let them take our farm or our house. I certainly won't let you and the children starve. We just have to hold on a little longer."

Disaster Everywhere Robert Keller was not alone. His worries were shared by every farmer in the Southside, Virginia's main tobacco-growing area. They were shared by nearly every American. All worried about their jobs and about feeding and clothing their families. Many feared losing their homes.

Soup kitchens and bread lines helped feed the hungry people during the Great Depression.
► Who do you think provided food for the soup kitchens?

Franklin Roosevelt used the radio to deliver his "fireside chats."
▶ What is on the desk in front of Roosevelt?

The situation Americans were facing is called a **depression** (dee-PRESH un). A depression is a time when many people have no jobs and very little money. The depression that began in 1929 was so terrible that it became known as the Great Depression. Many offices, factories, and banks throughout the nation had to close. For farmers, crop prices dropped to an all-time low.

Getting Worse Moreover, the nation was caught in a **drought** (drout). A drought is a long spell of dry weather. Crops did not grow without the water they needed. Cattle starved to death because the grasslands had dried up. Hundreds of farmers lost their land. Many families did not have enough to eat.

The Great Depression was especially hard on women and blacks. These two groups were the first to lose their jobs. Many black-owned businesses had to close. However, Maggie Lena Walker's St. Luke's Penny Savings Bank in Richmond continued to do business as usual.

Recovering Then in 1932, Franklin Delano Roosevelt held out a hope of better times. He was running for President. He promised that if elected, he would help the nation recover from the Great Depression. He believed it was the duty of government to help those in need.

Roosevelt won the presidential election and kept his promise. He started a government program called the New Deal that was meant to help people in need. The New Deal helped provide starving Americans with food and money. President Roosevelt also started work programs that provided jobs for many people.

B. Virginia's Progress

Some parts of Virginia were hit hard by the depression. The closing of factories lessened the need for Virginia coal. Mines closed, and many miners in southwestern Virginia lost their jobs. Many Southside farms were hurt as well because the price of tobacco had dropped so low. Some Virginians got help from government programs that President Roosevelt started.

Even so, at that time conditions in Virginia were better than in much of America. The United States Navy kept people working at the Newport News shipyards. Virginians who worked for the federal government in Washington, D.C., kept their jobs. The state's black farmers also did well. In the late 1930s they grew

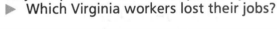

During the depression, conditions in some parts of Virginia were better than in other parts. Shipyards, such as the one in Newport News, stayed open and workers kept their jobs.
▶ Which Virginia workers lost their jobs?

about one third of the nation's tobacco and corn crops.

During the depression, leaders in Virginia's government looked for ways to help Virginians. In 1932 Governor John Garland Pollard cut government spending in several areas. He even reduced his own **salary**. A salary is the money a person gets paid to do a job. Many Virginians were given work repairing county roads.

C. Virginia and the Arts

Writers and Poets During the Great Depression, some Virginians chose to spend their time on other activities. Many of these people later went on to become famous writers, actors, and musicians.

The writer Ellen Glasgow of Richmond wrote stories about the Virginia of her day. She earned the Pulitzer (POOL iht sur) Prize in 1941 for one titled *In This Our Life*. The Pulitzer Prize is one of the highest honors a writer can receive. Another Pulitzer Prize–winning storyteller from Virginia was Willa Cather. Born in Gore, Virginia, Willa Cather moved to Nebraska with her family when she was ten years old. Her neighbors in Nebraska were from Germany, Russia, and Sweden. They were all struggling to build a new life in a new land. In Cather's stories,

Willa Cather, born in Virginia, was a famous American writer.
▶ What kind of people did Cather write about?

she wrote about the strength of these prairie pioneers, especially that of the women.

Anne Spencer, a black poet who wrote during the depression, lived in Lynchburg. Many important black poets of the 1920s and 1930s were guests in her home. Spencer wrote until she died in 1975 at the age of 93. She also helped start a local branch of a national group that helps black people.

Trade for Tickets Theater in Virginia also improved during the depression. In 1932 a man named Robert Porterfield opened a theater in Abingdon for out-of-work actors. Knowing that people did not have much money, Porterfield allowed customers to use barter to buy tickets for plays. Barter is goods given in return for services or other goods. People would arrive at the theater with armloads of fruits, vegetables, and cakes. Because of the unusual way in which the theater sold tickets, it became known as the Barter Theatre.

Today people pay money for their tickets to the Barter Theatre.
▶ How did the theater get its name?

327

Many young Virginians served during World War II. These are men from the 1st and 2nd Armored Division.
► What are the soldiers in this picture doing?

D. World War II

Cruel Dictators Because of Virginia's pay-as-you-go plan, the state was able to recover quickly when the depression ended. For some states, the hard times dragged on for many more years.

The countries of Europe were also having hard times. Italy and Germany, which had suffered most, fell under the rule of cruel and powerful men. These leaders took away the people's freedoms. They attacked other nations to spread their empires. Japan, a country in Asia, soon followed that example. It was clear that war would result.

The Nation at War America wanted to avoid entering the war. But by 1939, Americans understood that the actions of Germany and Italy threatened freedom everywhere. America began improving its own fighting forces. On December 7, 1941, Japanese warplanes dropped bombs on American ships at Pearl Harbor in Hawaii. The next day, America declared war on Japan.

During the war, many young men served in the United States Army, Navy, Air Force, Marines, and Coast Guard. Some women also served, although they were not involved in active fighting. By the end of the war, in 1945, about 300,000 Virginia men and women had served their country well.

The Home Front Women in Virginia also served in all kinds of jobs. Many did jobs once done only by the men who were away fighting. Some of the women drove tractors on farms. Others worked at the Newport News Shipyards. Some of them had jobs as **riveters** (RIHV iht urz). Those women worked to fasten metal plates to warships. In Lynchburg and in Radford, women worked in steel plants.

Black Virginians fought in the war and worked at home for the war. New laws had been passed that allowed blacks to join the armed forces. Many black Americans worked in wartime factories at home. But many blacks were still not treated fairly. Black soldiers were not allowed to fight side by side with white soldiers. Moreover, very few of the black soldiers were ever made officers.

When the war ended in 1945, black Virginians tried to get equal rights. Women in the state did the same. Both groups had helped bring peace and strength back to America. Both groups felt that they deserved equal treatment.

Women helped the war effort by making weapons and planes.
► What safety equipment is this woman wearing?

LESSON 2 REVIEW

THINK AND WRITE

A. What did Franklin Roosevelt promise the American people?
B. Why were conditions in Virginia during the depression better than in many other states?
C. How did the Barter Theatre get its name?
D. During the war, what jobs did women and blacks have?

SKILLS CHECK

THINKING SKILL
Think about the effect that America's entry into the war had on the work force at home. Then think about some of the long term effects of women taking jobs outside the home. Do you think this was a change for the better or for the worse? Give reasons for your answer.

Virginia's Rapid Change

THINK ABOUT WHAT YOU KNOW
How can a place change for the better? In what ways have you seen that happen?

STUDY THE VOCABULARY
service industry   segregation

FOCUS YOUR READING
What changes took place in Virginia between 1950 and 1970?

A. A Different Virginia

Time Travel Imagine that someone invented a time machine. This machine would enable you to travel through time. As you step into the time machine, you program the years you want to travel to.

The first stop is the year 1900. You get out of the time machine. You step onto a dusty road surrounded by farms. A car or two goes by, spitting out smelly smoke. Most people are traveling by horse and wagon. Much of the land is planted with tobacco. Down the road, children are helping to pick apples in the orchards. They spend a lot of time helping on farms since they go to school only four months of the year. You are surprised how different everything is. You are ready to leave so that you can get to your next stop.

Fifty Years Later The next stop is the year 1950. You cannot believe how much things can change in just 50 years! Everything is different. The roads are better. Cars are very popular. Many Virginians have moved to cities. Much of the land that was once covered with farms is now covered with factories. The farms that do exist are bigger than they used to be. Machines have been invented. With their help, one farmer can do the work of ten. Dairy farms are becoming popular. You get back into the time machine and head to 1970.

> This bar graph shows the state's urban and rural populations.
> ▶ Which population grew more between 1900 and 1950?

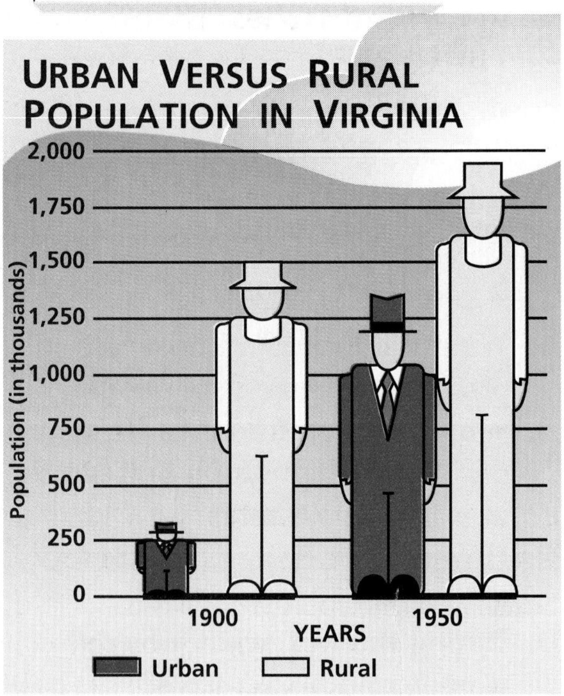

URBAN VERSUS RURAL POPULATION IN VIRGINIA

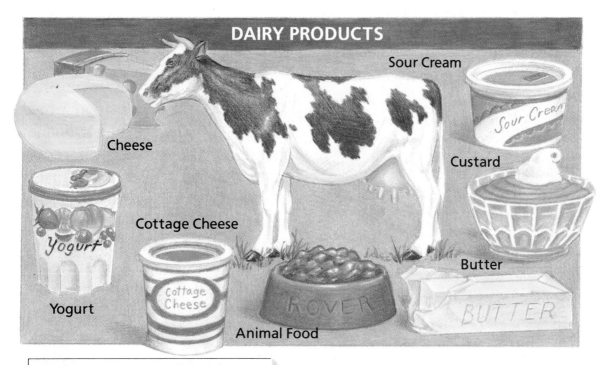

DAIRY PRODUCTS

Sour Cream

Cheese

Custard

Cottage Cheese

Yogurt

Butter

Animal Food

More than half of Virginia's farm income comes from livestock and livestock products.
▶ What are other dairy products?

Changing Industries By 1970 both beef cattle and dairy cows were important in most of Virginia. They had taken the place of tobacco as the most important farm product. Apple growing had decreased even though parts of the hill country were still thick with orchards.

Other natural resources grew in importance between 1950 and 1970. Trees, used for lumber and paper, became a big business. So did fishing. Virginia's rich supply of seafood earned over $20 million for the state.

Even though coal was not used as much as the cheaper and cleaner natural gas, it still remained a major industry. Between 1950 and 1970 the amount of coal Virginia produced increased. At the same time, however the number of miners decreased because machines could now do their jobs.

After World War II, coal continued to be an important resource.
▶ How much coal was produced in Virginia in 1960?

COAL PRODUCTION IN VIRGINIA, 1950-1970

Years	Short Tons	Metric Tons
1950	17,667,000	16,023,969
1955	23,508,000	21,321,756
1960	29,000,000	26,303,000
1965	34,053,000	30,886,071
1970	35,016,000	31,759,512

B. Industrial Change

New Industries Between 1950 and 1970, Virginia became an industrial power. Farming and processing tobacco, cutting lumber, and fishing were major industries. Coal and water were sources of energy for Virginia's factories.

By 1970 the chemical industry had become the new giant industry in Virginia. Chemical plants, which had made products to further the American war effort, now made synthetics. Do you remember what synthetic fibers are? They are fibers not found in nature.

During these years, the **service industries** also grew. Service industries offer services rather than goods. The many Virginians employed by the federal government hold service jobs. Doctors, lawyers, bankers, and people in the tourism business also provide services.

Tobacco, a leading industry for hundreds of years, also grew through the early 1960s. Machines produced 4,000 cigarettes a minute. But in the mid-1960s, the industry was hurt when it was discovered that smoking and chewing tobacco harm people's health.

Urban Changes Many people moved to Virginia after 1950. They brought with them many cars. This meant that Virginia needed to build more and better roads. In the 1950s Virginians used federal money to build Shirley Highway in northern Virginia. In 1964 the great Chesapeake Bay Bridge – Tunnel opened. It connects the Eastern Shore with other parts of Virginia. Because of new and better roads, Virginians could live farther from their places of work. This caused cities to grow. Land that was once pasture and woodland was now covered with houses and office buildings. Virginia had definitely changed.

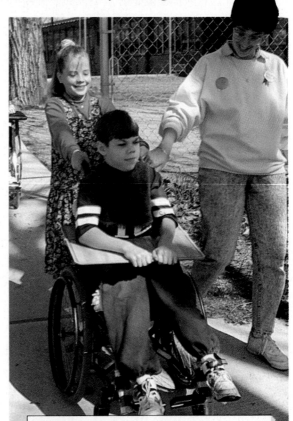

Many people work in service industries.
▶ What are some other jobs in service industries?

The Chesapeake Bay Bridge-Tunnel is more than 17 miles long.
► Why was the bridge-tunnel built?

C. Education in Virginia

Separate Schools The battle over education that Thomas Jefferson started in the 1800s had not ended by the early 1950s. The people were still arguing over the quality of Virginia's public education. A big part of the argument concerned the practice of sending black children and white children to separate schools. This practice, known as **segregation** (seg ruh GAY shun), angered many people. Some groups fought against segregation. They said that teachers in black schools were paid less than teachers in white schools. They also pointed out that black students often attended school in buildings that were old and in poor condition.

At the Supreme Court Virginia's government took small steps to correct these problems. Then in 1954 the United States Supreme Court made an important decision. The case centered on a black girl from Kansas who lived 4 blocks from a white school. The girl had been forced to travel 20 blocks to a black school. The Supreme Court ruled that this treatment was unfair. Soon after, the Supreme Court ordered an end to segregation.

Some Virginia leaders disliked the Supreme Court decision. They made sure that only a few blacks went to white schools. Other leaders openly favored segregation. One of them, Senator Harry F. Byrd, got a new law passed. Under this law, Virginia's governor had to close any school that followed the Supreme Court order. In 1958 and 1959 many public schools in Virginia closed their doors. Some stayed closed for four years.

Reactions It did not take long for Virginians to realize how much harm was being done to their children. Parent groups, community groups, and teachers called for an end to the closings of schools.

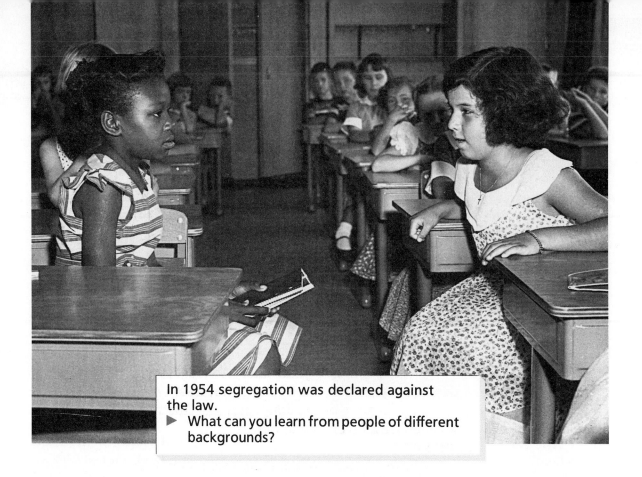

In 1954 segregation was declared against the law.
▶ What can you learn from people of different backgrounds?

Virginia's business leaders were also upset. They were afraid that the school closings would hurt business growth. They met with the governor, J. Lindsay Almond. On January 19, 1959, the Virginia Supreme Court outlawed school closings. A month later, segregation in most of Virginia's schools ended. Most Virginians went along quietly with the new ruling. For the first time ever, black students and white students were able to sit side by side in classrooms.

LESSON **3** REVIEW

THINK AND WRITE

A. What changes took place on Virginia's farms?
B. What are some jobs that are part of service industries?
C. How did the battle over education end in 1959?

SKILLS CHECK

THINKING SKILL

Look carefully at the photograph on this page. How do you think the two girls in the front feel about being in the same classroom?

"I HAVE A DREAM . . ."

Dr. Martin Luther King, Jr., was one of the most famous civil rights leaders in America. In 1963, King participated in the largest civil rights demonstration in history. King's "I Have a Dream" speech was the high point of the day.

Five score [one hundred] years ago, a great American . . . signed the Emancipation Proclamation. This . . . decree came as a great beacon light of hope to millions of Negro [black] slaves. . . .

But one hundred years later, we must face the tragic fact that the [black] is still not free. . . .

. . . In spite of the difficulties and frustrations of the moment I still have a dream. . . .

I have a dream that one day this nation will rise up and live out the true meaning of its creed: "We hold these truths to be self-evident; that all men are created equal."

Understanding Source Material

On a separate sheet of paper, answer the questions in complete sentences.

1. What was Dr. King's dream?
2. In what year were the slaves emancipated, or freed?
3. What words would you use to describe Dr. King?

Reforms in Virginia

THINK ABOUT WHAT YOU KNOW
How do you feel when you have
been treated unfairly?

STUDY THE VOCABULARY
heritage   **profession**
candidate

FOCUS YOUR READING
How have blacks and women in
Virginia brought about change?

A. Civil Rights for Blacks

Ending Segregation   In the 1960s,
many black people began calling
themselves African Americans.
They did this because they wanted
to keep their heritage alive. A heritage is something that is handed
down from earlier generations or
from the past. Even today, the term
African American is widely used.

Putting an end to school segregation was a first step toward equality for Virginia African Americans.
The next step was ending segregation in restaurants, hotels, parks,
and other places.

Although slavery had been
done away with nearly 100 years before, black people were still mistreated in many parts of the country.
In most of the South, they could not
drink at water fountains that white
people used. They could not swim in
the same swimming pools or sit at
the front of the bus. By the 1960s
African Americans began to take action against that unfairness and to
demand their civil rights.

Leading the Fight   Dr. Martin
Luther King, Jr., led the struggle for
civil rights. Dr. King was a minister
from Atlanta, Georgia. He urged
black people to make their demands
in peaceful ways.

One such peaceful event took
place in Richmond. However, the re-

It took many years to end the
segregation of public places.
► How do you think segregation
made black people feel?

action of the police was not peaceful at all. A photograph of the event appeared in *Life* magazine in March 1960. The picture showed a 58-year-old grandmother being dragged from a department store lunchroom by Richmond police officers. The woman, Ruth Tinsley, had been sitting in a restaurant where only white people were allowed.

Virginians and Americans were upset by these actions. White people began to see how unfairly black people were being treated. Many store and restaurant owners began to serve all people regardless of color.

A New Law In 1964 the United States Congress passed the Civil Rights Act. Black people were given their civil rights at last. In Virginia, state law was brought into agreement with the federal civil rights laws in 1970. Governor Mills E. Godwin, Jr., was responsible for that change in the state constitution. He also was responsible for a section added to the Virginia bill of rights. It stated that state and local governments in Virginia could not treat anyone unfairly on the basis of color, sex, national origin, or religion. National origin means the country a person comes from.

The Governor's Example The next governor, A. Linwood Holton,

Governor A. Linwood Holton sent his daughter to a black school.
▶ Why were white children transported to black schools?

was also concerned about equality for black people. Governor Holton's goal was "to make today's Virginia a model of race relations."

The following story shows how he and his family encouraged blacks and whites to go to school together by their good example.

It was the first day of the school year at Richmond's John F. Kennedy High. Like many students, Roy Kitt waited outside for the first-period bell to ring.

As Roy enjoyed the morning sunshine, something surprising happened. Roy asked his friend Cal, "Do you know who *that* is?" Roy was looking at two people — a man and a young girl — walking toward them.

"No," Cal said. "Who is it?"

"That's Governor Holton!" Roy replied. "And that must be his daughter Tayloe."

They had two reasons to be surprised that Governor Holton was bringing his daughter to Kennedy High. First, they were surprised because he was the governor and he did not live nearby. Second, they were surprised because Governor Holton was white.

Though segregation had ended, many schools, like Kennedy, were still mostly black. Other schools in Virginia were mostly white. In 1970 the Supreme Court had ordered schools to begin transporting white children, like 13-year-old Tayloe Holton, to black schools. Black children would be driven to white schools. The purpose was to make the schools more equal. It was another step toward equality among black and white people.

Before becoming governor of Virginia, Douglas Wilder served as lieutenant governor of the State.
▶ What was Douglas Wilder's first elected office?

B. Blacks in Government

Still another step was the involvement of black people in state government. During Governor Godwin's first term in office, he appointed about 35 black Virginians to important positions in the state government. Governor Holton was known for appointing more black people to government positions than any previous governor.

One black man's story began in Richmond. As a teenager, L. Douglas Wilder shined shoes and washed windows to help his parents and nine brothers and sisters. He paid his way through the local black col-

338

lege by pouring cups of coffee at the Hotel John Marshall. After college he became a hero in the Korean War. He was a hero again in the civil rights struggle in Virginia. In 1969 the people of Richmond elected him to the Virginia State Senate.

Twenty years later, Douglas Wilder, grandson of a slave, became the governor of Virginia. This was a very close election and a very important one. It was the first time in the history of the United States that an African American won election to a state's highest office.

Black Virginians also became involved in local government. In 1973 Hermanze E. Fauntleroy, Jr., became the first black person to be in charge of a city government in Virginia. He was elected mayor of Petersburg. Charles Barbour of Charlottesville and Charles Charlton of Radford became mayors of their cities in 1974.

In November 1976, Noel C. Taylor became the first black mayor of Roanoke. On the same day, Lawrence A. Davies became the first black mayor of Fredericksburg. Since 1976, black mayors have served in the cities of Richmond, Portsmouth, and Newport News. In 1984 Florence Farley became the first black woman mayor of a Virginia city, Petersburg.

C. Civil Rights for Women

Changes for Women During World War II, many women worked in factories and on farms. After the war, some wanted to continue to work. However, many people felt that women belonged back in the home. And the men who came back to the United States claimed their old jobs. Any jobs that were available for women were low-paying and uninteresting. Women felt that their time for civil rights had come.

During the 1950s and 1960s, some changes took place that helped women. Most important, they got involved in state government. In 1953 Kathryn H. Stone was elected to Virginia's General Assembly. In 1957 Dorothy S. McDiarmid became the head of the powerful Education Committee. She worked hard to improve Virginia's schools.

Today more Virginia women are working outside the home.
▶ How has the percentage of working women changed since 1950?

PERCENTAGE OF WOMEN IN THE VIRGINIA WORK FORCE, 1950-1990

| 25% 1950 | 31% 1960 | 36% 1970 | 44% 1980 | 44%* 1990 |

*Estimate

In 1970 McDiarmid had another success. She was the first woman from Virginia chosen to run as a **candidate** for the United States Congress. A candidate is a person who seeks an office.

Professional Women More women were working throughout the state of Virginia. Some of them worked in **professions.** A profession is a job, such as doctor, dentist, lawyer, or architect, that requires many years of special training and education. This change was in part due to the fact that more colleges were allowing women to attend.

Political Women In the 1970s and 1980s, women in Virginia continued to make progress in their fight for equality. When the Virginia General Assembly met in January 1989, 14 women were there. McDiarmid, in her twenty-fourth year there, continued to be a powerful leader.

Mary Sue Terry was a part of the General Assembly from 1978 to 1985. In 1985 she became the first woman ever elected attorney general of Virginia. Mary Sue Terry was reelected in 1989.

"A woman's place," Mary Sue Terry once said, "is where she wants it to be." In Virginia today, women work in business, industry, professions, and government.

D. Other Reforms

Clean Air and Water In the 1970s and 1980s, Virginia's government leaders worked to make more improvements in their state. One of the biggest issues was pollution. Governor Holton worked with the General

Here is the James River after the cleanup.
▶ Why was it important to clean the James River?

Assembly to pass tougher laws to control and prevent air pollution and water pollution.

When the next governor, Mills E. Godwin, Jr., was faced with a chemical disaster, he took quick action. It had started when a dangerous chemical leaked into the air and into the James River from a factory in Hopewell. Godwin closed the river to fishing so that people would not eat the affected fish. At his request, the federal government helped pay for cleaning up the James River. He asked the General Assembly to give the state environ-

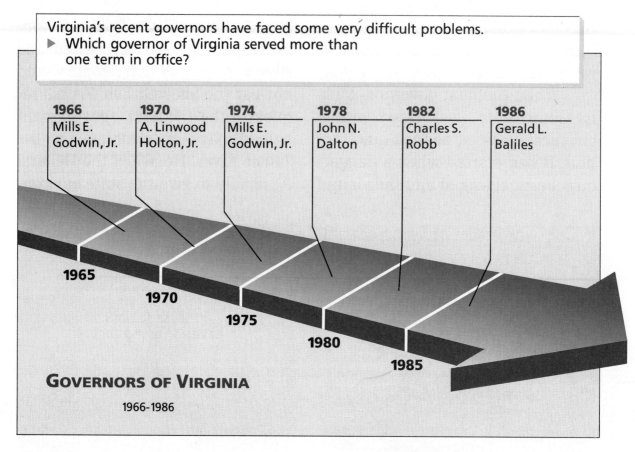

Virginia's recent governors have faced some very difficult problems.
► Which governor of Virginia served more than one term in office?

1966	1970	1974	1978	1982	1986
Mills E. Godwin, Jr.	A. Linwood Holton, Jr.	Mills E. Godwin, Jr.	John N. Dalton	Charles S. Robb	Gerald L. Baliles

1965
1970
1975
1980
1985

GOVERNORS OF VIRGINIA
1966-1986

mental protection agencies the power to oversee the production and storage of dangerous chemicals.

The next governor, John N. Dalton, continued the efforts begun by Godwin to protect the environment. He got the General Assembly to pass a new law to help prevent further chemical spills. That law required state inspections, or examinations, of safety measures in chemical manufacturing plants.

Improving Education Another issue that continued to occupy Virginia's leaders was education. When Charles S. Robb was elected gover-

nor in 1981, he had one thing on his mind: quality education for every Virginia student. During his term, he and the General Assembly poured state money into Virginia's schools and colleges. They especially helped poor schools. Later, Robb became a United States Senator.

Modern Methods The next governor, Gerald L. Baliles (buh LYLZ), was also very concerned with making improvements in Virginia's schools. He improved training programs for teachers. He brought modern learning tools such as computers into the classroom.

E. Virginians in Arts and Sports

Today, many Virginians shine as stars in the arts and in sports. William Styron, a best-selling author, was born in Newport News. His book *The Confessions of Nat Turner* tells of the 1831 slave uprising. Another of his books, *Sophie's Choice,* was made into a successful movie in the early 1980s.

Actor George C. Scott of Wise County has acted on the stage and in movies. One of his most famous roles was that of George Patton, a colorful World War II general.

Shirley MacLaine and Warren Beatty were born in Arlington. MacLaine became a dancer and later won an Academy Award for her acting in the movie *Terms of Endearment.* Beatty has starred in the movies *Shampoo* and *Reds.*

Many fine writers, exciting performers, and great athletes came from Virginia.
► Which of these famous Virginians have you heard about?

Tennis great Arthur Ashe, Jr., was born in Richmond. In 1968 he became the first black to win the United States men's national singles tennis championship. Seven years later, he became the first black person to win England's Wimbledon singles tennis championship. Ashe also wrote a book titled *A Hard Road to Glory*. This three-volume work traces the struggles of black athletes in America.

Virginia has produced leaders in government, education, writing, art, entertainment, and sports. It continues to be a beautiful place where millions of people live together in peace. It is a place to enjoy and care for. You have studied Virginia's geography, natural resources, industry, history, and people. Aren't you proud to be from the great state of Virginia?

Arthur Ashe helped his team win the Davis Cup in 1968 and 1972.
► What did Arthur Ashe do for black athletes?

LESSON 4 REVIEW

THINK AND WRITE

A. Why were people upset about the photograph of Ruth Tinsley in *Life* magazine?

B. Which governors helped blacks become involved in state government?

C. What was the most important change that took place for women during the 1950s and the 1960s?

D. How did Governors Robb and Baliles improve education?

E. Who are two famous Virginians working in the arts?

SKILLS CHECK

THINKING SKILL

How did involvement in state government help the blacks and women fight for equality?

10 PUTTING IT ALL TOGETHER

USING THE VOCABULARY

pay-as-you-go	riveter
depression	service industry
New Deal	segregation
salary	heritage
barter	candidate

On a separate sheet of paper, write the best word to complete each sentence. Choose your answers from the vocabulary words above.

1. In the 1930s President Franklin Roosevelt had a plan called the _____ that helped people.
2. During the _____, many people were out of work.
3. A person who seeks a government office is a _____.
4. The practice of sending black children and white children to separate schools is known as _____.
5. Trading goods for goods or services is called _____.

REMEMBERING WHAT YOU READ

Write your answers in complete sentences on a separate sheet of paper.

1. What was Harry F. Byrd's pay-as-you-go plan?
2. What is Antarctica?
3. What happened to farms and farmers during the drought?
4. What special subject did Willa Cather write about?
5. Which were the three countries that Americans fought against in World War II?
6. What are three industries that became important in Virginia between 1950 and 1970?
7. What was the important United States Supreme Court decision that was made in 1954?
8. What was Dr. Martin Luther King, Jr., famous for?
9. What was the name of the governor who added a section to the Virginia Bill of Rights in 1970?
10. What position has Mary Sue Terry held since 1985?

TYING LANGUAGE ARTS TO SOCIAL STUDIES: WRITING TO LEARN

Entertainment has always been an important part of the lives of Virginians and people everywhere. Most people enjoy reading or watching movies or television programs. Write a report about something you have seen or read recently. It could be a movie, a play, a television show, a book, or a poem. Your report should include things you liked about your subject as well as things you did not like. Share your report with the class.

THINKING CRITICALLY

Write your answers in complete sentences on a separate sheet of paper

1. In what ways does the history of the Byrd family remind you of the history of Virginia?
2. Why were times hard during the Great Depression?
3. How did World War II affect the way black people and women in Virginia felt about their rights?
4. Why did many people believe that education in the 1950s was not fair?
5. What issues concerned Virginia's leaders in the 1970s and 1980s?

SUMMARIZING THE CHAPTER

On a separate sheet of paper, draw a graphic organizer that is like the one shown here. Copy the information from this graphic organizer to the one you have drawn. Under the main idea for each lesson, write three statements that support it. The first one has been done for you.

CHAPTER THEME

In the 1900s Virginians dealt with changes, problems, and reforms.

LESSON 1

The Byrd family made important contributions to Virginia.

1. William Byrd—one of the first European settlers in Virginia
2. Harry F. Byrd—a powerful state senator, governor, and United States senator
3. Richard E. Byrd—an explorer

LESSON 2

The depression and World War II brought times of hardship as well as times of accomplishment.

1. _____
2. _____
3. _____

LESSON 3

Rapid changes took place in Virginia between 1950 and 1970.

1. _____
2. _____
3. _____

LESSON 4

Black people and women in Virginia brought about change.

1. _____
2. _____
3. _____

3 *REVIEW*

COOPERATIVE LEARNING

In this unit you learned about several Virginians who became famous in the arts. Now you are going to work with some of your classmates to learn more about one of these people.

REMEMBER TO:
- Give your ideas.
- Listen to others' ideas.
- Plan your work with the group.
- Present your project.
- Discuss how your group worked.

PROJECT

- Working in groups of five, decide which writer or actor you will learn more about.
- One member of the group should look for information on the person's family and early life.
- One member of the group should look for items about the person's work.
- Another member of the group will use the information to write a report about the person.

PRESENTATION AND REVIEW

- Once the report is written, still another member will present the group's work to the rest of the class in an oral report.
- The fifth group member should write five questions to ask the audience. Following the report, this person will copy the questions on the chalkboard. Then he or she should call on students for answers.
- Here are some sample questions. Was the report clear? What questions do you have about this person that were not answered in the report?

A. WHY DO I NEED THIS SKILL?

As the name suggests, the main idea is the most important idea, or topic, being discussed. In a paragraph, the main idea is often stated in the first sentence. The main idea is sometimes called the topic sentence. The remaining sentences in the paragraph support or give more information about the main idea. They are called supporting sentences. It is important to identify the main idea of a paragraph in order to know what topic is being discussed.

B. LEARNING THE SKILL

Usually the main idea is stated in the first sentence of a paragraph. In some cases, however, it may be stated in the second or third sentence of the paragraph. No matter where the main idea appears in the paragraph, it should be clear to the reader. Read the paragraph below and identify the main idea.

Virginia has many beautiful and interesting places for people to visit. Luray Caverns is a favorite of visitors to Virginia. Located in northwestern Virginia, the limestone cave covers almost a square mile. Rooms inside the cave are over 300 feet high. Some of the rooms have stalactites and stalagmites that are 50 feet in length. The cave has several small pools of water, but no fish live in them. Each year many people visit this fascinating underground attraction. They come to enjoy the beautiful formations and colors inside the cave.

To identify the main idea, ask yourself the following question. What topic does nearly every sentence give information about?

If you need to, read the paragraph again. At first, you may think the paragraph is about the interesting and beautiful places for people to visit in Virginia. But as you continue to read, you will see that nearly every sentence is about Luray Caverns. In this paragraph, the main idea was stated in the second sentence.

C. PRACTICING THE SKILL

Turn to page 195 (Chapter 6, Lesson 1, "Colonists in Rebellion"). Read each heading in the lesson and the paragraphs below it. What is the main idea of each section under the heading? List two supporting details that add to the main idea. Write your answers on a separate sheet of paper.

D. APPLYING THE SKILL

Choose three paragraphs from another section of your social studies textbook. Copy them onto a separate sheet of paper. Number the paragraphs from 1 to 3. Then answer the following questions about the three paragraphs.

1. What is the topic sentence, or main idea, of the first paragraph?

2. What details about the main idea are given in the supporting sentences in the second paragraph?
3. How many supporting sentences are there in the third paragraph that you chose?

A. WHY DO I NEED THIS SKILL?

Some statements that you hear or read are statements of *fact*. They can be proved. Others are statements of *opinion*. They tell you how the speaker or writer feels. Opinions may be of great value. However, it is very important that you learn to tell the difference between facts and opinions. It will help you determine the correctness of what you hear and read.

B. LEARNING THE SKILL

There are ways to tell the difference between facts and opinions. Look at the two sentences below.

1. When a goal is scored in soccer it counts for one point. (Fact)
2. Football is a more dangerous game than soccer. (Opinion)

You can prove the first statement by reading a soccer rule book or by looking at the scoreboard when a goal is made. The second statement is difficult to prove because it is what the person thinks or feels.

Sometimes you can spot opinions by clue words, such as *believe, think,* or *feel*. Other times, opinions are not as easy to spot. They may be stated like facts, as in the following sentence.

The Piedmont Plateau is the prettiest area in Virginia.

This statement sounds like a fact, but it is an opinion. Watch out for words like *most, best,* or *prettiest* that signal personal judgments. Even if you agree, it is still an opinion, not a fact.

C. PRACTICING THE SKILL

Write the numbers 1 through 10 on a separate sheet of paper. Then read the following statements. Next to each number, write *F* if the statement is a fact or *O* if the statement is an opinion.

1. The name of the state bird of Virginia is the cardinal.
2. Virginia's summer temperatures are very pleasant.
3. Carpetbaggers were very helpful to the South after the Civil War.
4. Coal mining is an important industry in southwestern Virginia.
5. James Madison is called the Father of the Constitution because many of his ideas are included in it.
6. I think the plays performed at Barter Theatre are the best.

7. The first blacks came to the state of Virginia in 1619.
8. Virginia is also the name of a city in northeastern Minnesota.
9. The Apple Blossom Festival held at Winchester every spring is worth seeing.
10. The best apples are grown in the state of Virginia.

D. APPLYING THE SKILL

Write a short essay describing your favorite place in Virginia. Include in your essay five facts that you know about the place you have chosen. Include also five opinions that you have about the place. Be very sure that you know the difference between a fact and an opinion.

351

ATLAS

THE WORLD: POLITICAL

0 — 1,500 miles
0 — 1,500 kilometers

WEST INDIES

0 — 200 — 400 miles
0 — 200 — 400 kilometers

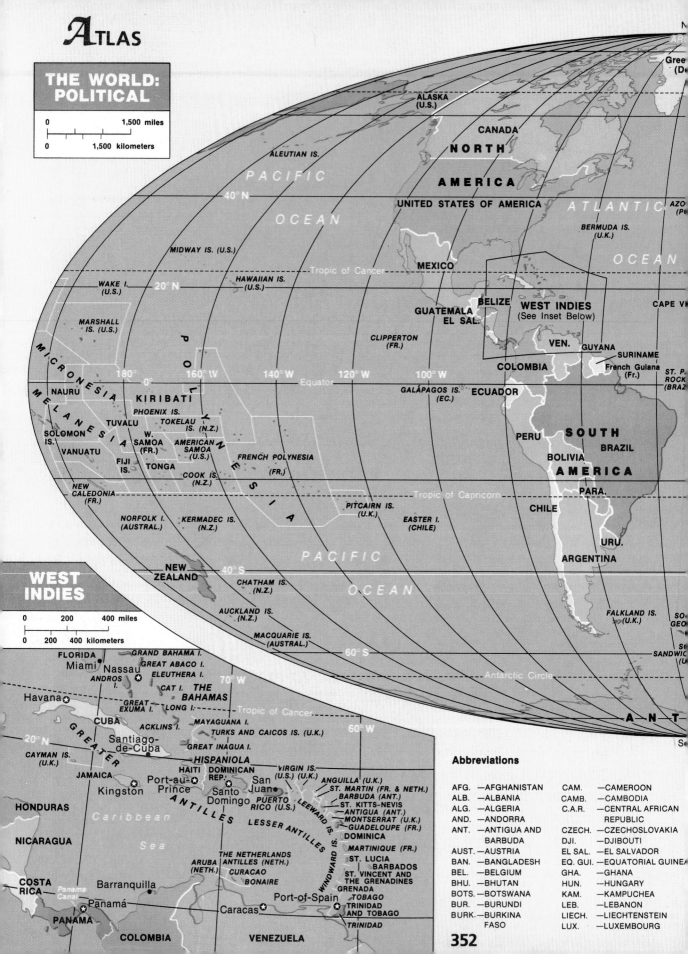

Abbreviations

AFG.	—AFGHANISTAN	CAM.	—CAMEROON
ALB.	—ALBANIA	CAMB.	—CAMBODIA
ALG.	—ALGERIA	C.A.R.	—CENTRAL AFRICAN
AND.	—ANDORRA		REPUBLIC
ANT.	—ANTIGUA AND	CZECH.	—CZECHOSLOVAKIA
	BARBUDA	DJI.	—DJIBOUTI
AUST.	—AUSTRIA	EL SAL.	—EL SALVADOR
BAN.	—BANGLADESH	EQ. GUI.	—EQUATORIAL GUINEA
BEL.	—BELGIUM	GHA.	—GHANA
BHU.	—BHUTAN	HUN.	—HUNGARY
BOTS.	—BOTSWANA	KAM.	—KAMPUCHEA
BUR.	—BURUNDI	LEB.	—LEBANON
BURK.	—BURKINA	LIECH.	—LIECHTENSTEIN
	FASO	LUX.	—LUXEMBOURG

352

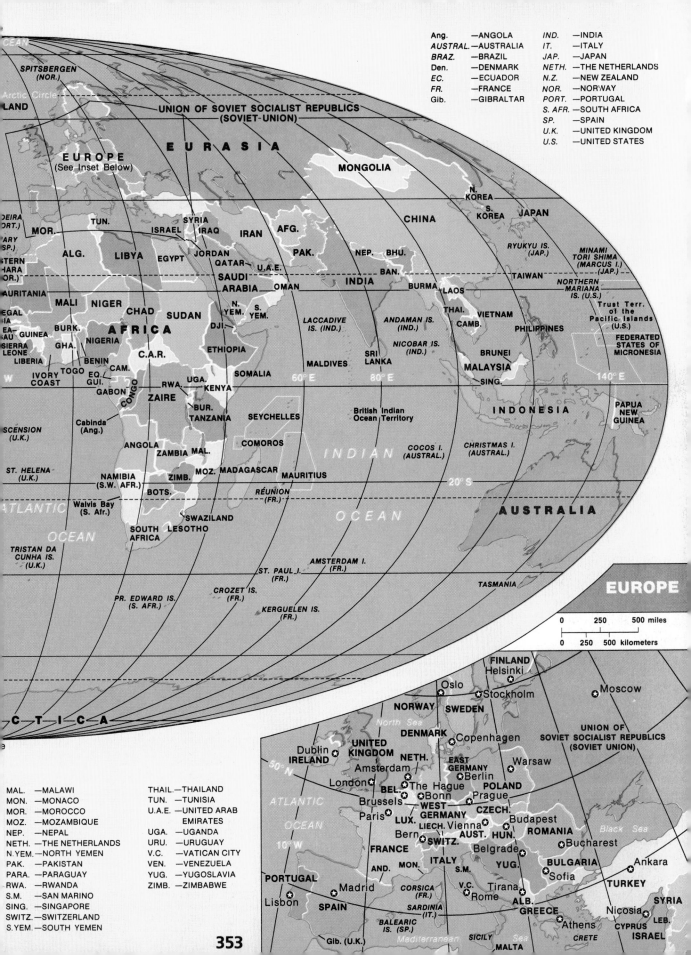

Ang. —ANGOLA
AUSTRAL. —AUSTRALIA
BRAZ. —BRAZIL
Den. —DENMARK
EC. —ECUADOR
FR. —FRANCE
Gib. —GIBRALTAR

IND. —INDIA
IT. —ITALY
JAP. —JAPAN
NETH. —THE NETHERLANDS
N.Z. —NEW ZEALAND
NOR. —NORWAY
PORT. —PORTUGAL
S. AFR. —SOUTH AFRICA
SP. —SPAIN
U.K. —UNITED KINGDOM
U.S. —UNITED STATES

SPITSBERGEN (NOR.)
Arctic Circle
EUROPE (See Inset Below)
UNION OF SOVIET SOCIALIST REPUBLICS (SOVIET-UNION)
EURASIA
MONGOLIA
N. KOREA
S. KOREA
JAPAN
MADEIRA (PORT.)
MOR.
TUN.
SYRIA
ISRAEL
IRAQ
IRAN
AFG.
CHINA
RYUKYU IS. (JAP.)
MINAMI TORI SHIMA (MARCUS I.) (JAP.)
CANARY (SP.)
ALG.
LIBYA
EGYPT
JORDAN
QATAR
U.A.E.
PAK.
NEP.
BHU.
TAIWAN
WESTERN SAHARA (MOR.)
SAUDI ARABIA
OMAN
INDIA
BAN.
BURMA
LAOS
NORTHERN MARIANA IS. (U.S.)
MAURITANIA
MALI
NIGER
CHAD
SUDAN
N. YEM.
S. YEM.
DJI.
THAI.
VIETNAM
CAMB.
PHILIPPINES
Trust Terr. of the Pacific Islands (U.S.)
SENEGAL
GUINEA-BISSAU
GUINEA
BURK.
NIGERIA
AFRICA
C.A.R.
ETHIOPIA
LACCADIVE IS. (IND.)
ANDAMAN IS. (IND.)
FEDERATED STATES OF MICRONESIA
SIERRA LEONE
LIBERIA
GHA.
BENIN
TOGO
CAM.
EQ. GUI.
GABON
CONGO
ZAIRE
RWA.
UGA.
BUR.
KENYA
SOMALIA
NICOBAR IS. (IND.)
MALDIVES
SRI LANKA
BRUNEI
MALAYSIA
SING.
IVORY COAST
60° E
80° E
140° E
ASCENSION (U.K.)
Cabinda (Ang.)
TANZANIA
SEYCHELLES
British Indian Ocean Territory
INDONESIA
PAPUA NEW GUINEA
ST. HELENA (U.K.)
ANGOLA
ZAMBIA
MAL.
COMOROS
MOZ.
MADAGASCAR
MAURITIUS
COCOS I. (AUSTRAL.)
CHRISTMAS I. (AUSTRAL.)
INDIAN
NAMIBIA (S.W. AFR.)
ZIMB.
BOTS.
RÉUNION (FR.)
20° S
TRISTAN DA CUNHA IS. (U.K.)
Walvis Bay (S. Afr.)
SWAZILAND
SOUTH AFRICA
LESOTHO
OCEAN
AUSTRALIA
ATLANTIC
OCEAN
AMSTERDAM I. (FR.)
ST. PAUL I. (FR.)
PR. EDWARD IS. (S. AFR.)
CROZET IS. (FR.)
KERGUELEN IS. (FR.)
TASMANIA
A-R-C-T-I-C-A

EUROPE

0	250	500 miles
0	250	500 kilometers

FINLAND
Helsinki
Oslo
Stockholm
Moscow
NORWAY
SWEDEN
North Sea
DENMARK
Copenhagen
UNION OF SOVIET SOCIALIST REPUBLICS (SOVIET UNION)
Dublin
UNITED KINGDOM
NETH.
EAST GERMANY
Warsaw
IRELAND
Amsterdam
Berlin
London
The Hague
BEL.
Bonn
Prague
POLAND
ATLANTIC
Brussels
WEST GERMANY
CZECH.
50° N
Paris
LUX.
LIECH.
Vienna
Budapest
ROMANIA
OCEAN
Bern
SWITZ.
AUST.
HUN.
10° W
FRANCE
Belgrade
Bucharest
AND.
MON.
ITALY
YUG.
BULGARIA
Black Sea
Ankara
S.M.
PORTUGAL
Madrid
CORSICA (FR.)
V.C.
Tirana
Sofia
TURKEY
Lisbon
SPAIN
Rome
ALB.
Nicosia
SYRIA
SARDINIA (IT.)
GREECE
LEB.
BALEARIC IS. (SP.)
Athens
CYPRUS
ISRAEL
Gib. (U.K.)
SICILY
Mediterranean Sea
CRETE
MALTA

MAL. —MALAWI
MON. —MONACO
MOR. —MOROCCO
MOZ. —MOZAMBIQUE
NEP. —NEPAL
NETH. —THE NETHERLANDS
N.YEM. —NORTH YEMEN
PAK. —PAKISTAN
PARA. —PARAGUAY
RWA. —RWANDA
S.M. —SAN MARINO
SING. —SINGAPORE
SWITZ. —SWITZERLAND
S.YEM. —SOUTH YEMEN

THAIL. —THAILAND
TUN. —TUNISIA
U.A.E. —UNITED ARAB EMIRATES
UGA. —UGANDA
URU. —URUGUAY
V.C. —VATICAN CITY
VEN. —VENEZUELA
YUG. —YUGOSLAVIA
ZIMB. —ZIMBABWE

353

CANADA

Seattle

WASHINGTON

Olympia ⊛

Spokane

Portland
Columbia   River
Salem ⊛

Eugene

Great Falls

Helena ⊛   MONTANA

Missouri   River

Grand Forks

NORTH DAKOTA

Bismarck ⊛

Fargo

OREGON

IDAHO

Billings

Boise ⊛

Idaho Falls

Snake
River   Pocatello

WYOMING

SOUTH DAKOTA

Pierre ⊛

Rapid City

Sioux Falls

NEVADA

Great
Salt
Lake

West Valley

Salt Lake
City ⊛
Provo

Casper

Laramie
Cheyenne

NEBRASKA

Grand Island

Omaha

Sacramento ⊛

Reno

Carson City ⊛

UTAH

Lincoln

Oakland
San Francisco
San Jose

Denver ⊛ Aurora
COLORADO
Colorado
Springs

Topek

KANSAS

Fresno

CALIFORNIA

Las
Vegas

Colorado   River

Arkansas
River

Wichita

35° N

Los Angeles Anaheim
Long Beach   Riverside
Santa Ana

San Diego

ARIZONA

Phoenix ⊛

Mesa

Santa Fe

Albuquerque

NEW MEXICO

OKLAHOMA

Oklahoma City ⊛

Lawton

Tul

Tucson

Las Cruces

El Paso

Arlington
Fort Worth   Dall

Red   River

Brazos   River

TEXAS

PACIFIC

OCEAN

30° N

120° W

HAWAII

Kailua

Pearl City   Honolulu

PACIFIC

20° N   OCEAN

0   100 miles

0   100 kilometers

160° W   155° W

ARCTIC   OCEAN

U.S.S.R.

Yukon   River

Fairbanks

ALASKA

CANADA

180°

0   200 miles

0   200 kilometers

55° N

354

170° W

Anchorage

Juneau ⊛

150° W

PACIFIC   OCEAN

140° W

Austin ⊛

Hous

San Antonio

Corpus
Christi

MEXICO

Rio   Grande

CANADA

MINNESOTA
Duluth

MICHIGAN

Minneapolis
St. Paul — Green Bay
WISCONSIN
MICHIGAN

IOWA
Madison
Milwaukee
Cedar
Rapids
Rockford
Des
Moines
Davenport
Chicago
Gary
Fort Wayne
ILLINOIS
INDIANA
Indianapolis
Columbus

Grand
Rapids
Lansing
Detroit

Toledo
Akron
OHIO
Wheeling

Cleveland
PENNSYLVANIA
Harrisburg
Pittsburgh

Rochester
NEW YORK
Buffalo

Springfield
WEST
VIRGINIA
Huntington
Frankfort
Lexington
Louisville

Cincinnati

WASHINGTON, D.C.

Charleston

KENTUCKY

Kansas City
St. Louis
Jefferson City
MISSOURI

ARKANSAS
North
Little Rock
Fort
Smith
Little Rock

Nashville
TENNESSEE
Memphis

Knoxville

Richmond
VIRGINIA
Norfolk
Virginia Beach

Raleigh
Greensboro
NORTH CAROLINA
Charlotte

Columbia
SOUTH CAROLINA
North Charleston
Charleston
Savannah

Atlanta
GEORGIA
Columbus

Birmingham
MISSISSIPPI
ALABAMA
Meridian
Montgomery
Jackson

Shreveport

LOUISIANA
Baton Rouge
New Orleans

Mobile
Biloxi

Jacksonville

Tallahassee
FLORIDA
Tampa
St. Petersburg

Miami

Gulf of Mexico

MAINE
Augusta
Montpelier
Lewiston
Burlington
VERMONT
Portland
Rutland
Concord
NEW HAMPSHIRE
Manchester
Nashua
Albany
Boston
Worcester
MASSACHUSETTS
Springfield
Pawtucket
Hartford
Providence
Warwick
New Haven
RHODE ISLAND
Bridgeport
CONNECTICUT
Jersey City
New York
Newark
Trenton
NEW JERSEY
Philadelphia
Wilmington
Baltimore
Newark
Rockville
Dover
Washington, D.C.
DELAWARE
Annapolis
MARYLAND

St. Lawrence River

ATLANTIC

OCEAN

40° N

35° N

30° N

25° N

Tropic of Cancer

THE UNITED STATES
OF AMERICA

～ Rivers
✪ National capital
✫ State capitals
• Other cities

0   100   200 miles
0   100   200 kilometers

75° W   70° W

90° W   85° W   80° W

355

VIRGINIA: A Road Map

Expressways

Major Highways

Other Roads

Interstate Highways

U.S. Highways

State Highways

Points of Interest

National Parks

Public Camping Areas

Elevation Points

Mileage Between Points

State Capital

0   25   50 kilometers

0   25   50 miles

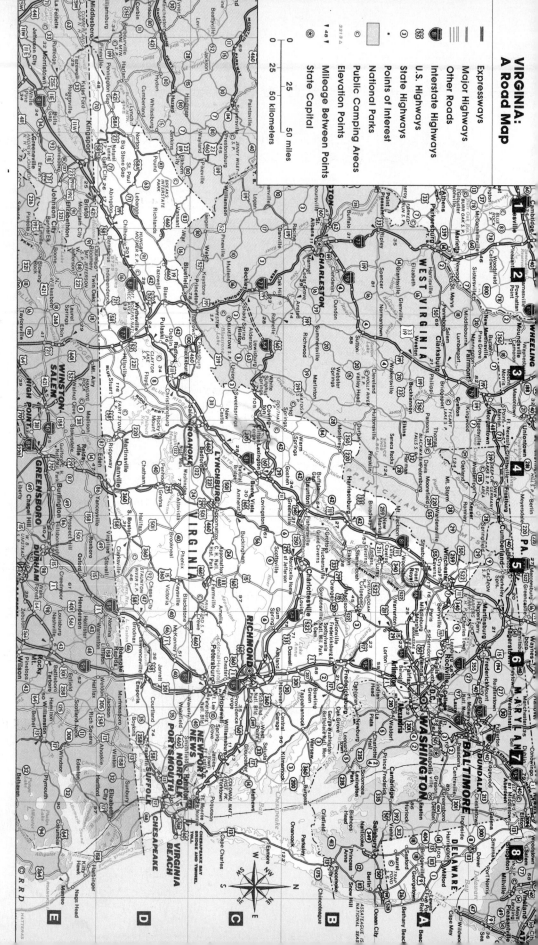

Gazetteer

Some words in this book may be new to you or difficult to pronounce. Those words have been spelled phonetically in parentheses. The syllable that receives stress in a word is shown in small capital letters.

For example: **Chicago** (shuh KAH goh)

Most phonetic spellings are easy to read. In the following Pronunciation Key, you can see how letters are used to show different sounds.

PRONUNCIATION KEY

a	after	(AF tur)										
ah	father	(FAH thur)	y	hide	(hyd)	u	taken	(TAY kun)	ng	long	(lawng)
ai	care	(kair)	ye	lie	(lye)		matter	(MAT ur)	s	city	(SIH tee)
aw	dog	(dawg)	oh	flow	(floh)	uh	ago	(uh GOH)	sh	ship	(shihp)
ay	paper	(PAY pur)	oi	boy	(boi)	ch	chicken	(CHIHK un)	th	thin	(thihn)
e	letter	(LET ur)	oo	rule	(rool)	g	game	(gaym)	thh	feather	(FETHH ur)
ee	eat	(eet)	or	horse	(hors)	ing	coming	(KUM ing)	y	yard	(yahrd)
ih	trip	(trihp)	ou	cow	(kou)	j	job	(jahb)	z	size	(syz)
eye	idea	(eye DEE uh)	yoo	few	(fyoo)	k	came	(kaym)	zh	division	(duh VIHZH un)

The Gazetteer is a geographical dictionary. It shows latitude and longitude for cities and certain other places. Latitude and longtiude are shown in this form: (37°N/80°W). This means "37 degrees north latitude and 80 degrees west longitude." The page reference tells where each entry may be found on a map.

Africa. The earth's second largest continent. p. 7.

Albemarle Sound. An arm of the Atlantic Ocean that extends into northern North Carolina. p. 356. (AL buh mahrl sound)

Alexandria (39°N/77°W). Independent city surrounded by Fairfax County. It is a Fall Line city located on the Potomac River. It is the eighth most populated city in Virginia. p. 57.

Allegheny Mountains. Part of the Appalachians. They extend from Pennsylvania to Virginia and West Virginia. p. 65.

Antarctica. The earth's third smallest continent. p. 7.

Appalachian Mountains. Chain of mountains stretching from Canada to Alabama. The highest peak is Mt. Mitchell at 6,684 feet (2,037 m). p. 65. (ap uh LAY chun MOUNT unz)

Appomattox (37°N/79°W). Site in Virginia where General Lee surrendered to General Grant during the Civil War. p. 356.

Arctic Ocean. Large body of salt water north of the Arctic Circle. p. 7.

Arlington (39°N/77°W). A county and urban area that surrounds Washington, D.C., and is in the northern Piedmont Region of Virginia. p. 57.

Asia. The earth's largest continent. p. 7.

Assateague Island. Located in Maryland and in Accomack County. It separates Chincoteague Bay from the Atlantic Ocean. p. 47.

Atlantic Ocean. Large body of salt water separating North America and South America from Europe and Africa. p. 7.

Australia. The earth's smallest continent. Also the name of the country that covers the whole continent. p. 7.

Blue Ridge Mountains. Range of mountains located in the eastern part of the Appalachians. They stretch from Pennsylvania through Virginia to Georgia. p. 65.

Blue Ridge Parkway. A highway that extends some 470 miles (756 km) from the southern end of the Shenandoah National Park in Virginia to the Great Smokey Mountains National Park in North Carolina. p. 356.

Boston (42°N/71°W). Capital of and most populated city in Massachusetts. Located on Massachusetts Bay. p. 355.

Buggs Island Lake. Largest artificial lake in Virginia. Located along the North Carolina border. Also called Kerr Reservoir. p. 87.

Canada. The largest country in North America and the second largest country in the world. p. 352.

Cape Henry (37°N/77°W). Point of land located at the entrance to Chesapeake Bay. Opposite Cape Charles. In 1607 the Jamestown settlers led by Captain Newport landed here before deciding to move inland on the James River. p. 47.

Caribbean Sea. Part of the Atlantic Ocean bounded by South America on the south; Central America on the west; and Cuba, Puerto Rico, and other islands on the north and east. p. 352. (kar uh BEE un see)

Charlottesville (38°N/78°W). Independent city surrounded by Albemarle County. Located on the Rivanna River. It is the home of the University of Virginia. Monticello, the home of Thomas Jefferson, and Ash Lawn, the home of James Monroe, are nearby. p. 57.

Chesapeake Bay. Inlet of the Atlantic Ocean in Virginia and Maryland. It is about 190 miles (306 km) long. The Potomac, Rappahannock, James, and York rivers empty into it. p. 47.

Chesapeake Bay Bridge–Tunnel (37°N/76°W). A 23-mile (37 km) transportation system of bridges, tunnels, and causeways that connects the Eastern Shore of Virginia with other parts of the state. p. 356.

Chesterfield County. County located in central southeastern Virginia and the area of Virginia's first coal beds. p. 36.

Chincoteague Island. Located in Chincoteague Bay. p. 47. (shihng kuh TEEG EYE-lund)

Clifton Forge (38°N/80°W). Independent city located in Allegheny County in western Virginia. p. 356.

Clinch River. Starts in Tazewell County. Flows into the Tennessee River in Tennessee. p. 87.

Columbia River. Major river of the western United States and Canada that carried Lewis and Clark in 1805 to the Pacific Ocean. p. 232.

Cowpasture River. Starts in Highland County. Joins the Jackson River near Iron Gate to form the James River. p. 87.

Craney Island. Small island in the Elizabeth River, just west of Norfolk. During the War of 1812, Virginia soldiers beat back the English at a battle fought here. p. 237.

Cumberland Gap (37°N/84°W). Natural pass through the Cumberland Mountains. Located at the point where Virginia, Tennessee, and Kentucky meet. p. 65.

Danville (37°N/79°W). Independent city surrounded by Pittsylvania County. Located on the Dan River near the Virginia–North Carolina border. An important textile center. p. 57.

Dismal Swamp Canal. Connects Hampton Roads and Chesapeake Bay with Albemarle Sound. It was completed in 1828. p. 257.

Eastern Hemisphere. The half of the earth east of the Prime Meridian. It includes Australia and most of Europe, Africa, and Asia. p. 16.

Eastern Shore. Part of the Tidewater Region located along the eastern shore of Chesapeake Bay. It includes all of the land in Maryland and Virginia east of Chesapeake Bay. p. 47.

Elkton (38°N/79°W). Town in Rockingham County. Located on the South Fork of the Shenandoah River. p. 65.

Endless Caverns (39°N/79°W). Natural caves in the Ridge and Valley Region where people can see beautifully shaped stalactites and stalagmites. p. 65.

Equator. A line, drawn on maps, that circles the earth halfway between the two poles. It is labeled 0° latitude. p. 15.

Europe. The earth's second smallest continent. p. 7.

Fairfax (39°N/77°W). The county seat of Fairfax County and part of the heavily populated northern Piedmont Region that surrounds Washington, D.C. p. 57.

Fairfax County. The most populated Virginia county, located in the northeastern region of the state. It is the home of George Washington's plantation, Mount Vernon. p. 36.

Fall Line. A series, or line, of small waterfalls and rapids. It separates the Tidewater and Piedmont regions. The falls along the Fall Line are 40 to 70 feet (12 to 21 m) high. Many cities are located along the Fall Line. Alexandria, Fredericksburg, Richmond, and Petersburg are all Fall Line cities. p. 46.

Falls Church (39°N/77°W). Town in Fairfax County and part of the heavily populated northern Piedmont Region that surrounds Washington, D.C. p. 57.

Fort Cahokia (39°N/90°W). Today a village in St. Clair County, southwestern Illinois. In 1778 George Rogers Clark and 175 Virginia frontiersmen captured the English fort at Cahokia. p. 212. (kuh HOH kee uh)

Fort Kaskaskia (38°N/90°W). Today a village in Randolph County, southwestern Illinois. In 1778 George Rogers Clark and 175 Virginia frontiersmen captured the English fort at Kaskaskia. p. 212. (ka SKAS kee uh)

Fort Monroe (37°N/76°W). Located on the north shore of Hampton Roads. Built by President James Monroe in 1819. p. 237.

Fort Vincennes (39°N/88°W). Today a city in Knox County, Indiana. In 1779 an important fort at Vincennes was captured from the British by George Rogers Clark. p. 212.

Fredericksburg (38°N/77°W). Independent city surrounded by Spotsylvania County. Located on the Rappahannock River. The Confederate army won a famous battle over the Union army here in 1862 during the Civil War. Home of John Paul Jones. p. 57.

Gordonsville (38°N/78°W). Town in Orange County. Terminus of the first railroad to cross the mountains in Virginia. p. 257.

Grand Caverns (38°N/79°W). Natural caves in the Ridge and Valley Region where people can see beautifully shaped stalactites and stalagmites. p. 65.

Great Dismal Swamp. Swamp located in southeastern Virginia and northeastern North Carolina. p. 47.

Great Lakes. Five large lakes that are located in east central North America. They are Lake Superior, Lake Michigan, Lake Huron, Lake Erie, and Lake Ontario. p. 355.

Great Salt Lake (41°N/112°W). Located in Utah. An inland saltwater lake with no streams flowing out of it. p. 354.

Great Valley. Name given to all the flatter land located between the Blue Ridge and Allegheny mountains. Also called the Valley of Virginia. p. 65.

Greenwich (51°N/0° long.). A place in London, England, designated as 0° longitude. The Prime Meridian runs from the North Pole through Greenwich to the South Pole. p. 16.

Halifax County. Southern county in Virginia and an important textile center. p. 36.

Hampton (37°N/76°W). Independent city located on Hampton Roads. It is the sixth most populated city in Virginia. Settled in 1610 by colonists from Jamestown. p. 47.

Hampton Roads (37°N/76°W). One of the world's finest natural harbors. It is the waterway through which the James, Elizabeth, and Nansemond rivers flow into Chesapeake Bay. The port of Hampton Roads includes the harbors of Newport News, Norfolk, and Portsmouth. p. 47.

Healing Springs (38°N/80°W). Natural hot springs located in Bath County. p. 65.

Holston River. Starts in Tennessee. Joins the French Broad River near Knoxville to form the Tennessee River. p. 87.

Hopewell (37°N/77°W). Independent city surrounded by Prince George County. Located at point where the Appomattox River flows into the James River. p. 47.

Hot Springs (38°N/80°W). Natural mineral springs located in Bath County. p. 65.

Indian Ocean. Large body of salt water between Africa and Australia. p. 7.

Jackson River. Starts in Highland County. Joins the Cowpasture River near Iron Gate to form the James River. p. 87.

James River. Starts in Botetourt County where the Jackson and Cowpasture rivers join to form it. It flows into Chesapeake Bay at Hampton Roads. Ships can sail on the James River as far as Richmond. It was named after King James of England. p. 87.

Jamestown (37°N/77°W). First permanent English settlement in America. Settled on May 13, 1607. Located on the James River. p. 356.

Lake Drummond. Largest natural lake in Virginia. Located in the Great Dismal Swamp near North Carolina border in southeastern corner of Virginia. p. 87.

Lake Erie. Located along the border between Canada and the United States. Second smallest of the five Great Lakes. p. 189.

Leningrad (60°N/30°E). Second most populated city in the Soviet Union. Located on the Gulf of Finland. p. 16. (LEN un grad)

Luray Caverns (39°N/78°W). Natural caves in the Ridge and Valley Region where people can see beautifully shaped stalactites and stalagmites. p. 65.

Lynchburg (37°N/79°W). Independent city surrounded by Campbell County. It is the tenth most populated city in Virginia. Located on the James River. It is an important manufacturing center. p. 57.

Manassas (39°N/77°W). County seat of Prince William County and part of the heavily populated northern Piedmont Region that surrounds Washington, D.C. p. 57.

Manassas Park (39°N/77°W). City in Prince William County and part of the heavily populated northern Piedmont Region that surrounds Washington, D.C. p. 57.

Martinsville (37°N/80°W). Independent city surrounded by Henry County and an important textile center. p. 57.

Massanutten Caverns (38°N/79°W). Natural caves in the Ridge and Valley Region where people can see beautifully shaped stalactites and stalagmites. p. 65. (mas uh NUT un)

Massanutten Mountain. Mountain ridge in Blue Ridge Mountains. Located between the North Fork and South Fork of the Shenandoah River. p. 65.

Maury River. Starts in Augusta County. Flows

into the James River near Glasgow in Rockbridge County. p. 87.

Middle Peninsula. One of four peninsulas in the Virginia Tidewater Region. Located between the Rappahannock and York rivers. p. 47.

Mississippi River. The longest river in the United States. Rises in northern Minnesota and flows into the Gulf of Mexico near New Orleans, Louisiana. p. 232.

Missouri River. The second longest river in the United States. Rises in western Montana and flows into the Mississippi River near St. Louis, Missouri. p. 232.

Mount Rogers (37°N/82°W). The highest point in Virginia. Located in Grayson County near the North Carolina border. It is 5,729 feet (1,746 m) high. p. 65.

Mount Vernon (39°N/75°W). Home and burial place of George Washington. Located on the Potomac River in Fairfax County. p. 148.

Mountain Lake (37°N/82°W). Well-known natural lake in Giles County. p. 87.

Natural Bridge (37°N/83°W). A natural bridge formed by a stream (Cedar Creek) cutting through tons of stone over millions of years. It is 215 feet (65 m) high, 50 to 100 feet (15 to 30 m) wide, and 90 feet (27 m) long. p. 65.

Natural Chimneys (38°N/79°W). Seven tall gray stone towers in Augusta County. These towers, or chimneys, were caused by the wearing away of softer stone. Every August a jousting tournament is held here. p. 65.

New Market (39°N/79°W). Town located in Shenandoah County in northern Virginia. p. 356.

New River. Starts in North Carolina. Flows north through Virginia into West Virginia where it joins the Gauley River to form the Kanawha River, which empties into the Ohio River. p. 87.

New York City (41°N/74°W). Most populated city in the United States. Located at the mouth of the Hudson River in the state of New York. It was the first capital of the United States. p. 355.

Newport News (37°N/76°W). Independent city located at the mouth of the James River at the entrance to Hampton Roads. It is the fourth most populated city in Virginia and a major shipbuilding and ship-repairing center. p. 47.

Norfolk (37°N/76°W). Independent city located on the Elizabeth River south of Hampton Roads. It is the second most populated city in Virginia. p. 47.

North America. The earth's third largest continent. Our country is in North America. p. 7.

North Pole. The most northern place on the earth. p. 15.

Northern Hemisphere. The half of the earth that is north of the Equator. p. 15.

Northern Neck Peninsula. One of four peninsulas in the Virginia Tidewater Region. Located between the Potomac and Rappahannock rivers. p. 47.

Norton (37°N/83°W). A coal mining town surrounded by Wise County, in southwestern Virginia. p. 356.

Ohio River. Formed at Pittsburgh, Pennsylvania, by the joining of the Allegheny and Monongahela rivers. Flows into the Mississippi River at Cairo, Illinois. Forms part of the boundary of five states. p. 189.

Ohio Valley. An area west of the Allegheny Mountains and of dispute during the French and Indian War and Revolutionary times. The valley is named after the Ohio River. p. 355.

Pacific Ocean. The earth's largest body of water. It stretches from the Arctic Circle to Antarctica and from the western coast of North America to the eastern coast of Asia. p. 7.

Peninsula, The. One of four peninsulas in the Virginia Tidewater Region. Located between the York and James rivers. p. 47.

Petersburg (37°N/77°W). Fall Line city located on the Appomattox River. Ships can sail up the Appomattox to Petersburg. A famous battle was fought here during the Civil War. Virginia State College is located here. p. 57.

Philadelphia (40°N/75°W). City in Pennsylvania. Located at the point where the Delaware and Schuylkill rivers join. One of eight cities in the United States with more than 1,000,000 people. p. 355. (fihl uh DEL fee uh)

Piedmont Plateau. An upland area of rolling hills extending from the Fall Line on the east to the Blue Ridge Mountains on the west. From north to south, it stretches from the Hudson River to Alabama. Also called the Piedmont Region. p. 57.

Piedmont Region. An upland area of rolling hills extending from the Fall Line on the east to the Blue Ridge Mountains on the west. From north to south, it stretches from the Hudson River to Alabama. Also called the Piedmont Plateau. p. 57.

Pittsylvania County. The largest Virginia county in area. Located in the southern part of the state. p. 36.

Portsmouth (37°N/76°W). Independent city located on the Elizabeth River and Hampton Roads. It is the seventh most populated city in Virginia. p. 47.

Potomac River. Starts in West Virginia and flows into Chesapeake Bay. Washington, D.C., is located on this river. p. 87.

Prime Meridian. 0° line of longitude. It divides the earth into the Eastern Hemisphere and the Western Hemisphere. p. 16.

Rappahannock River. Starts in the Blue Ridge Mountains and flows into Chesapeake Bay. Ships can sail up the Rappahannock as far as Fredericksburg. p. 87. (rap uh HAN uk)

Richmond (38°N/77°W). Independent city. State capital of Virginia. Located on the James River at the Fall Line. It is the third most populated city in Virginia. p. 57.

Ridge and Valley Region. Land west of the Piedmont, made up of a line of hills or mountains with valleys between them. The two main mountain ranges in this region are the Blue Ridge Mountains on the east and the Allegheny Mountains on the west. Both are part of the Appalachian Mountains. p. 65.

Roanoke (37°N/80°W). Independent city surrounded by Roanoke County. Located on the Roanoke River. It is the ninth most populated city in Virginia. p. 65.

Roanoke River. Starts in Montgomery County. Flows through Roanoke and through Buggs Island Lake (Kerr Reservoir) into North Carolina. Flows into Albemarle Sound. p. 87.

Rockingham County. County in northern Virginia that leads all other Virginia counties in cattle raising. p. 36.

Rocky Mountains. Longest mountain chain in the United States. Stretches from Alaska to Mexico. Highest Peak is Mt. Elbert, with an elevation of 14,433 feet (4,399 m). p. 354.

St. Louis (39°N/90°W). Second most populated city in Missouri. Located on Mississippi River near the point where it is joined by the Missouri River. The Lewis and Clark expedition left from St. Louis in 1804 to explore the Louisiana Territory. p. 232.

Salem (37°N/80°W). Independent city near Roanoke and surrounded by Roanoke County. Located on the Roanoke River. p. 65.

Shenandoah National Park. Large protected area of forest land in northern Virginia. p. 18.

Shenandoah River. Starts in Warren County where the North Fork and the South Fork of the Shenandoah join. It empties into the Potomac River at Harpers Ferry. p. 87.

Shenandoah Valley. Beautiful valley through which the Shenandoah River passes. Located between the Allegheny and Blue Ridge mountains. It is about 110 miles (177 km) long and about 25 miles (40 km) wide. p. 65.

Smithfield (37°N/77°W). Town in Isle of Wight County. Located on the James River. Famous for its peanuts and Smithfield hams. p. 47.

South America. The earth's fourth largest continent. p. 7.

South Boston (37°N/79°W). Independent city surrounded by Halifax County. Located on the Dan River. A major textile center. p. 57.

South Hill (37°N/78°W). A town surrounded by Mecklenburg County and an important tobacco center. p. 57.

South Pole. The most southern place on the earth. p. 15.

Southern Hemisphere. The half of the earth that is south of the Equator. p. 15.

Southside. Name given to the Tidewater land in Virginia that is south of the James River. p. 47.

Staunton (38°N/79°W). Independent city surrounded by Augusta County. Birthplace of Woodrow Wilson. p. 65. (STAWNT un)

Suffolk (37°N/77°W). Independent city. Located on the Nansemond River. p. 47.

Tazewell (37°N/81°W). County seat of Tazewell County. Located in a coal mining area. p. 27.

The Peninsula. *See* Peninsula, The.

Tidewater Region. Lies along the Atlantic Ocean. It is a coastal plain made up of low, flat land. p. 47.

Valley of Virginia. Name given to all the valleys located between the Blue Ridge and Allegheny mountains. Also called the Great Valley. p. 65.

Virginia Beach (37°N/76°W). Independent city located on the Atlantic Ocean. It is the most populated city in Virginia. p. 47.

Warm Springs (38°N/79°W). Natural hot springs located in Bath County. p. 65.

Washington, D.C. (39°N/77°W). Capital of the United States since 1800. Located on the Potomac River. p. 47.

Waynesboro (38°N/79°W). Independent city surrounded by Augusta County. Located on the South River. Terminus for the first railroad to cross the mountains in Virginia. p. 65.

Western Hemisphere. The half of the earth west of the Prime Meridian. Includes all of North America and South America. p. 16.

Williamsburg (37°N/77°W). Independent city surrounded by James City County. Located on peninsula between the James and York rivers. It was the capital of Virginia from 1699 to 1780. p. 356.

Winchester (39°N/78°W). Independent city surrounded by Frederick County. Located in the Shenandoah Valley. It is the oldest city in the Great Valley. Home of Daniel E. Morgan. p. 65.

Wise County. Southwestern county in Virginia and an important coal mining center. p. 36.

Woodstock (39°N/79°W). County seat of Shenandoah County. Located near the North Fork of the Shenandoah River. Home of John Peter Muhlenberg. p. 356.

York River. Starts at West Point in King William County. There it is formed by the joining of the Pamunkey and Mattaponi rivers. It flows into Chesapeake Bay. p. 87.

Yorktown (37°N/77°W). County seat of York County located on the York River. The Americans won a decisive victory over the British here during the War for Independence. After this defeat the British were ready to make peace. p. 87.

Glossary

The page references in each entry tell where the term is first used in the text.

abolitionist. A person who worked to bring about the end of slavery in the United States. p. 278.

agriculture. Farming; the raising of crops or livestock. p. 78.

architect (AHR kuh tekt). A person who draws up a plan for buildings or structures. p. 215.

artificial lake. A lake made by people, not by nature. p. 87.

ballot. A piece of paper or other object used in voting. p. 248.

barrel stave. A strip of wood used to make a barrel. p. 257.

barter. Goods given in return for services or other goods. p. 327.

bay. A part of a large body of water that reaches into the land. p. 46.

Bill of Rights. Part of the United States Constitution; it lists the basic rights granted to all Americans by the Constitution. p. 217.

boundary. A line that separates one state or one country from another. p. 11.

burgess. A representative who made new laws for the people of Virginia. p. 154.

Cabinet. A group of advisors to the President of the United States. p. 227.

candidate. A person who seeks an office in the government. p. 340.

capital. A city where a state's or country's government leaders get together to make laws. p. 154.

capitol. A building in which government leaders meet. p. 168.

carpetbagger. A person who moved to the South from the North and who carried belongings in suitcases made of carpeting. p. 303.

cash crop. A crop that a farmer could sell in large amounts. p. 306.

chart. A sailor's map of the sea or other bodies of water. p. 267.

chief justice. The head of the Supreme Court of the United States. p. 243.

civil rights. The basic rights to which all Americans are entitled. p. 312.

climate. The kind of weather a place has over a long period of time. p. 89.

coastal plain. A large area of flat or gently rolling land that is bordered by a large area of water. p. 45.

colony. Land that is settled far from the country that governs it. p. 144.

Committee of Correspondence. A colony-wide group set up to help Virginia protect itself against trouble from the English. p. 198.

compass. A tool for finding directions. p. 12.

compass rose. A drawing that shows where north, south, east, and west are on a map. p. 12.

coniferous (koh NIHF ur us). A type of tree that bears cones and usually remains green year-round. Coniferous trees are also called evergreens. p. 84.

conservation. Using natural resources wisely so they are not wasted or destroyed. p. 95.

constitution. A set of laws by which a country is governed. p. 216.

Constitutional Convention. The meeting in May 1787 during which a stronger plan of

United States government was drawn up. p. 216.

continent. A very large body of land. p. 7.

Continental Congress. The name given to the meetings of the group of representatives from the American colonies. p. 199.

contour line. A line on a map showing a certain distance above sea level. All places on a contour line are the same distance above sea level. p. 41.

county. The largest part of a state with a local government. p. 36.

cover crop. A crop that is planted to protect the soil from erosion. The roots of the trees or plants drink the water and hold the soil in place. p. 95.

current. A steady flow of water moving in a certain direction in the ocean or in a sea or river. p. 266.

dam. A wall that holds back water. p. 79.

deciduous (dee SIHJ oo us). Shedding leaves in the fall. p. 85.

Declaration of Independence. A document that explained why the American colonists were breaking away from Great Britain. p. 204.

depression (de PRESH un). A time when many people have no jobs and very little money. p. 324.

dissenter. In colonial Virginia, a person who held religious beliefs different from those of the Church of England. p. 158.

drought (drout). A long spell of dry weather. p. 324.

elect. To choose leaders by voting. p. 225.

electronics (ee lek TRAHN ihks). The use of electricity to give us many products. p. 124.

elevation. The distance or height above sea level. p. 41.

emancipate (ee MAN suh payt). To free. p. 298.

Equator. The imaginary line on the earth that is halfway between the North Pole and the South Pole. p. 14.

Era of Good Feeling. The period following the War of 1812 (during the presidency of James Monroe) when the United States experienced peace and unity. p. 240.

erosion. The wearing away of the soil by rain, wind, ice, or waves. p. 94.

estimate. To figure out something, such as distance or location on a map or globe. p. 17.

explorer. A person who travels through little-known lands or seas to find out about them. p. 234.

extinct. No longer existing. p. 96.

Fall Line. A line of small waterfalls and rapids. In Virginia the Fall Line separates the Tidewater and Piedmont regions. p. 56.

federal. National. p. 215.

ferrier. The man who ran the ferryboat for the county. p. 183.

fertile. Able to produce crops and plants easily and plentifully. p. 78.

fertilizer. A substance, such as manure or chemicals, that is spread over the soil to help plants grow bigger and stronger. p. 113.

food processing. Preparing farm products for sale. p. 122.

fossil. The remains of a plant or animal that lived long ago. Fossils are often found in rocks or minerals. p. 80.

freedman. A black who was freed from slavery. p. 302.

free state. A Northern state of the Union in which slavery was forbidden. p. 291.

frontier. Land that is on the edge of unsettled country. p. 157.

fuel. Something that can be burned to make heat or power. p. 80.

fund. Money set aside for a special purpose. p. 263.

gap. A break or opening, such as a pass through mountains. A gap is usually made by running water over a long period of time. p. 61.

geography. The study of the earth and how people use it. p. 9.

globe. A sphere-shaped model of the earth. p. 6.

governor. The chief executive of a state. p. 153.

Great Wagon Road. An early road that began in Philadelphia and ran southwest into Georgia. Near Roanoke it connected with the Wilderness Road. p. 269.

grid. A system of crossing lines that form squares or boxes on a map or globe. p. 17.

harpoon. A special kind of spear that is used for catching whales. p. 255.

hemisphere. Half of the earth. p. 14.

heritage. Something that is handed down from earlier generations or from the past. p. 336.

history. The story of what happened in the past. p. 9.

hornbook. An early schoolbook made of a board with paper on both sides and covered with a thin sheet of animal horn through which the paper could be read. p. 159.

House of Burgesses. The elected representatives in the General Assembly of Virginia during colonial times. p. 154.

hydroelectric (hye droh ee LEK trihk) **power.** Electric power produced from falling water. p. 79.

indentured servant. A person who worked for a certain time in exchange for free passage to a foreign land. p. 151.

industry. Any kind of business or trade, such as fishing, farming, or printing. p. 103.

irrigation. The bringing of water to crops or other plants where it is needed. Irrigation is usually done through pipes, canals, or ditches. p. 88.

Jim Crow laws. Laws that kept black people from using certain facilities, such as restrooms and drinking fountains, that whites used. p. 312.

key. The part of the map that tells what the symbols stand for. p. 24.

landform. A type of land surface formed by nature. p. 45.

latitude. The lines that run across a map and represent the distance north or south of the earth's Equator. p. 14.

limestone. A stone used for building and for making lime. Limestone is formed mainly by tightly packed pieces of shell or coral. p. 68.

livestock. The name given to farm animals, such as cattle, sheep, and pigs. p. 119.

location. Where a place is compared with other places around it. p. 5.

longhouse. A long, low building made with a frame of bent young trees, and covered with grass, tree bark, or animal skins. Indians often lived in these buildings. p. 138.

longitude. The lines on a map that run from the North Pole to the South Pole. p. 16.

Louisiana Purchase. On April 30, 1803, the United States bought the territory of Louisiana from France for about $12 million. p. 233.

lumbering. The process of cutting down trees and cutting the wood into pieces. p. 106.

mainland. The main part of a continent. p. 46.

manufacturing. The making of goods by hand or by machine. p. 121.

map. A special kind of drawing that shows the earth or part of the earth on a flat surface. p. 5.

mechanic. A person trained to work with tools and to make, repair, and use machines. p. 263.

militia (muh LIHSH uh). Soldiers partly trained for war. In colonial Virginia, groups of soldiers trained to protect the colonists against outside attacks. p. 184.

mineral. A natural resource found in the earth, such as gold, copper, coal, or stone. Minerals can be mined and are used for various purposes. p. 80.

Monroe Doctrine. A message from President James Monroe to Congress, stating that European countries must stay out of the affairs of the Western Hemisphere. p. 242.

natural resource. A material found in nature that is useful to people. Such things as land, minerals, water, and forests are natural resources. p. 77.

navigator (NAV uh gayt ur). A person who maps out ocean routes. p. 174.

New Deal. A government program started by President Roosevelt that was meant to help people in need. p. 325.

oath of office. The words by which the President promises to do the job well. p. 227.

ocean. A large body of salt water. There are four oceans on the earth: the Arctic, Atlantic, Pacific, and Indian oceans. p. 6.

orchard. A field of fruit trees. p. 118.

Oregon Trail. A famous trail used by thousands of Americans moving westward across the country. It stretched 2,000 miles from Missouri to Oregon. p. 275.

patriot. A person who has a special love for his or her country and works for its good. p. 198.

pay-as-you-go. Senator Harry Byrd's motto, meaning that the senator did not like Virginia's plan to borrow money for road repairs. He wanted the money to come from a tax. p. 320.

peat. A black, sticky soil made up of partly rotted plants. p. 52.

peninsula. A piece of land that is almost surrounded by water and is connected to the main part of the land. p. 46.

plantation. A large farm, usually one on which one main crop is grown. p. 149.

planter. A person who owns or runs a plantation. p. 149.

plateau. A large, high, rather level piece of land that is raised above nearby areas. p. 61.

pollution. The result of harming any part of the earth's air, water, or land by making it dirty. p. 93.

population. The number of people living in a place. p. 34.

population density. The number of people per unit of area, such as per square mile or square kilometer. p. 34.

precipitation (pree sihp uh TAY shun). All forms of water that fall on the earth's surface. It includes rain, snow, sleet, and hail. p. 91.

Prime Meridian. The line of longitude that divides the Eastern and Western hemispheres. p. 16.

367

profession. A job, such as doctor, dentist, lawyer, or architect, that requires many years of special training and education. p. 340.

rapids. Places in rivers or streams where the water flows very quickly and roughly. p. 56.

rebellion (rih BEL yun). An uprising or fight against the ruling government. p. 158.

reclaim. To put something back the way it was. p. 104.

Reconstruction (ree kun STRUK shun). The time after the Civil War when the North and South had to struggle to put America back together again. p. 303.

reform. Change for the better. p. 310.

refuge. A place of shelter or protection, such as a wildlife refuge, where wild animals can live in safety. p. 97.

relief map. A map that shows the heights of places. p. 41.

repeal. To take back. p. 196.

reservation. Land set aside by the government for a special purpose, such as for the Indians to use. p. 155.

reservoir (REZ ur vwahr). A place where water is collected and stored for use. p. 88.

restore. To bring something, such as a building, back to a former state or condition. p. 170.

ridge. A line of hills or mountains. p. 64.

riveter (RIHV iht ur). A woman who worked to fasten metal plates to warships during World War II. p. 328.

rotate. To turn something around in a circle. p. 13.

rural. Of or relating to the country. p. 38.

salary. The money a person gets paid to do a job. p. 326.

scale. The size of a map or model compared with what it represents. p. 26.

secede (sih SEED). To leave an organization or union. p. 291.

segregation (seg ruh GAY shun). The practice of sending black children and white children to different schools. p. 333.

seminary. A school especially for young women. p. 263.

service industry. An industry that offers services instead of goods. p. 332.

sharecropper. A person that farmed a small part of someone else's land in return for a share of the crops. p. 301.

shingle. A thin piece of wood that is used with others to cover the roofs and sides of buildings. p. 257.

slave state. A Southern state in the Union that allowed slavery. p. 291.

specialized farming. The growing or raising of only one thing. p. 112.

sphere. An object that is round like a ball. p. 6.

stable. A building where horses or cattle are kept or fed. p. 168.

stalactite. An icicle-like shape that hangs down from the walls and ceilings of caves. Stalactites are formed over a long period of time by dripping water that contains lime. p. 69.

stalagmite. A lime formation shaped like a cone that is built up from the floor of a limestone cave. p. 69.

Stamp Act. A law passed by England in 1765 that required Americans to buy special tax stamps to put on newspapers, pamphlets, legal documents, and certain articles for sale. p. 196.

statesman. A wise government leader. p. 218.

steamboat. A boat that moves by steam power. p. 255.

Supreme Court. The most important court in the United States. The Supreme Court settles questions having to do with the Constitution and the country's laws. p. 243.

surface mining. A type of mining in which huge power shovels scoop out dirt and rock to get to minerals that are near the earth's surface. p. 103.

surrender. To give up something, such as a battle. p. 189.

surveyor. A person who measures land for size, shape, position, and boundaries and uses this information to make maps. p. 188.

symbol. On a map, something that stands for a real place or thing on the earth's surface. p. 24.

synthetic fiber. A fiber, such as nylon or rayon, that is not made from natural materials but rather from chemicals. p. 121.

tax. Money that people must pay to support their government. p. 191.

technology (tek NAHL uh jee). All the ways people have of making and using the things they need and want. p. 253.

temperature. The degree of hot or cold, such as of the air. p. 90.

term. The length of time for which a person is elected to hold an office. p. 227.

textile (TEKS tyl). Industry in which cloths and fabrics are made. p. 122.

thermometer. An instrument that is used to measure temperature. p. 90.

tide. The rise and fall of the ocean and other large bodies of water connected to the ocean. p. 46.

timber. Trees that are cut and used for wood. p. 106.

time line. A tool that shows when certain things happened and the order in which they happened. p. 161.

time zone. Any of the regions into which the earth is divided for measuring standard time. p. 20.

toll road. A road that a driver had to pay to use. p. 308.

tourism. Providing services for people who travel for pleasure. p. 110.

Townshend Acts. Laws that said that Americans had to pay a tax when they bought certain goods from England. p. 197.

treasury. The place where a country keeps its money. p. 195.

treaty. An agreement between two groups, such as two nations. p. 179.

Treaty of Paris. A peace treaty that leaders from England and the United States signed in Paris, France. In it, England said that the United States was a free nation. p. 213.

tribe. A group of people held together by family ties, geography, and customs. p. 137.

Union. Another name for the early United States. p. 291.

urban. Of or relating to a city. p. 38.

Vagrancy (VAY grun see) **Law.** A law that allowed people to arrest any stranger without a job who arrived in their town. p. 302.

Virginia Convention. The meeting held on May 6, 1776, in Williamsburg, during which Virginia patriots met to work for colonial independence. p. 204.

Virginia Declaration of Rights. A part of the Virginia constitution that stated that no one could take away the rights of any Virginian. p. 217.

Virginia Statute for Religious Freedom. A paper drawn up by Thomas Jefferson that stated that all people must be free to worship God in any way they please. p. 214.

wetland. Low, flat land where water is always close to the surface; land containing many marshes and swamps. p. 50.

wigwam. An Indian home made of bent, young trees and covered with grass, bark, or animal skins. A wigwam is smaller than a longhouse. p. 139.

GEOGRAPHICAL DICTIONARY

Barrier Island

A barrier island is formed over time by waves moving sand into a huge sand bar that rises above the ocean surface. Barrier islands protect the coast from being worn away by the ocean waves.

Cape

A cape is a point of land that projects noticeably into a lake, sea, or ocean. Capes are often at tips of islands or continents. Capes can be formed by sand or rock.

Coast

A coast is land along the edge of a large body of water. The people on the east coast live next to the Atlantic Ocean. The people on the west coast live next to the Pacific Ocean.

Coastal Plain

A coastal plain is an area of low land that borders a large body of water. In Virginia the coastal plain is called the Tidewater, because tidal waters flow through it.

Continent

The earth's land surface is divided into seven parts called continents. Therefore, a continent is a huge body of land on the earth's surface. One of the earth's seven continents is shown here. What is the name of the continent?

Gorge

A gorge is a narrow valley, that is often steep and rocky. Gorges are usually formed by swiftly flowing streams and rivers.

Gap

A gap is a narrow valley or a narrow pass through the mountains. A gap is often formed by a stream across a mountain ridge.

Island

An island is a body of land that has water all around it. It is smaller than a continent. The largest island in the world is Greenland.

GEOGRAPHICAL DICTIONARY

Lake

A lake is a body of water with land all around it. Virginia has only a few natural lakes. Its largest is Lake Drummond in the Great Dismal Swamp.

Mountain

A mountain is a piece of land that rises steeply from the land around it. The top of a mountain can be peaked or round. The Appalachian Mountains are in Virginia.

Marsh

A marsh is a wetland where tall grasses, bullrush, and cattails grow. Marshes can be covered by either fresh or salt water. They provide needed food and shelter for many kinds of fish and animals.

Ocean

An ocean is a very large body of salt water. There are four oceans. They are the Atlantic Ocean, the Pacific Ocean, the Indian Ocean, and the Arctic Ocean. Locate these oceans on the map on pages 352–353.

River

A river is a long, narrow body of water that flows through the land. Where a river begins is called its source. Where a river ends is called its mouth. The Rappahannock River flows through northern Virginia into the Chesapeake Bay.

Swamp

A swamp is a low, wet, land where shrubs and trees grow. Water hardly ever drains away from a swamp. Swamps are usually found in lowland areas, coastal areas, and near slowly flowing rivers. The Dismal Swamp in Virginia is very beautiful.

Shoal

A shoal is a sandbank, sand bar, or ledge of rock or coral that makes the water shallow. Sometimes ships run aground on shoals.

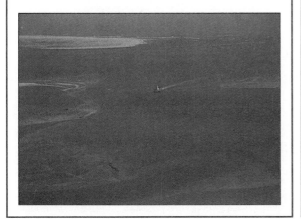

Valley

A valley is a long, low place between hills or mountains. Valleys are areas in the mountains where farming can be done. Virginia's valley land lies between the Blue Ridge and the Allegheny Mountains.

SOME IMPORTANT PRODUCTS MANUFACTURED IN VIRGINIA

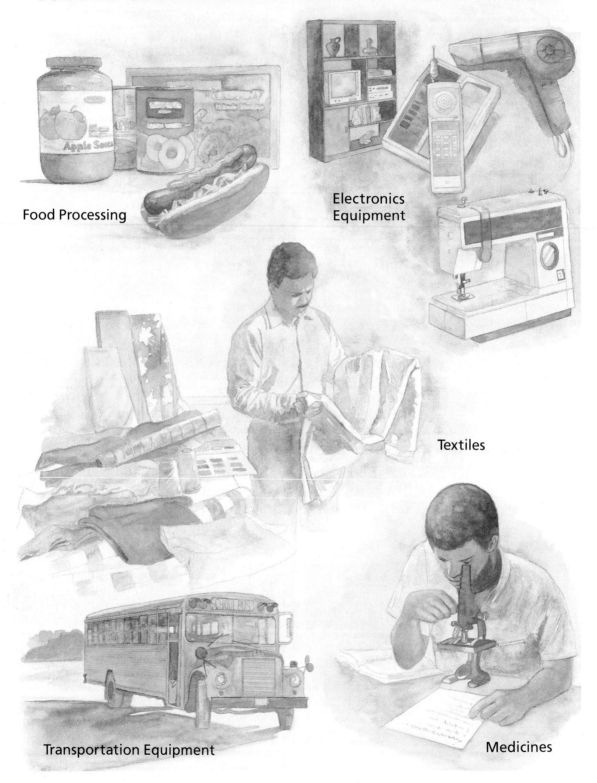

Food Processing

Electronics Equipment

Textiles

Transportation Equipment

Medicines

SOME IMPORTANT VIRGINIA FARM PRODUCTS

Cattle and Milk

Chickens and Turkeys

Soybeans

Apples and Peaches

Peanuts

Wheat Products

GRAPH APPENDIX

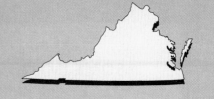

VIRGINIA: FIVE MOST POPULATED COUNTIES

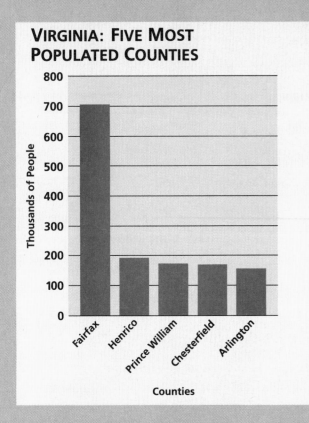

VIRGINIA: FIVE MOST POPULATED CITIES

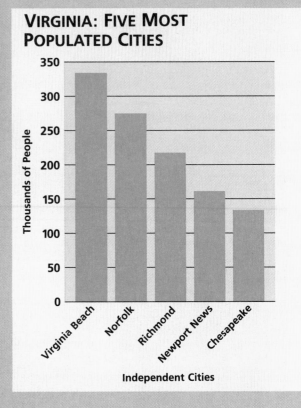

VIRGINIA: POPULATION BY AGE GROUPS

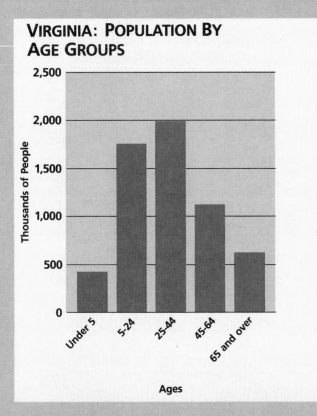

THE UNITED STATES: LEADING PRODUCERS OF FISH

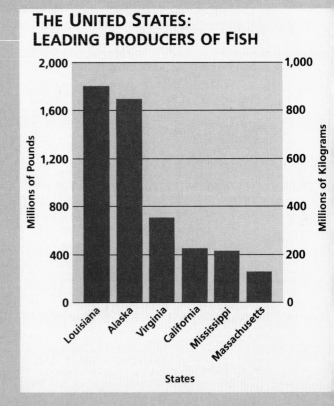

VIRGINIA: INCOME FROM MINERAL PRODUCTION

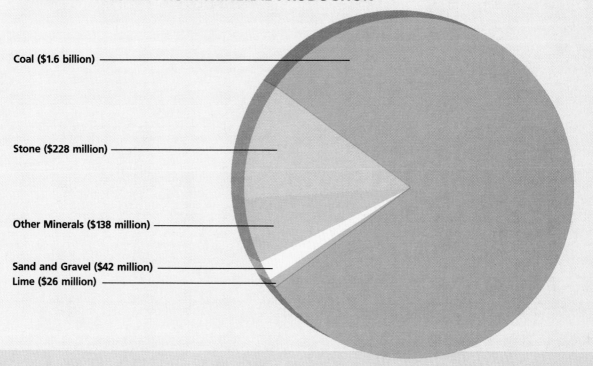

Coal ($1.6 billion)

Stone ($228 million)

Other Minerals ($138 million)

Sand and Gravel ($42 million)

Lime ($26 million)

VIRGINIA: BEEF CATTLE PRODUCTION, 1985-1990

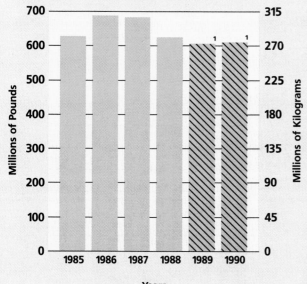

Millions of Pounds

Millions of Kilograms

Years

Estimated   [1]U.S. projection figures from Economic Research Service

VIRGINIA: WINTER WHEAT PRODUCTION, 1984-1989

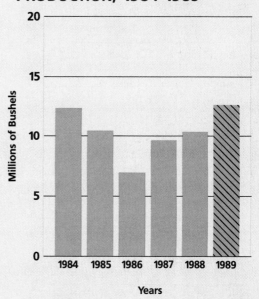

Millions of Bushels

Years

Estimated

Average Monthly Precipitation

Richmond

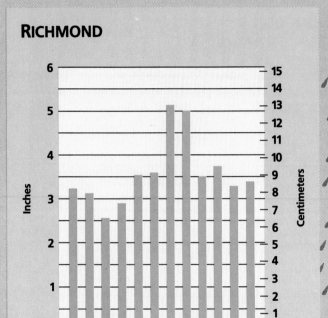

Inches

Centimeters

Months

Norfolk

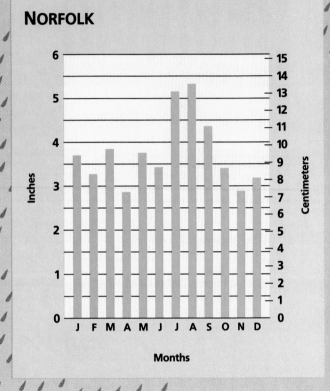

Inches

Centimeters

Months

Lynchburg

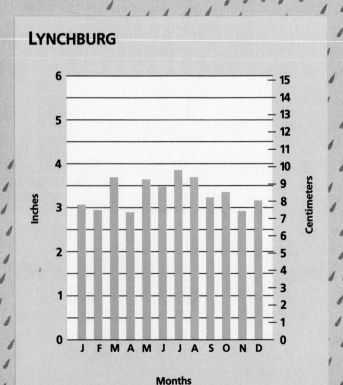

Inches

Centimeters

Months

Roanoke

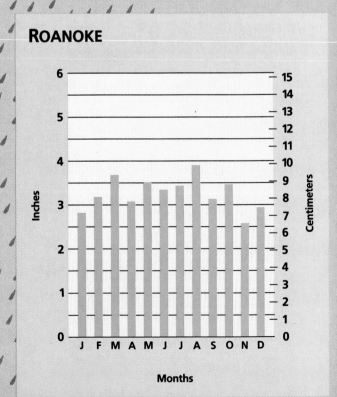

Inches

Centimeters

Months

AVERAGE MONTHLY TEMPERATURES

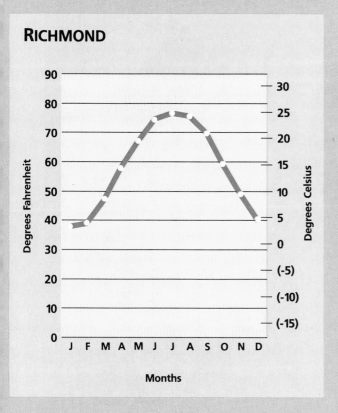

RICHMOND

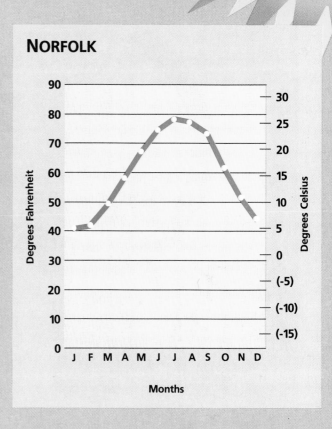

NORFOLK

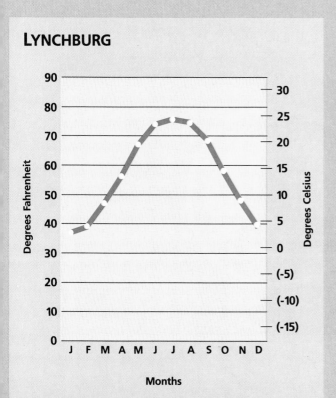

LYNCHBURG

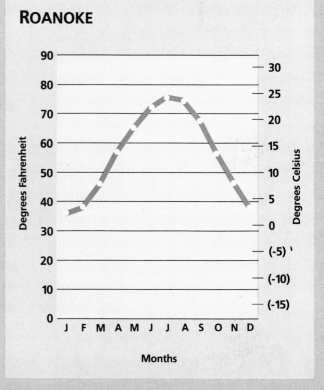

ROANOKE

Emblems of Our State

State Seal

State Bird — *Cardinal*

State Flower — *American Dogwood*

State Tree — *American Dogwood*

State Flag

Virginia's Independent Cities

City Name	City Population	Population Rank	Area in Square Miles (Square Kilometers)
Alexandria	107,800	8	15 (39)
Bedford	6,300	37	7 (18)
Bristol	18,000	25	12 (30)
Buena Vista	6,500	36	3 (8)
Charlottesville	41,100	13	10 (27)
Chesapeake	134,400	5	340 (881)
Clifton Forge	5,100	38	3 (8)
Colonial Heights	16,500	26	8 (20)
Covington	7,900	30	4 (11)
Danville	44,700	12	17 (44)
Emporia	4,700	39	2 (6)
Fairfax	19,900	21	6 (16)
Falls Church	9,700	29	2 (5)
Franklin	7,600	31	4 (10)
Fredericksburg	19,500	22	6 (16)
Galax	6,900	35	8 (21)
Hampton	126,000	6	51 (133)
Harrisonburg	27,000	15	6 (16)
Hopewell	24,100	16	10 (27)
Lexington	7,000	33	2 (6)
Lynchburg	68,000	10	49 (128)
Manassas	20,100	20	8 (21)
Manassas Park	7,100	32	2 (5)
Martinsville	18,700	23	11 (28)
Newport News	161,700	4	65 (169)
Norfolk	274,800	2	53 (137)
Norton	4,700	40	7 (18)
Petersburg	39,800	14	23 (60)
Poquoson	10,100	29	17 (44)
Portsmouth	111,000	7	30 (77)
Radford	13,700	27	7 (19)
Richmond	217,700	3	60 (156)
Roanoke	101,900	9	43 (112)
Salem	23,700	17	14 (37)
South Boston	7,000	34	5 (14)
Staunton	21,500	18	8 (22)
Suffolk	51,300	11	409 (1,060)
Virginia Beach	333,400	1	256 (663)
Waynesboro	18,100	24	8 (20)
Williamsburg	11,400	28	5 (13)
Winchester	21,200	19	9 (24)

Source: U.S. Department of Commerce, Bureau of the Census

facts About Virginia Counties

County Name	County Seat	County Population	Population Rank	Area in Sq. Mi. (Sq. Kilo.)	Area Rank	Year Formed
Accomack	Accomac	31,600	30	476 (1,232)	32	1634
Albemarle	Charlottesville	60,900	10	725 (1,878)	6	1744
Alleghany	Covington	13,900	62	446 (1,156)	37	1822
Amelia	Amelia Courthouse	8,500	85	357 (924)	53	1734
Amherst	Amherst	29,000	33	479 (1,241)	28	1761
Appomattox	Appomattox	12,400	65	336 (870)	57	1845
Arlington	Arlington	158,700	5	26 (67)	95	1847
Augusta	Staunton	51,900	14	989 (2,561)	2	1738
Bath	Warm Springs	5,200	93	538 (1,393)	16	1790
Bedford	Bedford	39,300	23	747 (1,936)	5	1753
Bland	Bland	6,400	89	359 (929)	52	1861
Botetourt	Fincastle	24,700	42	545 (1,411)	15	1769
Brunswick	Lawrenceville	16,000	58	563 (1,459)	13	1720
Buchanan	Grundy	35,800	26	504 (1,305)	24	1858
Buckingham	Buckingham	12,300	67	583 (1,511)	12	1761
Campbell	Rustburg	47,200	18	505 (1,309)	23	1781
Caroline	Bowling Green	19,000	51	535 (1,386)	17	1727
Carroll	Hillsville	27,300	37	478 (1,237)	30	1842
Charles City	Charles City	6,500	88	181 (470)	86	1634
Charlotte	Charlotte Courthouse	11,800	70	477 (1,235)	31	1764
Chesterfield	Chesterfield	172,400	4	434 (1,125)	40	1748
Clarke	Berryville	10,300	71	178 (462)	88	1836
Craig	New Castle	4,200	94	330 (854)	59	1851
Culpeper	Culpeper	24,300	43	382 (989)	48	1748
Cumberland	Cumberland	7,900	86	300 (776)	65	1748
Dickenson	Clintwood	19,800	48	331 (858)	58	1880
Dinwiddie	Dinwiddie	21,100	46	507 (1,313)	22	1752
Essex	Tappahannock	8,900	81	263 (680)	75	1691
Fairfax	Fairfax	710,500	1	394 (1,020)	46	1742
Fauquier	Warrenton	42,000	20	651 (1,686)	8	1759
Floyd	Floyd	11,800	71	381 (987)	50	1831
Fluvanna	Palmyra	10,700	73	290 (751)	68	1777
Franklin	Rocky Mount	37,200	24	683 (1,770)	7	1785
Frederick	Winchester	36,900	25	415 (1,075)	43	1738
Giles	Pearisburg	17,600	54	362 (938)	51	1806
Gloucester	Gloucester	28,300	34	225 (583)	81	1651
Goochland	Goochland	12,600	64	281 (729)	69	1727
Grayson	Independence	16,600	57	446 (1,155)	37	1792
Greene	Stanardsville	8,700	84	157 (406)	89	1838
Greensville	Emporia	10,400	75	300 (778)	67	1780
Halifax	Halifax	29,900	31	816 (2,114)	4	1752
Hanover	Hanover	54,100	13	467 (1,210)	34	1720
Henrico	Richmond	195,500	2	238 (617)	78	1634
Henry	Martinsville	56,200	11	382 (990)	48	1776

Source: U.S. Department of Commerce, Bureau of the Census and the World Almanac.

County Name	County Seat	County Population	Population Rank	Area in Sq. Mi. (Sq. Kilo.)	Area Rank	Year Formed
Highland	Monterey	2,800	95	416 (1,077)	42	1847
Isle of Wight	Isle of Wight	24,100	44	319 (827)	61	1634
James City	Williamsburg	26,600	38	153 (397)	90	1634
King and Queen	King and Queen Courthouse	6,400	90	317 (821)	63	1691
King George	King George	12,000	69	180 (466)	87	1720
King William	King William	10,300	78	278 (719)	71	1701
Lancaster	Lancaster	11,100	72	133 (344)	92	1652
Lee	Jonesville	26,600	36	437 (1,133)	39	1792
Loudoun	Leesburg	66,800	7	521 (1,350)	19	1757
Louisa	Louisa	19,100	50	497 (1,286)	25	1742
Lunenburg	Lunenburg	12,200	68	432 (1,120)	41	1746
Madison	Madison	10,700	74	322 (833)	60	1792
Mathews	Mathews	8,800	82	87 (226)	94	1790
Mecklenburg	Boydton	29,800	32	616 (1,596)	9	1764
Middlesex	Saluda	8,700	83	134 (347)	91	1673
Montgomery	Christiansburg	66,100	8	390 (1,009)	47	1776
Nelson	Lovingston	12,300	66	474 (1,228)	33	1807
New Kent	New Kent	10,400	76	213 (551)	83	1654
Northampton	Eastville	14,500	60	226 (585)	80	1634
Northumberland	Heathsville	10,200	79	185 (478)	85	1648
Nottoway	Nottoway	14,900	59	316 (818)	64	1788
Orange	Orange	19,800	49	342 (886)	55	1734
Page	Luray	20,000	47	313 (811)	65	1831
Patrick	Stuart	17,600	55	481 (1,246)	27	1790
Pittsylvania	Chatham	65,600	9	995 (2,577)	1	1766
Powhatan	Powhatan	13,100	63	261 (677)	76	1777
Prince Edward	Farmville	17,400	56	354 (916)	54	1753
Prince George	Prince George	26,200	39	266 (688)	74	1702
Prince William	Manassas	175,400	3	339 (879)	56	1730
Pulaski	Pulaski	34,200	27	318 (824)	62	1839
Rappahannock	Washington	6,200	92	267 (692)	73	1833
Richmond	Warsaw	7,200	87	193 (499)	84	1692
Roanoke	Salem	74,500	6	251 (650)	77	1838
Rockbridge	Lexington	17,600	53	603 (1,562)	10	1778
Rockingham	Harrisonburg	54,400	12	865 (2,240)	3	1778
Russell	Lebanon	32,200	29	479 (1,241)	28	1786
Scott	Gate City	25,500	40	535 (1,386)	17	1814
Shenandoah	Woodstock	28,200	36	512 (1,327)	21	1772
Smyth	Marion	33,000	28	452 (1,171)	36	1832
Southampton	Courtland	18,000	52	603 (1,562)	10	1748
Spotsylvania	Spotsylvania	39,400	22	404 (1,046)	45	1720
Stafford	Stafford	50,100	16	271 (702)	72	1664
Surry	Surry	6,300	91	281 (729)	69	1652
Sussex	Sussex	10,100	80	491 (1,272)	26	1753
Tazewell	Tazewell	50,400	15	520 (1,347)	20	1799
Warren	Front Royal	23,300	45	217 (563)	82	1836
Washington	Abingdon	47,300	17	562 (1,456)	14	1776
Westmoreland	Montross	14,400	61	227 (587)	79	1653
Wise	Wise	44,800	19	405 (1,048)	44	1856
Wythe	Wytheville	25,600	41	465 (1,204)	35	1789
York	Yorktown	40,400	21	113 (293)	93	1634

Source: U.S. Department of Commerce, Bureau of the Census and the World Almanac.

1. Patrick Henry	1776–1779	
2. Thomas Jefferson	1779–1781 (resigned)	
3. William Fleming (acting)	June 4–12, 1781	
4. Thomas Nelson, Jr.	June 12–Nov. 30, 1781	
5. Benjamin Harrison	1781–1784	
6. Patrick Henry	1784–1786	
7. Edmund Randolph	1786–1788	
8. Beverley Randolph	1788–1791	
9. Henry Lee	1791–1794	
10. Robert Brooke	1794–1796	
11. James Wood	1796–1799	
12. Hardin Burnley (acting)	Dec. 7–11, 1799	
13. J. Pendleton (acting)	Dec. 11–19, 1799	
14. James Monroe	1799–1802	
15. John Page	1802–1805	
16. William H. Cabell	1805–1808	
17. John Tyler, Sr.	1808–1811	
18. George W. Smith (acting)	Jan. 15–19, 1811	
19. James Monroe	Jan. 19–April 3, 1811	
20. George W. Smith (acting)	April 3–Dec. 6, 1811	
21. George W. Smith (governor)	Dec. 6–26, 1811	
22. Peyton Randolph (acting)	Dec. 27, 1811–Jan. 4, 1812	
23. James Barbour	1812–1814	
24. Wilson Cary Nicholas	1814–1816	
25. James Patton Preston	1816–1819	
26. Thomas Mann Randolph	1819–1822	
27. James Pleasants	1822–1825	
28. John Tyler, Jr.	1825–1827 (resigned)	
29. William B. Giles	1827–1830	
30. John Floyd	1830–1834	
31. Littleton Waller Tazewell	1834–1836 (resigned)	
32. Wyndham Robertson (acting)	1836–1837	
33. David Campbell	1837–1840	
34. Thomas W. Gilmer	1840–1841 (resigned)	
35. John M. Patton (acting)	March 20–31, 1841	
36. John Rutherford (acting)	1841–1842	
37. John Munford Gregory (acting)	1842–1843	
38. James McDowell	1843–1846	
39. William Smith	1846–1849	
40. John Buchanan Floyd	1849–1852	
41. Joseph Johnson	1852–1856	
42. Henry A. Wise	1856–1860	
43. John Letcher	1860–1864	
44. William Smith	1864–1865	
45. Francis H. Pierpont (provisional)	1865–1868	
46. Henry H. Wells (provisional)	1868–1869	
47. Gilbert C. Walker (provisional)	Sept. 21–Dec. 31, 1869	
48. Gilbert C. Walker (governor)	Jan. 1, 1870–Jan. 1, 1874	
49. James L. Kemper	1874–1878	
50. Frederick W. M. Holliday	1878–1882	
51. William Evelyn Cameron	1882–1886	
52. Fitzhugh Lee	1886–1890	
53. Philip W. McKinney	1890–1894	
54. Charles T. O'Ferrall	1894–1898	
55. James H. Tyler	1898–1902	
56. Andrew Jackson Montague	1902–1906	
57. Claude A. Swanson	1906–1910	
58. William Hodges Mann	1910–1914	
59. Henry Carter Stuart	1914–1918	
60. Westmoreland Davis	1918–1922	
61. Elbert Lee Trinkle	1922–1926	
62. Harry F. Byrd	1926–1930	
63. John G. Pollard	1930–1934	
64. George C. Peery	1934–1938	
65. James H. Price	1938–1942	
66. Colgate W. Darden, Jr.	1942–1946	
67. William M. Tuck	1946–1950	
68. John S. Battle	1950–1954	
69. Thomas B. Stanley	1954–1958	
70. J. Lindsay Almond, Jr.	1958–1962	
71. Albertis S. Harrison, Jr.	1962–1966	
72. Mills E. Godwin, Jr.	1966–1970	
73. A. Linwood Holton, Jr.	1970–1974	
74. Mills E. Godwin, Jr.	1974–1978	
75. John N. Dalton	1978–1982	
76. Charles S. Robb	1982–1986	
77. Gerald Baliles	1986–1990	
78. L. Douglas Wilder	1990–	

1607	First English settlers arrive in Jamestown.
1612	John Rolfe introduces the cultivation of tobacco in Virginia.
1619	First women arrive in Jamestown. First blacks arrive in Jamestown. First meeting of the Virginia House of Burgesses.
1622	Indians attack English settlements.
1624	Virginia becomes a royal colony.
1634	First eight counties are created in Virginia.
1676	Nathaniel Bacon leads a rebellion.
1693	College of William and Mary is founded.
1699	Williamsburg becomes capital of Virginia.
1736	Newspaper is published in Williamsburg.
1753	Thomas Walker finds Cumberland Gap.
1754	French and Indian War begins.
1763	Treaty ending French and Indian War is signed.
1765	England passes Stamp Act. Patrick Henry makes famous speech.
1767	England passes Townshend Acts.
1773	Virginia forms colony-wide Committee of Correspondence.
1774	First Continental Congress meets.
1775	Second Continental Congress meets.
1776	Virginia Convention calls for independence. Declaration of Independence is signed. Virginia becomes a commonwealth and adopts its first constitution.
1780	Virginia government moves to new capital at Richmond.
1781	Americans win battle of Yorktown.
1783	Treaty of Paris is signed.
1786	Virginia Statute for Religious Freedom becomes law.
1787	Constitutional Convention meets.
1788	Virginia adopts U.S. Constitution.
1789	Washington is elected first President of the United States.
1792	Kentucky formed from three of Virginia's western counties.
1799	George Washington dies.
1800	Washington, D.C., becomes capital of the United States.
1801	Thomas Jefferson becomes President. John Marshall becomes chief justice of the United States Supreme Court.
1808	James Madison becomes President.
1812	America goes to war with England.
1814	British burn Washington. Peace treaty is signed with England.
1817	James Monroe becomes President.
1821	First free blacks leave Virginia for Liberia.
1823	President Monroe announces the Monroe Doctrine.
1825	University of Virginia opens.
1831	Nat Turner leads slave revolt.
1833	First steam-driven railroad is built in Virginia.
1836	Virginia's first cotton mill is built.
1839	Virginia Military Institute is founded.
1841	William Henry Harrison, a Virginian, becomes President of the United States. Upon his death a month later, Vice President John Tyler, another Virginian, becomes President.
1845	Matthew Fontaine Maury begins his wind and current charts of the ocean.
1846	War with Mexico begins.
1849	Zachary Taylor becomes President.
1850	Virginia Constitutional Convention meets in Richmond to resolve serious disagreements within the state.
1859	John Brown leads raid at Harpers Ferry
1861	Virginia secedes from the Union. Civil War begins.
1863	Lincoln issues the Emancipation Proclamation. Confederate victory at Chancellorsville.
1865	General Lee surrenders at Appomattox Court House. Civil War ends.
1869	Virginia ratifies new constitution.
1899	Horseless carriage arrives in Virginia.
1908	First child labor laws in Virginia are passed.
1917	United States enters World War I.
1929	The Great Depression begins.
1932	The Barter Theatre opens.
1958	Public schools in Virginia close to avoid integration.
1959	School integration begins.
1973	Hermanze E. Fauntleroy, Jr., becomes first black mayor of a Virginia city.
1989	L. Douglas Wilder elected first black governor of Virginia.

Some Annual Events in Virginia

January

Stonewall Jackson's Birthday
 Celebration. Lexington
Robert E. Lee's Birthday. Stratford
Lee Birthday Celebrations.
 Alexandria

February

George Washington's Birthday
 Celebration. Washington's
 Birthplace
George Washington's Birthday
 Celebration. Mason Neck
George Washington's Birthday.
 Fredericksburg

March

Kite Festival. Gunston Hall
 Plantation. Lorton
Opening of Oatlands Plantation.
 Leesburg
Military Through the Ages.
 Williamsburg

April

Annual Easter Sunrise Service.
 Natural Bridge
Annual Daffodil Show. Franklin,
 Gloucester
International Azalea Festival. Norfolk
Historic Garden Week. Statewide
Spring Wildflower Pilgrimage.
 Booker T. Washington National
 Monument, Franklin County
Barter Theatre's Spring Production.
 Abingdon
Annual Vinton Folklife Festival.
 Vinton
Annual Wildflower Pilgrimage.
 Roanoke
Annual Azalea Festival. Alexandria

May

Annual Reenactment of the Battle of
 New Market. New Market
Annual Battles of Wilderness and
 Spotsylvania. Fredericksburg
Patowmack Canal Festival. Great
 Falls
Kenbridge Strawberry Festival.
 Kenbridge
Annual Memorial Day Jazz Festival.
 Alexandria

June

Festival-in-the-Park. Roanoke
Virginia Pork Festival. Emporia
Annual Potomac River Festival.
 Colonial Beach
Hampton Jazz Festival. Hampton
Harborfest. Norfolk
Annual James River Batteau
 Festival. Columbia

July

July 4th Celebration. Washington's
 Birthplace
19th Century Craft Days. New Market
Tuskegee Institute Day. Booker T.
 Washington National Monument,
 Franklin County
Shenandoah Music Festival. Orkney
 Springs
Annual Pony Roundup and Penning.
 Chincoteague
Games from the Past. Williamsburg
Annual Pork, Peanut and Pine
 Festival. Surry
Civil War Life. Chantilly

August

Annual Old Fiddlers Convention.
 Galax
Annual Jousting Tournament.
 Natural Chimneys Regional Park,
 Mt. Solon
Annual Festival of Nations. Norfolk
Lucketts' Annual Country Fair.
 Lucketts

September

Virginia Peanut Festival. Emporia
Annual Craft Show. Occoquan
State Fair of Virginia. Richmond
Annual Virginia Beach Neptune
 Festival. Virginia Beach
Annual Draft Horse and Mule Day.
 Leesburg
Annual Traditional Frontier Festival.
 Staunton
Fall Festival. Mouth of Wilson

October

Oyster Festival. Chincoteague
Historic Appomattox Railroad
 Festival. Appomattox
Festival of Leaves. Front Royal
Aldie Harvest Festival. Aldie
Yorktown Day Celebration. Yorktown
Suffolk Peanut Festival. Suffolk
Sorghum Molasses Festival. Clifford
Apple Harvest Festival. Syria

November

Virginia Thanksgiving Festival.
 Berkeley Plantation, Charles City
 County
Thanksgiving Hunt Weekend.
 Charlottesville
Annual Urbanna Oyster Festival.
 Urbanna
Food and Feasts in 17th-Century
 Virginia. Williamsburg
Joy from the World. Richmond

December

Annual Scottish Christmas Walk.
 Alexandria
Old Town Christmas Candlelight
 Tour. Alexandria
Carols by Candlelight. Gunston Hall
 Plantation, Lorton
The Merrie Old England Christmas
 Festival. Charlottesville
Annual Old Town Christmas.
 Petersburg
Anniversary of the Battle of
 Fredericksburg. Fredericksburg
Civil War Christmas. Newport News

Index

CREDITS